HOW TO RAISE A HAPPY CHILD

HOW TO RAISE A HAPPY CHILD

EFFECTIVE STRATEGIES TO ENSURE THE WELL-BEING OF YOUR CHILD FROM BIRTH TO ADULTHOOD

JAVAD H. KASHANI, M.D.

DONNA V. MEHREGANY, M.D.

WESLEY D. ALLAN, M.A.

KATE KELLY

VERMILION
London

1 3 5 7 9 10 8 6 4 2

First published in the United States in 1998 by Three Rivers Press, a division of Crown Publishers, Inc.

First published in the United Kingdom in 2000 by Vermilion
an imprint of Ebury Press
Random House, 20 Vauxhall Bridge Road, London SW1V 2SA

Random House Australia (Pty) Limited
20 Alfred Street, Milsons Point, Sydney, New South Wales 2061, Australia

Random House New Zealand Limited
18 Poland Road, Glenfield, Auckland 10, New Zealand

Random House (Pty) Limited
Endulini, 5A Jubilee Road, Parktown 2193, South Africa

The Random House Group Limited Reg. No. 954009

www.randomhouse.co.uk

A CIP catalogue record for this book is available from the British Library.

Design by Cindy LaBreacht

ISBN 0 09 182761 2

Papers used by Vermilion are natural, recyclable products made from wood grown in sustainable forests.

Printed and bound in Great Britain by Butler & Tanner Ltd, Frome, Somerset

To **SORAYA,**

an exemplary human being,

mother, wife, physician and academician

ACKNOWLEDGEMENTS

ACKNOWLEDGEMENTS

WE WOULD LIKE TO THANK our literary agent, Regina Ryan, for her tireless commitment, feedback and support. From the moment we first spoke about the project, she has given willingly of her time, and we greatly appreciate her devotion to our work.

We would also like to acknowledge the assistance of Ms. Julie Dahlmeier, Ms. Heather Shannon and Dr. Debora Bell-Dolan with various drafts of the book.

Finally, we owe a debt of gratitude to PJ Dempsey, who believed in the book from the beginning and who guided us in reorganizing and writing the material. Without her guidance the book would not have reached its full potential, and we deeply appreciate the time and energy she devoted to making it work.

Without the help of these people, we could not have written this book. Thank you.

CONTENTS

CONTENTS

Part Three MENTAL DISORDERS AND FAMILY DIFFICULTIES / 151

INTRODUCTION

introduction

TURN ON THE television and watch the news or read the local newspaper and you are sure to find reasons to worry – robberies, drug abuse, gangs, violence and murder. Many people are rightfully afraid to go out alone after dark, and some are fearful even in their own homes because of criminal activities in their community.

Problems within the family are also increasing. The divorce rate is almost 50 per cent for new marriages, children are in turmoil and have serious problems, crimes committed by youths are multiplying, and our environment seems a great deal less safe. Many people are asking themselves what is happening in our society and how changes can be made.

At times, raising mentally healthy children in our turbulent society seems quite difficult. Yet it is within the family that the solution lies.

WHAT IS WRONG with the current system that has led to an increase in children with serious problems? Why are children breaking laws, running away from home, using drugs and alcohol, and showing no respect for their parents? Why have the rates of youth suicide and homicide increased? Why have we seemingly accepted such a violent atmosphere?

Perhaps two of the most common reasons children develop problems and turn to crime are the lack of family values and the absence of a support system. Many of these troubled youngsters have endured experiences, such as mental or physical abuse, that destroyed their self-respect and their basic trust in other people.

Kids learn to respect other people by learning to respect themselves first, and this self-respect grows out of having adult caregivers who love and respect them. Without parental respect for the child, children cannot be expected to have respect for society.

Unfortunately, the news on how children are faring is not good. Increasingly, parents are finding themselves unable to handle the problems of their children without the help of mental health professionals. Between 1982 and 1992 the number of children who needed out-of-home care – in psychiatric hospitals and group homes, for example – increased an astounding 69 per cent.

About one adult in five has a psychiatric disorder such as depression, anxiety, or drug abuse. This statistic intrigued us, and we undertook a study of the number of youngsters in the US who display psychiatric disorders. The results of our research show that almost one in every five adolescents is impaired with a psychiatric condition and could benefit from psychological treatment. The most common conditions in adolescents (with similar results shown for younger children) are anxiety, depression and conduct disorder (often called juvenile delinquency), and Dr. Kashani was the first clinician in the US to document a case of major depression in a preschooler. Given the prevalence of such disorders, even in very young children, parents are becoming increasingly interested in ways to prevent or cope with the mental difficulties their children face.

We wrote this book because we wanted to help. Regularly we are confronted by worried parents asking one simple question: 'How can I make sure my child will turn out okay?' Having a stable and supportive family is the foundation for raising a healthy and happy child.

The fact that you are reading this book indicates that you are interested, concerned and aware of the importance of your task. Your awareness of the significance of child-rearing and the love and acceptance you feel for your children are two crucial factors that will enable you to raise mentally healthy children.

We are here to guide you along this challenging and rewarding pathway. Our goal is to help you prevent serious problems with your children, handle everyday childhood problems, and reduce the number of parent-child conflicts. Good luck.

how to use this book

HOW TO USE THIS BOOK

HOW TO RAISE A HAPPY CHILD is divided into four parts.

Part One should be read in its entirety. The chapters in this section offer advice on everything from being a better parent by taking good care of yourself to reducing stress to create a better home life. Simply reading it should offer you relief!

Part Two concerns the day-to-day issues we hear about most frequently and that many parents want to know more about. The subjects covered range from building self-esteem and potty training to what to do when your teenager dyes his hair blue. When you have a question, you can simply turn to the page where that issue is discussed. This section of the book can be read straight through, but more likely, you'll enjoy reading it in small chunks.

Part Three provides information on mental health disorders and difficulties that can occur in children. You'll find answers to questions about attention deficit disorder, and you'll learn how to handle bed-wetting. Alcohol and drug abuse, phobias, mental retardation, eating disorders, and a host of other topics are covered in detail as well. Each topic is defined, the cause, if known, is explained, and solutions are offered.

In Part Four we introduce the mental health professionals who are working today. If your child has a problem, do you need a psychiatrist or can a psychiatric social worker help you? Part Four will answer these questions and many others.

A FEW NOTES ABOUT HOW THE BOOK IS WRITTEN

Please keep the following in mind. First, the pronouns 'he' and 'she' are used interchangeably. We made an effort to distribute equally the use of 'he' and 'she' by section to avoid giving the impression that one gender is more susceptible to a certain disorder or problem than the other.

Second, we often write as though all parents are married and have several children. We fully realize that many parents are not married or have only one child. However, it becomes awkward to write in a manner that takes into account all possible family configurations.

Third, we sometimes mention the findings of a particular researcher. These studies are cited in the notes at the end of the book.

part one

LAYING THE GROUNDWORK FOR A HAPPY FAMILY

chapter one
IS YOUR FAMILY HAPPY?

HAPPY PEOPLE are fun to be around. They are easygoing, secure in their lives, and generally healthier than unhappy individuals. They are also happier with themselves. All of us like to be around someone with a cheerful outlook on life. But what makes individuals happy? Are they born that way, or did their environment have something to do with it?

Family has a great deal to do with it. Happy people grow up in an atmosphere that helps them see the best in others and themselves, and during childhood they are instilled with a positive attitude that helps them cope with whatever life brings their way. As adults they are pleased with their accomplishments, their home, their job and their family. We know that happy people are those who are able to give themselves credit for what they do and see their admirable traits, such as being bright, compassionate, or in good physical shape. Happy people are able to accept other people's shortcomings as well as their own faults, and they don't try to control the lives of others, including family members. Since happy people don't harbour a lot of resentment or bitterness toward others, they don't waste their energy getting even. As a result, they can spend energy on the more pleasant aspects of life.

Happy people do their best to strengthen their weak points and live up to their own expectations, but they are not overly harsh with themselves. They realize that change is sometimes gradual and requires a great deal of work. With others, they gently and tactfully offer constructive comments in a helpful way.

GUIDELINES FOR CREATING A HAPPY FAMILY

1. Set limits without being angry or cruel. Limits should be in the best interests of the children and should be clearly explained from the beginning.

2. Reduce angry interactions at home. While everyone gets upset sometimes, your home should primarily be viewed as a place for love and support.

3. Demonstrate the importance of dedication. Whether you work hard at your job or contribute time to church or community, your devotion to something will serve as a useful example for your children. They will learn to incorporate this type of behaviour in their own lives by working hard at school and knowing the value of community service.

4. Enrich your life through others. Make friends feel welcome in your home and expose your children to people you like, thus demonstrating the strength you receive from others.

5. Encourage open communication. Family members should always be allowed to talk about what's bothering them and to share happy news.

6. Praise your children whenever you have an opportunity. Noticing your child doing something good and acknowledging it is one of the most loving things you can do.

7. Spend time together. Establish a family mealtime or playtime when you can all be together to share on many levels.

8. Encourage thoughtfulness. Demonstrate the importance of helping others. Children raised in this environment become thoughtful and caring adults.

9. Respect your children. Children who are respected will learn to respect you and others in return.

IF YOU CAN incorporate these guidelines into your lifestyle, you are more likely to create a 'happy family'. Your kids will be given the opportunity for success and will feel supported because they know you care.

MISTAKES THAT CREATE FAMILY UNHAPPINESS

To keep the balance on 'happy' rather than 'unhappy' you'll want to avoid making certain very natural mistakes. Any of these actions can undermine your attempts for raising a happy child:

1. Showing no respect for each other or your children.
2. Allowing ridicule to be an accepted part of your family's life.
3. Using threats and punishment to control each other and your children.

4. Demanding control; using anger and rage to get your way.
5. Complaining frequently.
6. Forcing or manipulating children to take sides in parental arguments.
7. Emphasizing the importance of making money over spending time together as a family.
8. Discouraging open communication.
9. Failing to praise your children when they do well.
10. Seeking revenge when things go wrong.

chapter two
THE BASIC NEEDS AND FEELINGS OF PARENTS

WE ALL GET so busy with our day-to-day lives and the needs of our children that it's difficult to remember that in addition to being parents, we are also human beings with our own needs, desires and feelings.

In order to raise a happy child, you should first be aware of your own basic needs. Parents who are comfortable with themselves and their lives have a direct, positive impact on the happiness and mental health of their children. Parents who are content and satisfied have more energy to devote to child-rearing, and as a result, they create a more pleasant atmosphere in which their family can grow.

If you're in close touch with your own feelings, you can achieve a level of satisfaction which will help you realize that no matter what your external achievements, you can be a success in your own life.

UNDERSTANDING YOUR FEELINGS

Although each of us is unique, some basic feelings are common to everyone. We all acknowledge feelings like happiness or sadness, but we tend to ignore or deny some of our other feelings, like the tendency to worry or to feel competitive. For that reason, it is helpful to know that these feelings are perfectly normal.

Perhaps the best way to begin, then, is to help you better understand who you are and why you sometimes feel the way you do. Having a better understanding of basic human emotions will also help you understand the motivations and behaviour patterns of others as well. This is part of being human.

The Need to Be Liked and Loved

It is normal for people to want to be told that they are valued and loved by significant others such as their spouse, children, parents, relatives, friends, neighbours, co-workers and supervisors. We all need to hear compliments like 'You are a good person' regularly.

This basic need is present even in the toughest individuals. Directly or indirectly, even the office bully is looking for praise and wants people to indicate that something about him is likeable – the way he talks, for example, or his knowledge, his experience, or the way he tells jokes.

Being able to tell your spouse, your children and your friends that they are worthy people and you love them is very helpful. Doling out generous doses of love will help you get what you need in return.

The Need for Acceptance

We all want and need respect, approval and acceptance. Feeling that you will be approved of regardless of your behaviour and beliefs is necessary for your self-esteem. It makes you feel good to know that someone likes your taste in clothing, your cooking, the way you manage your department, or the way you relate to children.

Acceptance by those we love and respect is very important, and lack of acceptance by others can be hurtful. Haven't you ever been hurt when you weren't invited to a party – but then, when you thought about it, realized that you didn't know the host that well and that the party guests were members of a group to which you didn't belong? That sort of thing happens to all of us occasionally. With maturity comes the ability to think only momentarily about slights from those you don't know (the shop assistant who acts as if you've ruined her day by returning something) or don't like (your aunt Tildy, who never has anything nice to say about anybody, so why should what she says about you be significant?). This need for outside acceptance isn't a sign of neediness or dependency. All human beings want their behaviour, their work and their efforts to be recognized, acknowledged and appreciated.

Remember, too, that just as you want approval and acceptance, so do the people around you. Either through direct compliments ('I like your tie') or by other means (a complimentary note in a birthday card, for example) let others know how much you admire them or enjoy working with them.

If you've ever heard the expression, 'What goes around comes around', then you'll know the effect this will have on you. The more praise you offer people, the greater the likelihood that you will receive praise in return.

The Need to Feel Special

Everyone wants to feel special and important, whether that means being smart, being well educated, owning a nice car, or having a great haircut. It can be amusing to watch how people try to prove that they are special and unique. Scientists say, 'Our group was the first to discover that...' and a rich man's son may say, 'My dad is the wealthiest man in town.'

Wanting to feel special is normal and healthy. When assessing what is special about yourself it's best to concentrate on character traits like intelligence and kindness. These are permanent forms of specialness because no one can take them away from you. External qualities such as beauty or material possessions can and do change over the years.

Sometimes we get so busy with self-improvement and working on our weaknesses and bad habits that we dismiss what we do well. An excellent way to focus on what people like about you and what you're good at is to make a list.

Write down all the things you like best about yourself. This can include anything from the shape of your hands to your taste in clothes. Once you've acknowledged that you actually have some very lovely qualities, think next about the accomplishments you're proudest of. This positive reinforcement is a valuable tool for adults and children. At certain times in your life you will need to be your own cheering squad, and having the facts written down will help.

Remember, too, that claiming something special about yourself needn't mean denigrating someone else. For example, saying 'I've got a great sense of humour,' is preferable to saying 'I'm a lot wittier than my brother.'

You'll also find that if you make others feel special, they will learn to return that favour to you. When you notice that a friend does something particularly well, tell her so! Your wife wants to hear that she is the best lover, the best cook, most beautiful or generous or moral person you know. Your children, relatives, co-workers and friends also love hearing what you especially value in them. Generally, they will pick up on your cues, and you'll soon find them occasionally pointing out what is special about you.

It goes without saying that children have a strong need to be special in their parents' eyes. If you have three children, your work is more than tripled because each of them wants to be special. Ideally, it is wonderful if you recognize each child through specific interests or activities, so they don't feel that they have to compete with each other. However, make sure they know you also appreciate their efforts in many areas, as you don't want them to feel labelled. We all have friends who have suffered because one of their siblings was 'the smart one' or 'the athlete'. While each child has his or her strengths, it's important to convey the message that hard work can help them succeed at almost anything they really want to do.

The Feeling of Selfishness or Self-Interest

Selfishness – thinking first of ourselves – is one of the most fundamental feelings. It is this need at its most basic that leads to self-preservation, or survival. It is therefore perfectly normal to be selfish, because if we don't look after our own interests, who will?

Babies are born thinking that they are the centre of the universe. Gradually, a baby comes to acknowledge his mother and other caregivers, but he sees them only in their roles of servants of his interests. As the child grows older, he begins to see that there are others – siblings, for example – and that his needs can't always come first. As he matures, he learns to postpone gratification and to take turns and to respect other people's rights.

As you've likely observed, adults demonstrate all levels of self-centredness; some still need to be pampered constantly and need people to focus on their lives; others can postpone gratification and do a great deal for others. Even the most giving people, however, have a deep and abiding need to protect themselves. It is important to realize that thinking of yourself first is not pathological; it's simply human nature.

As a parent, part of thinking of yourself first means doing things that make you happy. For example, you might exercise, go bowling, listen to music, or spend money on yourself. You must satisfy your own needs before you will be ready to address the needs of others. If you don't do what makes you happy, you'll feel deprived and become resentful towards or impatient with family members.

Volunteerism and altruism actually grow out of a type of selfishness or self-interest. Altruistic people have been raised with a family value that has made them want and need to do good. Their sacrifice brings them pleasure, satisfaction and a sense of accomplishment and pride. It makes them feel they are doing something for humanity. So while these people are serving others, they are also doing something for themselves. While sacrifice and service are admirable, it is important to realize that it's also fine to do things that make you happy.

The Need to Compete with Others

Being competitive and having rivalries with other people is also normal. Competition can actually be healthy because it pushes us to work hard and do better.

Try not to let your self-worth depend on the outcome of competitions. Though you may feel disappointed if you lose at something, you should be able to put the loss behind you quickly with your ego still intact. You can attribute the failure to an off day – everyone has those – or you can find a new way to view your loss. For example, if you played in a tennis tournament and made it to the semifinals, you can tell everyone you were a finalist, which you were, or share with them your ultimate rank; you needn't announce that you lost the last game if that makes you feel bad.

Understanding that most people are competitive will help you when someone is competing with you. If a co-worker is trying to block your promotion, for example, you may feel hurt by his actions, but you'll understand that for him to want to get ahead of you is a normal human reaction. By acknowledging it, perhaps you can smile a bit while also deciding to work harder to stay ahead of him. This way you needn't waste your time getting angry or planning to get even. Instead use your energy to advance yourself further.

Competition becomes destructive when people try to win at someone else's expense. Some parents, for instance, put each other down in front of their children to make themselves feel better or to encourage the children to take sides. This is a destructive form of competition that should be discouraged.

Most successful people are competitive, but they focus solely on self-improvement, not on trying to prevent others from succeeding.

The Need to Compare Ourselves to Others

Beginning in childhood, individuals become familiar with concepts such as good versus bad, beautiful versus ugly, and rich versus poor. And starting during these early years, hearing about someone else's success is usually paired with hearing about your own failure. For example, a child who gets poor marks might be asked by his father, 'Why can't you get good marks like your brother Jerry?' Thus people grow up learning that when they have not done so well, they are likely to hear about another person who does better.

As a result, some people may even infer the reverse: when others are bad, then I am good. This happens when individuals want to build themselves up at the expense of others. When they hear about other people's accomplishments, they cope with their frustration by becoming restless, feeling annoyed, getting headaches, wanting to change the subject, or leaving the room.

This reaction, you might see, partially accounts for gossip. Spreading unpleasant gossip about someone allows a person to feel good temporarily because he feels that he is above that sort of thing. This also happens between families, when the Jones family says unkind things about the Smith family, and even among competing countries, when the people of one nation make fun of the food, attitudes, behaviour, language and culture of the other country. As a result, the members of one cultural group feel better about themselves because they have found reasons to believe they are superior to another nationality. (Nationality jokes are a prime example of human need.) Within one's own family, this type of put-down can be very hurtful. A husband may make cruel comments about his wife's job, intelligence, or parenting skills.

Remember that your success does not hinge on someone else's failure, nor are you likely to fail simply because someone else is good at something. If your spouse or a friend or co-worker always implies that his successes are greater than yours, you need to come up with a reply that will break the cycle: 'I'm delighted that the Acme Agency liked you so much, Bert, but that doesn't mean my department didn't handle the account well. We helped them with all of their projects.'

To learn more about yourself, try gauging your own reaction to comments you hear. The next time you hear something good about another person, consider your reaction. If you feel uncomfortable, examine the reasons why you feel that way. Don't compare yourself with this person and conclude that you aren't as good as he is. That will make you mad at yourself, and later on, you may take your anger out on other people or your family members. Accept the fact that this person about whom you have heard good things has done a good job. Contemplate what you can do to reach the same level of competence or even to do better. If the other person is a true expert, however, accept your limitations and remind yourself of your own successes. It is crucial to be aware that another person's success does not diminish your achievements.

Feelings of Fear, Worry and Anxiety

Rejection, failure and loneliness can cause fear, worry and anxiety. Certain events can trigger these upsetting emotions in each of us.

For some people, the world is a fearful place. Most of the time, the fears have to do with the future. For example, a student may fear failing an exam, an employee may fear losing her job, a parent may worry about the well-being of her children, or a middle-aged person may worry about retirement and growing old.

Facing your fears is generally the best way to overcome them. Admit that you are concerned, worried, or scared. Don't think that it is a sign of weakness if you acknowledge a particular worry or fear. If you sit down and think for a few minutes about whatever is troubling you, you will then be able to confront what is upsetting you. By denying your fears or resisting thinking of them, you deny yourself the opportunity to work on diminishing their impact. You'll find that once you confront fear it will be much easier for you to overcome it. (Also see the five-step coping strategy in Chapter 5 for understanding anxiety.)

Feelings of Self-Blame

Self-blame is much more common than you might imagine. People who are impatient with the mistakes of others are generally impatient and critical of their own faults as well. In general, when people start to blame themselves, they become less effective and cannot do things well because they doubt their abilities, and this wastes their energy.

What causes self-blame? We have found that people who engage in self-blame come from a background in which either they have been criticized excessively or they have witnessed others being criticized. These people then begin to blame themselves as a way of coping with problems.

Admitting that you made a mistake is different from blaming yourself. If you can admit to your mistakes, you will be able to learn from the experience and then move on with your life.

Self-blame is something to fight against

because it is very destructive. When you condemn yourself, you may lose sleep, be disappointed with yourself and become angry with yourself, your spouse, children, co-workers, neighbours and friends. Dr. Kashani has found this process of self-blame to be so debilitating that he hung a sign in his office that reads, 'Be a *noncritical* observer of self.' Over the years, hundreds of people have related to this sign. They have reported that they are very critical observers of themselves, rather than noncritical or nonjudgmental.

If you can stop blaming yourself for your mistakes, including dumb ones, you will enjoy life more. In becoming a noncritical observer of your emotions, your thoughts and your behaviour, you will find that it is easier to accept yourself and others.

The Need for Fantasy

We all occasionally need to escape from the real world through fantasy, especially when we are having problems. Fantasies can involve anything, from lying on a beach to aggressive ways to get back at someone who has upset you.

For children, fantasies are common. Your youngsters may have imaginary friends, and this can be helpful and healthy. Through their imaginary friends, children can solve problems and think about issues that are bothering them.

Although it seems as though we have no control over our fantasies, that isn't true. A married man may fantasize about having an affair, for example. If he acknowledges that it is just a fantasy and ends it, he will never act upon what could be very destructive thoughts. However, if he allows the fantasy to take control, he might actually have an affair. This would result in hurt feelings and possibly a divorce, causing his spouse and children to suffer the consequences of what started out as a fantasy.

Fantasizing becomes problematic if it takes too much of your time or intrudes on your responsibilities. For example, some people whose lives are very difficult, spend more of their time fantasizing than actually trying to improve their lives. They could do themselves a favour by developing reality-based fantasies about ways to make their lives better – things they could actually bring about, not far-fetched solutions like winning the lottery. If they then act upon them, they'll begin to view themselves as action-oriented individuals who can make change happen.

UNDERSTANDING THAT all of the feelings discussed above are perfectly normal and are shared by everyone will help you better understand yourself and others. This, in turn, will lead you to greater self-acceptance as well as an appreciation of others.

chapter three

MARITAL HAPPINESS LEADS TO FAMILY HAPPINESS

TO BECOME the best parent you can be, you need to be happy in your marriage. How content you are has a direct impact on the happiness of your child. Adults are more likely to be satisfied and have more energy to devote to parenting if they have dealt effectively with any problems in their marriage.

WHAT YOU DREAMED OF AND WHAT YOU GOT: HAVING REALISTIC EXPECTATIONS ABOUT MARRIAGE

Starting in childhood, people dream about the person they will eventually marry. As you matured, your views of marriage likely became more realistic, and perhaps you became attracted to someone who was compatible with you. Perhaps you shared basic values and beliefs, or maybe you really enjoyed the same activities and hobbies. It's also possible, however, that you were attracted to someone who was very different from you. Making the necessary adjustments and recognizing why you chose your partner is an important step in creating a marriage that works. Problems arise when people continue to search for the fairy-tale spouse of their childhood dreams.

If you have selected a spouse who has qualities that are still attractive to you, then you are fortunate. At the time you selected that person, you made an important step towards creating happiness for yourself and building a happy foundation for your children.

However, no matter how well you knew your spouse before you were married, you inevitably encountered some letdowns. Will he ever remember your anniversary without being reminded? Will she, just once, stop worrying about the kids all the time? Maybe he just can't abide the thought of having pets. Perhaps she never will understand why you enjoy spending Sunday afternoon watching a football game. And why must you spend *every* holiday with her parents?

New information about your spouse will continually surface during your marriage. You may be surprised, for example, at how totally shattered your spouse is when a distant relative dies.

Parenthood is almost certain to bring out new aspects of both of your personalities. Who would have guessed he could be so tender with a little baby? And who would have known that she would find mothering so gratifying? Yet there will also be moments of struggle: Must it always be the mother's job to get up every time the baby cries? Who takes care of investigating day-care centres or nursery schools? And who takes off from work when a child is sick?

Learning new and unpleasant things about your spouse can be disconcerting. It's not uncommon for a wife to feel angry when she learns that her husband has some characteristic she didn't know about before. Most people want a certain degree of stability and predictability in their lives.

It's helpful for couples to discuss their concerns about these changes. They can encourage growth while also voicing their feelings about new and different aspects of each another.

THE BEST MARRIAGES ARE NEVER ON TV

As family values change, we can witness their evolution as it is interpreted by the media. The image of parents in television families has also evolved over the last several decades. In the late 1950s Donna Reed and the Cleavers dominated our notion of what parents should be like. Whether or not our own mother stayed home all day cleaning and baking cookies, it always seemed that she *should* do so, because that was what June Cleaver and Donna Reed did. Of course, most families in those days had two parents, and both did all they could to see that the children received every benefit possible.

By the late1960s, though, the rosy glow of the 'normal' nuclear family was beginning to fade as one-parent families, like the one in *My Three Sons*, came onto the scene.

This trend continued in the 1970s as all-knowing and perfect parents were discarded in favour of parents like bigoted Archie Bunker and liberal Maude. By the 1980s, shows like *Dallas* and *Dynasty* portrayed families who would stab each other in the back to get ahead.

Today we watch programmes where parents constantly argue and marriage is seen as a battleground in which the only way to win is to cut your partner down at every turn. Further, if families are intact, which they rarely are on TV anymore, fathers may be depicted as bumbling fools while mothers have the final say in all matters and seem to have far more wisdom.

Because television is a major frame of reference, many couples, young couples especially, may unwittingly identify with the characters. As a result, they may base their relationships to some extent on what they see on television. While funny put-downs of friends and family may make television audiences laugh, they are no laughing matter when real people are involved. The key to a good marriage is establishing your own strong set of values, not mimicking the sometimes twisted values and relationships depicted on TV, which are intended to be entertainment, not a lesson in what is needed to keep a marriage stable and happy.

SACRIFICE IS PART OF ANY STRONG RELATIONSHIP: GIVING 51 PER CENT AND RECEIVING 49 PER CENT

Interestingly, sacrifice and doing things for other people are not often talked about much today. Today's goals are to make money and win in relationships, yet good relationships involve being generous to others.

Whether it's two friends, two spouses, or two business partners, giving and receiving in a relationship are not always equal. There will be times when it's 100 per cent to 0 per cent – for example, when one person is ill – but most often healthy partnerships balance out at 40–60 or 30–70; sometimes you'll receive a little more and sometimes you'll get a lot less. You simply have to believe that in the long run it will all even out.

Though this example comes from the business world, it is perfect because it illustrates how sometimes neither partner knows how heavy a load the other partner carries.

Howard, a successful businessman, told us that for several years he felt that he was doing more work than his business partner, Tim. Coming in early and staying late was always a part of Howard's schedule, but he enjoyed producing his best and tried not to get bogged down by petty concerns. One day he overheard a conversation that amazed him between a staff member, Lynn and Tim. Lynn asked Tim why he worked so hard for the company by travelling at odd hours and being away for so many days. 'Why don't you ask Howard to do his part in the upkeep of the out-of-town accounts?' she asked. Tim stated that he didn't mind doing a bit more and wouldn't let this minor issue get in the way.

Howard's first reaction was resentment: how could Lynn think Tim worked harder than he did when he was the one who kept the home office running smoothly? But as he thought about it, his respect for Tim grew, as did his appreciation of the way Tim handled the conversation. Howard further realized that Tim really was doing a lot for the company by undertaking so many unpleasant business trips, which interrupted his time with his family. Because Tim was away a great deal, Howard hadn't considered how very hard he worked while travelling. He felt a bit embarrassed for thinking that he did more work and for overlooking Tim's contribution.

In this situation, both partners were contributing everything they could to the company, and they felt no need to call for an hour-by-hour accounting of each other's time. Neither felt that he was being taken advantage of, cheated, or abused and as a result of their efforts, the company was a great success.

If you sit and wait to get back exactly what you have given to others, you will almost certainly be disappointed. Many times the receiver does not fully see or recognize the giver's contribution, and sometimes the receiver may not be capable of giving back at that time.

Some people think only about what they can milk from others as they strive to get more for themselves, but we have observed that people who are giving are less angry, feel better about themselves and have higher self-esteem.

There are people who are consistently willing to give 51 per cent or more and receive 49 per cent or less in relationships. These people, of course, can be assertive and stand up for what they believe. However, they consider doing things for other people to be a pleasure and a privilege – an act that is right and of which they can be proud.

APPROPRIATE ASSERTIVENESS

How best to communicate your needs? Use 'I' statements, and avoid confrontational phrases like 'You never . . .' 'You always . . .' 'You forgot . . .' or 'You really make me mad when you come home late.' Try rephrasing your statements to express what happened to you as a result of the other person's actions: 'I feel angry when you come home late without letting me know. I was trying to hold dinner so that we could eat together, but it got burned.'

Remember that your intention in being assertive is not to insult your spouse but to get your feelings across. Instead of attacking your mate with an accusation, you want to assert yourself by stating what happened to you and how it made you feel. Your spouse cannot argue about whether or not you feel angry, but he can argue about whether he was to blame. A marriage requires teamwork. If you blame your spouse all the time, you are dividing the team and weakening your bond.

Feelings need to be acknowledged and expressed, so let your spouse know how you feel when you're upset. If you bottle things up inside you, all your pent-up frustration will come out when you do finally blow up about something. That isn't fair to either of you. What happened in the past is over with, and all that should be under discussion is what is happening now.

Part of being assertive is considering and discussing any changes that might help your spouse improve the situation. Try following these guidelines:

- ➤ **BE REALISTIC.** Don't choose goals that are beyond your spouse's control.
- ➤ **EXPRESS YOUR WANTS AND NEEDS IN A CLEAR STATEMENT** – for example, 'I

would like you to take responsibility for the baby every Saturday morning so that I can go to the supermarket without having to take her along.'

➤ **AVOID VAGUE DEMANDS.** Don't make statements like 'Be a better husband',

➤ **MAKE SPECIFIC REQUESTS.** Say things like 'I would like you to call me if you're going to be more than thirty minutes late coming home from work.'

WHEN BABY MAKES THREE OR FOUR OR FIVE

'Which should I put first, my spouse or my child?' is a question frequently asked by parents. Your husband wants to go out, but the baby is sick. You want to coach your son's soccer team, but doing so will mean taking the team to out-of-town tournaments several weekends each year, leaving your wife at home with twins. Parents are often put in a position of having to choose between a spouse's needs and those of the child.

How you handle such a situation is important, yet there is rarely a right or wrong answer. This is a case where parents must simply try to make the best decision at the time.

New parents are often overwhelmed by the challenge of adjusting to a new lifestyle while maintaining the marital relationship. Couples need to talk about what they are going through. Husbands need to understand that helping out through this phase is the most loving thing they can do, but they will come to this task more readily if they have their wives' assurance that they are still number one, that this is just a time of transition as a family. Spouses who are made to feel wanted are likely to become more responsible and feel no resentment when sharing child-rearing tasks.

Assertiveness on the part of the parent who needs to speak up and good listening skills for both partners are vitally important as these discussions can be emotionally intense and will set the tone for future talks concerning each other's feelings. If your spouse talks about feeling neglected, take these comments seriously. Don't make fun of your spouse if she goes out on a limb and lets you know she feels neglected. Take her seriously and do your best to correct the problem.

If you love your baby or child completely, and if your own needs are nurtured by your spouse and by yourself some of the time, your child will flourish because love is all around him. Loving parents who openly care for each other and who also devote time to the family will create an environment that will nurture those who are a part of it.

PREVENTING A MARITAL BREAKUP

In today's 'me'–oriented society, couples are often told that if they are unhappy in a marital relationship they owe it to themselves to seek a divorce. However, divorce sends a very dangerous message to youngsters. Many children may observe that if Mum and Dad can end their relationship with each other so quickly, then parents may abandon them as well.

We firmly believe that it is wrong to take marriage lightly, particularly when children are involved. How strong the family unit is has an effect on a child's mental health, and a marital breakup can have an enormous impact on them.

Given the benefits of keeping the marriage together, we would like to offer some recommendations to help you and your spouse get along better, so let's talk now about the key skills that can help prevent divorce.

HOW TO STAY HAPPILY MARRIED

Here are seven rules for staying happily married:

Rule #1: Be willing to compromise, sacrifice and forgive.

Flexibility, good communication and the ability to compromise are crucial. Healthy communication involves listening and considering where the other person is coming from and what he believes. By being open to the other person and trying to understand the reasons for what he is asking, you'll be better prepared to work things out between you. Often, compromise or sacrifice will be necessary in reaching a solution.

Forgiveness is also vital to a healthy marriage. Though the two of you will undoubtedly disagree sometimes and do things that make each other angry, it's important to forgive. Harbouring anger over issues, large or small, will inhibit your ability to have a good marriage.

Rule #2: When you feel upset about something, discuss your concerns with your spouse rather than keeping your feelings to yourself.

While this skill is crucial when you're angry, it's also helpful when you're simply feeling overwhelmed.

When talking about their feelings directly, many people find it helpful to go through the following process. If your spouse is the cause of your being upset, then try articulating it this way: 'I feel _____ when you _____ because _____.'

For example, if you are angry with your husband because he constantly nags, don't let the anger build up until you explode and then tell him off. Instead, say, 'I feel irritated when you nag me to cook dinner because I can do it without being reminded.' In other words, state the problem and the feeling clearly without being confrontational or aggressive. If he forgets and nags you again, repeat how it makes you feel. Or you might suggest that the two of you fix dinner together, or suggest that he take over the task himself, since he seems to be ready to eat, whereas you're still busy helping the children with their homework.

At other times you may simply be irritable because of day-to-day home or office responsibilities. In situations like these, you should still try to explain yourself: 'I feel _____ because _____.'

If people understand what's bothering you, they'll be better prepared to offer comfort and support.

Think about how you would like your spouse to respond if you had a problem.

Would you like her to offer suggestions? Would you just want support or reassurance? Or would you want something else? Don't be afraid to tell your spouse what you need. You might say, for example, 'I really appreciate your advice, but right now I just want to talk.' Remember, your spouse can't read your mind and may not know what to do or how to support you.

Keep this in mind next time your spouse approaches you with a problem. Sometimes it's helpful just to listen and let her talk. She may simply want to vent her feelings and not receive any response at all. You might also ask your spouse how you can support her and make things easier.

Rule #3: Avoid constant arguments about unimportant issues.

If your arguments with your spouse usually involve unimportant details like putting the dirty clothes in the laundry basket or leaving the toilet seat up, you might ask yourself why these issues seem so important to you. This type of bickering may be based on marital examples of your parents, or it may be that unkind communication has simply become a bad habit. However, some couples fight about small stuff because they want to avoid talking about a bigger issue.

If you and your spouse are constantly arguing, wait to talk until you both feel calm and relaxed. Try to be honest and get to the root of what is really bothering you. If you are open about the problem, chances are good that you will find a satisfactory solution.

Petty arguments also crop up in marriages where one spouse has a desperate need to always be right. In cases like this, there has to be a winner and a loser, and no one likes to be the loser. If you are the one who always wants to win, you can improve your relationship by understanding that your spouse should sometimes have different opinions from yours. Within a marriage, it is a healthy sign when you don't push your spouse to agree with all of your views. If it is your spouse who always has to win, then try showing him or her this section of the book and explaining how you feel. If that doesn't work, your spouse could benefit from counselling. Most people who suffer this need have a deep-rooted sense of insecurity that stems from experiences that occurred long before marriage. Working with a professional could help in a case like this.

Rule #4: Always avoid putting down or undermining your spouse in front of other people, including your children.

Put-downs, even when they're presented as jokes, will only result in anger and resentment in your spouse. Instead of insulting your spouse in front of others, we recommend that you take the opposite approach and talk about what is terrific about your mate. Saying something nice will make your spouse feel good, and it will reflect well on you, too. You can enhance your relationship by being kind and complimentary to your spouse.

It is particularly important not to denigrate or reprimand your spouse in the presence of your children. At times this happens subtly.

As parents you should try to model

appropriate behaviour for your children by expressing respect and support for each other. By arguing in front of the children, you may also put your children in the middle and force them to choose between you and your spouse.

Rule #5:   Focus on the positive.

Thinking of all the things that bother you about your spouse is sometimes easier than concentrating on all the things that make you love each other. Think about what led the two of you to marry. Does he have a great sense of humour? Is she well read and intelligent? Do you love the fact that she's always ready to take on a new challenge? Were you attracted to his kindness? Did you find it easy to be good friends right from the start? Any of these qualities might be easily taken for granted or simply assumed to be part of the person's role in the relationship. Nevertheless, these traits are what make each person special and unique.

Use every available opportunity to compliment your spouse, and when you offer a compliment, use an 'I' statement, such as 'I think you're a wonderful parent.' This way, it is clear to your spouse that the compliment involves something that you believe. Also, look the person in the eye and smile. Finally, give compliments that are genuine so that your spouse will believe you. If you want to compliment your wife for the excellent dinner she served you, you could say, 'I think you made an excellent meal, and I appreciate your hard work.' This clear and direct compliment will make her feel terrific.

Rule #6:   Never try to make your spouse jealous, particularly by flirting with someone else.

This approach may have been effective in junior high school, but when taken by an adult, it becomes destructive and ineffective. Insecure people may flirt to see if they are still desirable, but this will seriously test the trust involved in the relationship and can have many destructive consequences. You've put a lot of time and effort into your marriage up to this point, so don't jeopardize it by flirting. Also, be aware that if your children become aware of your behaviour, they will be extremely upset, and you'll be modelling behaviour that is less than exemplary.

Our society looks down on people who are jealous. In reality, however, many people who are jealous have reason to be upset. If your spouse is flirting with someone else, you have every right to say that his behaviour hurts your feelings. Don't be afraid to talk about how it makes you feel.

Rule #7:   Remember the little gestures that make life special.

Periodically do special things for your spouse such as serving breakfast in bed, giving a back rub, bringing home flowers, or doing whatever else your spouse likes. These small signs of personal thoughtfulness can be more meaningful than expensive gifts.

Think back to the beginning of your relationship and focus on the things that you used to do for your spouse. The special attention you showed and the wonderful feelings you experienced during your courtship should be incorporated into your marriage.

For instance, instead of complaining that your spouse does not treat you as well as he used to, initiate a regular date night, perhaps twice a month, so you can be together and renew your relationship. This small step can lead to things gradually getting better.

Of course, these small demonstrations of affection should be in addition to remembering your spouse's birthday and your anniversary, as well as fulfilling your daily responsibilities.

There are some spouses for whom you will never be able to do enough. These people are unhappy and may need professional help. If you're living with someone like this, try to focus on what originally attracted you to this person and talk to him or her about how things have changed. If you can get your spouse to agree to counselling, alone or for the two of you, you may find that the situation can be improved. Also, if drinking, drug abuse, or mental illness has caused changes in your marriage, look for outside help. Even if your spouse won't attend counselling sessions, you may find relief and support for yourself.

THESE SUGGESTIONS are a few of the most important ones that we have seen used by spouses with strong marriages. We realize that these suggestions require a great deal of work on your part, but the benefits of using them are immeasurable.

chapter four

THE BENEFITS OF AN EXTENDED FAMILY

MARRIAGE DOES NOT just unite two individuals; it joins two different families. A common attitude in our society is that a marriage is strictly 'my business and not my parents' business'. This view is unrealistic because you are going to be interacting with your family and your spouse's family throughout your married life. In addition, your children are related to both families, and it is far better if all of you get along.

In-laws can be a great source of support, pitching in to help when needed, or just being friends to you and your kids. Many children's most cherished moments are spent with their grandparents. Many others identify with their grandparents and learn values and standards from them.

In-laws, however, can also be a source of stress in a marriage, particularly if they are critical of you or of the decisions you make for your family.

Ideally, before you were married, both of you got to meet and be approved by the other set of parents. Many people think that getting parental approval before marriage is old-fashioned and insulting, but even though it may not seem important initially, it will affect the marriage eventually. If your parents disapprove of your spouse, or if your in-laws don't like you, their disapproval will have an impact on your marriage because it will create family tension. This tension will filter down to your children, who will pick up immediately on the strained relationship.

If you find yourself in a situation where relationships are strained, talk it over with a trusted friend or mental health professional and come up with some solution. There is almost always something that can be done to make things better within the extended family.

BUILDING A STRONG RELATIONSHIP WITH IN-LAWS

Even if you have been married for a time, continue to work at getting to know your in-laws and always be considerate of them. Take the time to create a unique relationship with your in-laws, regardless of how you feel about your own parents.

The key to making any relationship work is good communication. If you have a problem with your in-laws, you should talk to them directly but tactfully. Don't put your spouse in the middle of the situation. This isn't fair to him or his parents.

Holidays are often a time of serious family stress, and families who manage them most successfully have generally developed a fair system of rotating where they spend the holidays. This helps to build family goodwill.

You must also be conscious of what you convey to your children about both sets of grandparents. All generations deserve the opportunity to build a relationship without the interference of other emotional messages.

Sometimes extended families encounter stress because of differences of opinion over child-rearing. Always remember that you do have the ultimate say about how your child is raised, and you should not go against your beliefs simply to make your in-laws happy. For example, if you know your in-laws believe in spanking, let them know before they take your child for the weekend that you do not want your child to be punished in that way. (Be respectful but firm when you make this request.) Be clear and state your reasons. If they cannot abide by your rules, you may have to limit their access to your child when you aren't present.

CREATING BONDS WITH OTHER MEMBERS OF THE EXTENDED FAMILY

Aunts, uncles and cousins can also provide social and emotional support for you and your children. This type of support is valuable and can enhance the mental health of all individuals, especially children. Unfortunately, many children see their relatives only at holidays or family reunions or talk to them on the phone occasionally. Not surprisingly, children have often told us that they wish they had more access to relatives.

Loneliness is common in our society. Our research shows that loneliness is reported by children as young as eight years old. Increasing contact with extended family members may be one way to help combat loneliness. While friends may drift away, relatives will always be there, since family relationships are more enduring.

Relationships with extended family members can teach a child how to get along with other people and work out problems. If your child gets into an argument with a cousin, you can use this as an opportunity to demonstrate how to solve problems. Resist stepping in to defend your child and instead point out ways that both children can compromise. Even if the cousin is bad news, encourage your child to be as nice as possible. In so doing, you demonstrate the virtues of forgiving. Later on, if you feel that your child was in the right, you can explain that for you a strong family value is to sacrifice, resisting the impulse to get even.

Despite the benefits of living near relatives, our society is becoming increasingly mobile, and it is common for families to move often. The ideal is to have both friends and family surrounding you.

RECONSIDERING FAMILY NORMS

Typically when a child turns eighteen or so, she moves out of her parents' home to make her own life. This process is thought to help a person become mature and independent. However, a number of factors make it increasingly unattractive for young adults to live on their own. In our work, we hear a lot about loneliness from adult children, parents and grandparents. Loneliness, sadness and anxiety are common feelings in people who live on their own and are unhappy. Unfortunately, many people in our society look down on or ridicule adults who live with their parents.

INTERGENERATIONAL GIVING

Sacrificing for our spouse, our children, our parents and our relatives is an important family value. Our society is preoccupied with assertiveness and getting your rights, but society would be better served if individuals considered the needs of others. How can we help? What can we do? What can we say that will make others feel good about themselves?

If we willingly do things for others, without feeling cheated or taken advantage of, the following things will happen:

➤ Our children will learn from our example.

➤ Our children will be the recipients of the love we are demonstrating, and as a result, they will feel well cared for and fulfilled rather than deprived.

➤ An increasing number of people will reciprocate, and consequently we will feel loved.

➤ By establishing closer relationships, we will gain love and support in our lives and in our careers.

➤ If we can be generous with others without feeling cheated, we will no longer harbour chronic anger, which can cause health problems. (People who feel less angry have a stronger immune system and have fewer physical illnesses.)

ALTHOUGH OUR society is perceived as wealthy, if we are not willing to sacrifice for the well-being of our family, then we are truly poor. Parents must make family the number one priority in their lives. If they do so, the likelihood of their children turning out well and reaching their potential is very high. Sacrificing for your children and your extended family should be a pleasure, and in return, you will raise children who will want to maintain strong family bonds.

chapter five

THE FAMILY GUIDE METHOD FOR COPING WITH STRESS

BEING A PARENT is one of the most stressful and demanding jobs a person can have. Parents encounter all the same challenges any other person faces – problems with a boss, colleagues, neighbours and relatives; financial difficulties; and health concerns. Added to all this, of course, they face the problems of any family, from an unexpected trip to the paediatrician because a child is sick to an out-and-out blowup with a teenager. All parents face stress at home over which they have very little control.

Stress is a perfectly normal, automatic reaction to a demand or a change. There are good forms of stress of course: our ability to rise to challenges, for example, grows out of a stress reaction. Too often, however, stress is negative because, when there is little relief from the stress, it can affect your mental and physical health. Stress can lead to headaches, high blood pressure, digestive problems, backaches, sleeping difficulties and other problems, including general irritability.

The key to managing stress is coping with the day-to-day problems that occur in life. While serious problems are best discussed with a counsellor, a clergy member, or a mental health professional, most people prefer to solve their problems themselves – but often they don't know how. As a result, their stress levels continue to build. The best solution is to face each problem directly and try to deal with it effectively. That's what this chapter is about.

FIVE STEPS FOR COPING WITH STRESS

The following strategies are presented as questions to ask yourself. Each one is accompanied by suggestions that will help you find the reasons for your stress. If you follow these instructions, you will be able to pinpoint and deal with stress. To begin, you'll need a pen and paper.

1. What *is* the problem?

If you've been feeling stress but aren't sure why, then you need to determine the cause. Examine honestly what you are worried about right now. Consider any problem that comes into your mind and write it down, no matter how trivial. Most people have many things – both serious and trivial – on their minds so feel free to list everything that's bothering you.

After writing down your problems, consider each one separately. As you work through the list, you may find that some of them interrelate. For example, perhaps you're irritated at your son because he's always late getting ready for school, and that

in turn makes you late to work, which is making your boss mad. Therefore, if your son gets ready on time, other problems will be solved as well.

2. What *might* happen to me and what is the *worst* that might happen to me?

Select the problem that seems to be the root of your current anxiety and write down all the possible outcomes to the problem. (While you may be tempted to do this in your head, you really must write it down. If you do this only as a mental exercise, you will go through this too quickly, and your feelings of uneasiness are likely to stay with you.) Again, let your mind be free and try to think of as many different consequences as possible. Some of your worries and fears may seem very silly, but write them down anyway. Although you are looking at only one problem, try to think of several negative outcomes, including the worst possible thing that could happen. Writing down everything will help you relax and gain peace of mind because you will have confronted your worst fears.

Your next task is to evaluate the likelihood that the outcomes you've noted will occur. You might even assign a rating – say 1 to 100 – for the probability of each consequence.

In most cases, you'll discover that most negative outcomes are not very likely. This fact, by itself, may automatically help to decrease your stress or anxiety because you will realize that your fears have been exaggerated.

3. What was my role in the development of this problem?

Be honest with yourself concerning your role in the problem. Don't try to minimize or exaggerate your contribution or simply blame the problem on someone else. Again, write down as many different ideas as you can. Also write down all of the things that you have done wrong. This will provide a list of actions to avoid in the future if you are again in a similar situation.

Once you admit your mistake, don't blame yourself or get angry at yourself for creating the problem. You should be a noncritical observer of yourself. Mistakes are a part of life, part of development, part of learning, and your job is to be supportive of yourself. Tell yourself that you are okay and that you have made a mistake but that you will probably not make that mistake again. Give yourself a second chance (or third) and remind yourself that you are only human. As time goes by, you will make this particular mistake less and less often.

Self-acceptance is vital to our well-being. How can you teach your children to be gentle with themselves if you are not gentle with yourself?

4. What are the solutions to the problem, and what are my alternatives?

This is your chance to troubleshoot and fantasize freely. Write down every solution you can think of that might improve your current situation. Some solutions are easier than others, but you should include all of the possibilities. As you go through your list you'll see that some of your fantasy solutions

(murdering your boss; bashing the face of your child's teacher) are unreasonable, and ultimately, you'll need to stay with the more practical possibilities (looking for a new job; scheduling a meeting with the principal to discuss the teacher's treatment of your child).

5. What actions should I take?

Critically evaluate the possible solutions that you have listed and decide which ones would be most likely to result in the outcome you want. There may be more than one way to solve a problem. Pick one or more changes that best suit your needs and then take the steps necessary to solve the problem.

You may find that you can't do much about a particular problem. For example, if your mother is in an advanced stage of cancer, your chances of bringing about a successful resolution will be limited. Of course you can spend as much time as possible with her, do things for her and make her life as pleasant as possible for the next few months or years, but you also have to accept that your mother is going to die and there is little you can do about it. Facing this reality may be painful, but it will help you manage your stress, because it will permit you to focus your energies on what you can do to be helpful. In the future you will never feel bad that you did not do your best.

WHENEVER YOU run into problems or feel a great deal of stress, take a few minutes and complete the steps outlined above. Remember, thinking them through in your head is not enough. There are two benefits to writing everything down: It slows the process, and this helps you think more clearly. It also allows you to gain a certain degree of perspective on the problem.

When you have more than one problem, you should tackle each problem separately and write down the five steps for each problem.

STRESS RELIEVERS FOR EVERY DAY

The five-step coping method outlined above is ideal to use when you know exactly what is causing your stress or anxiety. However, sometimes you may have general stress that cannot be eliminated right now. For example, you may not be able to reduce the amount of work you have at your job without quitting, and thereby risking more stress, or you may have other life stresses that just aren't going to go away anytime soon – a sick spouse, for example, high college bills for a child, or minor but annoying health problems of your own.

The following suggestions have been found helpful in managing everyday stress. Use whichever of these recommendations work best for you.

1. Exercise. Try to exercise three times a week for twenty or thirty minutes to help relieve stress. Evidence indicates that during exercise, a chemical called endorphin is released in your brain that causes your body to feel more relaxed.

2. Participate in pleasant activities. Sometimes people forget to have fun. Take time out from your hectic schedule to do things you enjoy that are stress-free. You might listen to music, do craft work, take pho-tographs, watch movies, read a good book or magazine, spend time with a friend, or go to a concert.

3. Pay attention to your health. You need to take care of your body to help minimize the effects of stress. Get enough sleep, eat well and practise good hygiene. You should also get regular medical checkups.

4. Employ time-management skills. If you are well organized, you will feel that your life is under your control. Make a daily list of every-thing you want and need to accomplish. Prioritize the tasks for each day and avoid working on too many projects at once. To avoid becoming overburdened, learn how to say no when people ask you to do additional or unnecessary work. Schedule enough time between appointments to prepare or to get where you need to go.

5. Express yourself. Express your feelings and opinions and cry when you need to cry. Scream when you need to scream (but not at your children). Don't make a habit of being unemotional, or you'll find that pent-up emotion will spill out inappropriately.

6. Ask for support. Turn to your spouse, children, relatives and friends for support. Talk to them when you are stressed. At the same time, avoid people who pull you down or make you feel bad.

7. Realize that you don't have to be perfect. Once you have relieved yourself of this burden, you'll find that life is more manage-able. Also, if your expectations are more reasonable, you won't often be disappointed in yourself.

8. Anticipate situations that will cause stress and do what you can to avoid them. If you know certain things drive you crazy, try not to get involved!

People find many different ways to handle stress, so experiment to see what works for you.

HELPING YOUR CHILDREN COPE WITH STRESS

Certainly by the time your children are teenagers, they can be taught to use the five-step method for themselves. (This method is not recommended for use with young children or preadolescents because the necessary writing and self-evaluation skills are too advanced for them to use effectively. However, preadolescents can learn the method gradually if an adult assists the child at each step.)

If your teenager comes to you with a school problem, ask her to describe the problem and to explain why she is concerned. To help her effectively you need to be noncritical and supportive as she talks through her problem. (For younger children, the process of writing it down is too daunting; talking it through with you will be helpful.) Ask about possible solutions and possible outcomes. Then help her select the best solutions and take action to solve the problem. Your child may not be able to complete all of the steps, but she will learn to stop and think before she reacts to a difficult situation. This ability is important and will help her confront and change troublesome situations in the future.

ALLEVIATING STRESS is particularly important for parents because it's difficult if not impossible to be a functional parent if you are feeling tense and anxious much of the time. Encountering stress is perfectly normal, but how you deal with the situation will make the difference in the outcome.

part two

PARENTING WISELY
FROM DAY TO DAY

chapter six

BRINGING OUT THE BEST IN YOUR CHILDREN

OUR PARENTS, our grandparents and the parents we have become all share one common goal: Bringing out the best in our children so that they can live happy and fulfilling lives.

For that reason, we start this section with the fun of parenting – all that you need to know to encourage your child to grow up to be a polite, independent, empathetic person who makes friends easily. In the process, your efforts will come full circle, and one day your children will be great parents, too.

This chapter, Bringing Out the Best in Your Children, includes:

Fulfilling the Basic Needs of Children

Being a Positive Role Model

Teaching Social Skills

Building Self-Esteem

Helping the Shy Child

Developing Creativity

Encouraging Competence

Fostering Independence

Nurturing Responsibility

Advocating Empathy

Preparing Your Child for Parenthood

Fulfilling the Basic Needs of Children

To be a good parent you need to understand your child's feelings and try to meet her needs. This isn't quite as easy as it sounds because some of the things children want and need are unique to being a child. Though you went through these stages at one time, it isn't always easy to remember what it felt like to be age five. Here are some of the things that make a child feel well cared for.

1. Children need to be respected. Show your respect by listening to your child when she is telling a story, talking about her day, or expressing an opinion, even if it differs from yours. It's not always easy to tune in to your child at the end of the day, but it's one of the most important things you can do.

2. Children need to be liked and loved. This is usually easy. Every kid we've ever met has likeable qualities. Find those characteristics and focus on them. Praise your child at every opportunity and tell her that you love her – say it several times a day. There are many ways to show a child affection, but parents are sometimes so busy and so overwhelmed by their own lives that they forget to express their love to their kids.

3. Children need to feel approved of and accepted by others. Approval and acceptance are the foundation of self-esteem and self-concept (how the child views himself). Because parents have the earliest influence on the development of a child's opinion of himself, they need to express love and offer praise. When your child misbehaves, you must separate the behaviour from the child. If you catch your fifteen-year-old daughter smoking a cigarette with some friends, you can certainly disapprove of the behaviour, but don't disapprove of your child. Even during the roughest times, it's important to convey understanding and support for your child.

4. Children are naturally self-centred. The infant is totally absorbed in his own needs; the nursery school child does not yet have the maturity to understand the feelings of others; and anyone who has ever seen a teenager react to a new pimple realizes that even at this age an enormous amount of energy is going into worrying about oneself. This egocentric behaviour lessens gradually, however, and as an individual matures, the capacity for empathy increases.

5. Children need time to play and to fantasize. Some adults regard play as a waste of time, but play is actually constructive for a young one. Kids learn through experimentation, and in play they learn to cooperate and to play by the rules. The companionship and pleasure of being with others and the excitement and learning that occur during play are also key elements in the development of a healthy child.

6. Children need to feel special. They feel more secure and loved when they feel that they bring a unique quality to the family. Always emphasize the accomplishments of each child, even if they aren't earth-shattering. For example, one child might be a great cook while another can stand on her head. Praise each generously.

7. Sibling rivalry is perfectly normal. To modify it, you need to be sure each child has private time with you and is made to understand her special role in the family. When you are with one child, focus on her achievements. A child may feel that you love a sibling more if you talk about or praise the other child more frequently. Parents should avoid favouritism and resist comparing children, as this breeds rivalry. Also be careful not to criticize one child while giving another child a compliment – 'You're a better cook than your sister.'

8. Children have real fears, worries and anxieties. The first fear many kids have is separation anxiety, and this fear may gradually transform itself into fear of the dark, animals, monsters and other things. Listen to your child and take her fears and worries seriously. Offer her reassurance and comfort.

9. Children tend to blame themselves unnecessarily. Since children are egocentric and assume that they are the centre of the world, they may think that when something bad happens it's their fault. Remember to reassure your youngster, even when something really was his responsibility. After all, breaking a plate by accident is very different from doing so on purpose, which is generally not the case. Reassure him that everything will be okay and that you know he didn't mean to do it.

IF YOU TRY to understand your child's needs and take them seriously, you'll be less irritated and more accepting of your child's behaviour. As a result, your youngster will be more likely to share his feelings and emotions with you. In the long run, you'll find that this is the cornerstone of a healthy parent-child relationship.

Being a Positive Role Model

Read the entries in the remainder of this chapter and refer also to Chapter 9, Parental Issues.

Observing and imitating role models can be a powerful source of learning for children. Children are more likely to imitate the behaviour of people they consider admirable, powerful, or similar to them, and as a result, they are most likely to imitate parents, teachers and other adults who are part of their lives.

This learning starts at birth and happens every day. Children watch us constantly, even when we're not closely watching our own behaviour.

Parents often want to know how they can make sure they are suitable role models for their children. The answer lies in making sure that your actions uphold the standards you set. This isn't always easy. For example, if you tell your child that smoking cigarettes is a health risk, you shouldn't smoke. And if you stress to your children the importance of not lying, it's important that you always tell the truth.

Modelling excellence is also key to helping a child develop those qualities. For example, you should be kind and willing to help other people and look for ways constantly to demonstrate this. By being a good role model, you will also influence your child's family values, religious beliefs, financial values, education and work ethic. Remember that children usually agree with and espouse most of their parents' values, particularly if they are proud of their family and feel like an integral part of it. Additionally, your child's values and beliefs will add to the strength of the family.

Although your child may follow in your footsteps and hold some of your values and beliefs, he will not do so completely. For this reason, being a role model involves demonstrating your own values and beliefs but being open to your child's values and beliefs, too. This will encourage an open and respectful attitude, and in the process, you may learn some valuable lessons from your child.

Teaching Social Skills

(Refer also to Nurturing Responsibility, p. 49; Advocating Empathy, p. 50; Speaking So Your Child Will Listen, p. 68; and Saying You're Sorry, p. 85.)

Social skills are the specific actions and rules people use when interacting with others – the things that make people feel comfortable with you, because you help them feel comfortable about themselves.

There are no classes in social skills. Youngsters need to see these skills modelled by the adults in their lives, and they need plenty of opportunity to practise them. The first time you introduce your preschooler to an old friend of yours, she won't have any idea how to behave. With some practice and some demonstrations by you, however, even a three-year-old can learn to look the new acquaintance directly in the eye,

extend a hand to be shaken and say, 'I'm pleased to meet you.' They learn all other social skills the same way – everything from answering the phone properly to using interesting speech patterns in conversation – by watching you and by practising the observed behaviour.

Perhaps the most important social skill that parents should teach is politeness. From the beginning, children should be encouraged to say 'thank you', 'please' and 'excuse me'. Most kids learn rapidly, especially if you praise them when they display appropriate good manners. Apologizing when one has done something wrong is also crucial. Be sure to model apologetic behaviour with your children (parents sometimes neglect to do this). If you've hurt her feelings or accidentally broken something she loved, say you're sorry. She'll learn it's important because you do it.

Making others feel good about themselves is an important social skill that people sometimes forget about. By teaching your child that compliments brighten other people's day, you'll find that the goodwill created generally comes back to you and your child. Most kids are warm, loving people who like to make others happy. By teaching them to give compliments, you're playing into their natural abilities. The first step in teaching this skill is to compliment your child. Be generous with your appreciative comments to others as well. For example, at dinner, compliment your spouse on the food she prepared, and when your mum arrives at your home in a new dress, tell her you think she looks great in it.

Carrying on a good conversation is sometimes difficult for both adults and kids. One way to encourage discussion is to ask open-ended questions that can't be answered with a simple yes or no. For instance, you might ask your child, 'What did you like about _____ (his or her favourite book)?' Eventually you may hear your child ask a friend, 'What do you like about _____ (the latest popular television show)?' instead of just 'Do you like _____?'

Good conversationalists don't just talk, they also listen, and listening and responding carefully to your child will teach this important skill.

Friendship, like a good conversation, is based on give-and-take, and children who learn good social skills will find it easier to find and keep friends. What's more, socially competent people are happier, probably because social support is essential to good health.

MODELLING A SPECIFIC SKILL

Children aren't born with good social skills, but don't be put off by the thought that you may have to teach explicitly some of the skills with which your child has difficulty. Let's look at how you would teach a shy child to make a request of an adult.

1. Define the skill. In this case, making a request is the skill, so let's say that your child was absent when the class went to the library and would like to ask her teacher for permission to go to the library and return her books.

2. Demonstrate the skill for your child. Pretend you are the child and your child is the teacher. You might ask, 'Ms. Richards, ı. please take my books to the library later this morning, since I was absent yesterday?' Be sure to model good eye contact and clear enunciation.

3. Have your child practise the skill. Pretend you are the teacher and let her ask the question. Tell her that this is just a practice and that she shouldn't be nervous.

4. Praise your child and make helpful suggestions. Start with compliments and point out to her what she did correctly. Perhaps your child spoke clearly and said the correct words, but if she looked down as she asked, you need to encourage her to make eye contact in order to master this skill. Frame your corrections as 'things we need to work on more'. For example, you could say, 'Wow, Joan! You did a great job of speaking clearly. I could understand everything you said. Now we can work on helping you look directly at the person you're talking to. Let's try it again.' Practise as many times as necessary, until she feels comfortable performing the skill. Encourage your child to try out the same skill – making a request – with other people. The next day, ask if she was able to make her request of the teacher. Praise her for her efforts when she has done so.

ULTIMATELY, the most important thing you can do to help your child acquire good social skills is to act as a role model by treating everyone you encounter with respect. If your child accompanies you to the supermarket, thank the person who bags your groceries. Listen attentively when you are youngster and speak to her ... ay you would to any good ... out other people with good ... and ask your child how he felt ... ng with this person. You may soon ... that your child displays the social skills of a future ambassador.

Building Self-Esteem

(Also see Helping the Shy Child, p. 44; Finding Quality Time, p. 53; Taking Special Joy in Parenting, p. 95; What to Do When You Dislike Your Child, p. 95; Avoiding Favouritism, p. 106; Putting an End to Scapegoating, p. 108.)

Self-esteem (respect for yourself) is one of the most important components of mental health. Our own research has shown a relationship between self-esteem and lack of psychiatric disorders. A recent study found that well-adjusted adolescents with high self-esteem were more likely to be free from psychiatric disorders and symptoms, reported significantly fewer stressful life events and had a greater number of people in their social support group than did adolescents with lower self-esteem. Adolescents with high self-esteem also reported less sadness and more pleasant emotions, were less inhibited and forceful and were more confident and respectful than other adolescents – all excellent building blocks for good mental health in adulthood.

HELPING TO BOOST SELF-ESTEEM

1. Make your child feel wanted. This strategy should begin as early as possible, but it's never too late to start. Repeatedly tell the child that since she was born, your life has never been better. Tell your child that you are happy to have him and that he is a source of great joy.

2. Cultivate a genuine respect for your child. Don't assume that children aren't capable of doing very much. If you pay attention, you'll be amazed at how much a toddler can do and how much little ones understand. Always treat a child with the same amount of respect and care that you expect him to give to you.

3. Set aside time to be with your child and attend his or her activities, performances and games. This will make your child feel special and deserving of attention. Education is particularly important, of course, so be sure to attend parents' night and other school activities.

4. Consider the age of the child when looking for praiseworthy milestones. Tasks that are simple for one age are very difficult for another. For example, a five-year-old's major new challenge is to go to school and stay there without crying. If you've got older children, this may not seem like much of an accomplishment, but if you're only five, it's an important milestone. Praise your child for everything that he does well – going willingly to school, greeting the teacher and letting you go without clinging or crying. If you praise him for what he does well, he will make more rapid progress.

5. Provide opportunities for your child to succeed. Create situations in which your child can achieve. Ask him to help you cook dinner and praise him for each small success such as stirring the batter or cracking the eggs. Doing well in small undertakings will allow your child to develop a sense of self-mastery, an important component of self-esteem.

6. Pay attention to your child's achievements. When your child tells you about something she did, listen carefully and praise her accordingly. Let her know how pleased you are with her. Tell other people about these accomplishments in front of her. For example, if your child received an A on a maths test, call your relatives and brag about it.

7. Tell positive stories about your child to others. Never make critical or sarcastic comments about your child to others as those comments will undercut his self-esteem.

8. Don't dwell on your child's mistakes. Discuss the problem briefly with your child and let her know that she made a mistake. Tell her that she can learn from mistakes and shouldn't be worried about them or ashamed of them. If she makes the same mistake again, say gently, 'You must have been so busy with other things that you didn't realize what you were doing. I'm sure that you won't make that mistake again.' Let your child learn from mistakes, even if it takes a while.

9. Downplay negative evaluations. If your child receives a bad grade, don't get upset or yell. Instead, discuss with your child what is difficult about school and try to fix that problem. It is hard for children to separate themselves from their behaviour, and if you get upset, your child will think she is bad.

10. Give your child an opportunity to state his case when the two of you disagree. Show your child that disagreements are a time for both people to voice their opinions calmly and decide which is best. This awareness can be very powerful and can increase a child's self-concept and help him trust his judgment.

11. Accept and approve of your child without question. No child is perfect, and there will be times when your child doesn't measure up to your expectations. However, withdrawing your love and approval would be counterproductive. You must constantly provide your youngster with a reason (your constant faith in him) to believe he can do better. Adolescence is a particularly trying time for parents when it comes to accepting a child's sense of self. Your teenager is working to form her identity, and she may do things you disapprove of. While you need to be watchful concerning unsafe behaviour, try to tolerate acts of rebellion like changes in hairstyles and clothing. Accepting your teenager will improve her self-esteem and give her greater faith in her own judgment, increasing the likelihood that she will steer away from risky behaviour.

12. Share good news with your child. Whenever you hear something good about your child from friends, neighbours, relatives, or other children, share the news with her. If your neighbour compliments you because your child never leaves toys on the pavement, pass the praise along to your child.

Keep up this practice even after your child becomes an adult.

Parenting a child who feels good about herself is a joy in itself; you'll find your own self-esteem rising because she finds such pleasure in being alive.

Helping the Shy Child

(See also Teaching Social Skills, p. 40; Building Self-Esteem, p. 42; Fostering Independence, p. 48; Overcoming Fears, p. 117.)

Shyness is very common in childhood and usually manifests itself in general discomfort in classroom and social situations. Shy kids shun the spotlight and hate to be the centre of attention. In the classroom they are unlikely to volunteer or speak out loud. Being quiet and avoiding eye contact, they rationalize, will make them more invisible and less likely to draw unwelcome attention to themselves. Because of their timid behaviour, shy kids are not normally picked on or openly rejected, but they are often ignored and neglected.

Some kids gradually outgrow their shyness. They may encounter a teacher who helps draw them out, or sometimes they are befriended by another not-quite-so-shy child and together the two of them gain social confidence.

Close relationships with peers and a feeling of belonging are essential for good mental health. Rather than waiting for your child to outgrow it, take the following steps to show your child that it's safe to put oneself forward to make friends.

1. Talk frequently with your child about his strengths and praise his achievements. Underlying the shyness is generally a fear of rejection, so the more you can do to make your child feel acceptable, the more likely he is to open up and be less shy. If children feel good about themselves, they will be more likely to assume that others will like them.

2. Create a comfortable, safe atmosphere. Try not to criticize your child and be patient with him if it takes time for him to warm up to situations.

3. Be an attentive listener. Sometimes kids don't talk much because they think that what they say is unimportant. Give your child your full attention when she wants to discuss something and comment appropriately. Avoid dismissive remarks like 'I'm sure everything will be okay, sweetheart.' Make comments that validate her experience: 'You must have really been surprised when that happened!'

4. Provide frequent hugs. Shy kids are often self-conscious about or uncomfortable with their bodies. Hugging and touching your child conveys the message that he is likeable and attractive.

5. Don't ridicule your child for being shy. Like many other parents, you may be embarrassed when your five-year-old stands behind you, rather than stepping forward to meet his new teacher, but don't cover your own embarrassment with teasing or ridicule. Shy kids fear criticism and rejection, so any harsh comments will simply make the situation worse. Don't say things like 'Come on, say hello – don't be so shy.' That will only make a shy child feel less likely to talk.

6. Help your child develop good grooming habits. Make sure that your child looks good each day. This will make him more appealing to others.

7. Help your child develop good social skills. The child who has had opportunities to practise meeting new people and conversing with adults will be better prepared to get along with others, despite her shyness.

8. Help your child increase his social circle. Shy kids frequently don't know how to make friends. Introduce him to neighbourhood children or to the children of your own friends and invite them to play. Over time, your child may feel more comfortable and find that he really enjoys some of the kids.

Signing your child up for a sports team or an after-school club will also expose her to more people. Ask her for suggestions. If your school puts out a brochure about after-school activities, read through it together and let your child pick one to try. If your child is reluctant to join any clubs or teams, make a deal with her. Insist that she attend at least five meetings or practices; then she can decide whether to continue or quit.

9. Discuss your child's shyness with her teacher. The teacher will be able to tell you how your child is faring at school and will almost surely help you find ways to draw her out.

10. Be a good role model. Shy kids may have parents who are shy or socially isolated. If necessary, follow our guidelines yourself to help you become less shy or make more friends. If you're in a new community and all of you are struggling a bit, you can approach this as a family project.

Developing Creativity

(See also Understanding the Importance of Play, p. 56.)

Creativity, the ability to innovate or discover new ways of doing things, is a wonderful quality in a child. It ranks neck-and-neck with intelligence in terms of helping a person create a life for herself. Creativity and intelligence aren't always linked, however. Some very bright kids aren't creative and some who struggled through maths and English in school are among the most creative people in the country.

Like intelligence, creativity can be influenced by the environment in which a child is raised. A child raised in an enriched environment is more likely to be creative because he has been encouraged and provided with the necessary resources. However, creativity can also come about in children who had no encouragement and who therefore had to be innovative in order to create a place for themselves.

Keep in mind that in developing your child's creativity, you're not necessarily trying to create the next Shakespeare or Rembrandt. You're simply trying to instill in your child the ability to see that life is filled with many possibilities, not just right and wrong answers.

Children who are creative have four basic

qualities, according to G. Cornelius and J. Casler in an issue of *Early Child Development and Care:*

1. A sense of wonder about the world. This can be encouraged by expressing wonder yourself. Take your child on walking trips, to the park or to any other places to explore and appreciate the world. And express your own joy when you see or hear something wonderful – a glorious sunset, perhaps, or an electrifying concert by a children's folksinger.

2. An openness to feelings and emotions. By being open about how you feel you convey an important message to your child. Often parents think that boys have to be little tough guys who don't express their feelings. Fortunately this attitude is slowly changing, and today's parents see the benefits of encouraging both boys and girls to be in touch with their feelings.

3. Curiosity. You can nurture your child's curiosity by encouraging her to ask questions and by expressing curiosity yourself. Then share with your child the fun of investigating something. Point out to your child how she can use all her senses when exploring. If you go to the beach, talk about how the beach looks, what you hear, how the sand and wind feel and even how the air tastes. Ask about what details she notices and probe if you see that she's missed something, such as the squishy feel of the wet sand between her toes.

4. Imagination. Make up stories together. You start one and let him finish it; next time let him start the story and you finish. You'll soon find that this is a lot of fun, and it can also get

you through a long wait at the paediatrician's office.

ENCOURAGING CREATIVITY starts with early parental tolerance, whether your child is experimenting with discordant noises on a toy piano or spending a long time putting dabs of muddy sand all around the sandbox. Parents who raise creative children are those who let them explore and experiment from the very start.

Time is the next ingredient in raising creative children – time spent reading and playing with them. By reading, you expose your child to other people's flights of fantasy; in playing together, you can draw out his personal creativity by encouraging him to imagine or innovate on his own. In addition, when you spend more time with your child you'll see what things interest her.

When your child is involved in a creative endeavour, offer praise and be specific. If he writes a story about a rabbit named Dolliver, don't just say, 'What a nice story.' Say something like, 'I love the name you chose for the rabbit. What a creative boy you are.' This response shows that you are paying attention to details of the story, and chances are your child will work very hard to come up with interesting names for all of his characters from now on.

Also look beyond traditional creative endeavours to catch your child being creative. For example, your daughter may be the only one in the house who can fix the vacuum cleaner when it's clogged. Tell her that it takes creative thinking to solve any type of problem and that you appreciate her creative approach to problem-solving. Similarly, praise your son's creativity when you're baking together and he suggests using raisins instead of chocolate chips in a cookie recipe.

Find 'real life' ways for your child to be creative, whether it's making a patchwork quilt, laying out your garden, creating birthday cards for family members, or decorating his own room with his collection of baseball paraphernalia. Let your child experiment through things that are practical and that he can share with others.

Helping develop your child's creativity is one of the greatest gifts you can give, and in the process, you may find some wonderfully imaginative parts of yourself, too.

Encouraging Competence

(See also Fostering Independence, p. 48; Nurturing Responsibility, p. 49.)

A competent child can manage a specific skill or challenge. Areas of competence grow one by one; a child may be competent at schoolwork but not yet competent to baby-sit for his sister, for example. Competent children can solve problems if they are allowed to think about them and tackle them on their own.

You can help your child develop competence by encouraging him when he tries new things. For example, when an infant tries to walk for the first time, you can give him a lot of verbal praise. Clap for him and say, 'Wow! You're trying to walk! That's great!' When an older child is learning to ride a bike, you could run alongside her, providing reassurance and encouragement. As soon as

a milestone has been reached, you should take pictures and offer praise. This encouragement will motivate her to try to succeed with the current task and future ones.

Focus on your child's success and not her failure when she is trying something for the first time. When you take your child on her first fishing trip, don't comment on the fact that she didn't catch any fish. Instead, praise her for sitting so quietly (a learned skill in fishing) or for the way she casts the line into the water.

Children who succeed will continue to look for new challenges. You can help instill feelings of success by asking your youngster to do things that you know she can do, with a little effort. For example, if your child knows how to read well, ask her to read a bedtime story to her little brother.

CAREFUL TEACHING INCREASES COMPETENCE

Some parents expect their children to learn how to do things by simply watching them. However, kids often need more explicit instructions for complex tasks. When teaching your child a new skill, you should follow this five-step process:

1. Be sure your child is dressed appropriately for the activity – in a helmet for biking, for example. Then define and explain the task.
2. Demonstrate the task.
3. Have your child practise. Make this practice session as risk-free as possible. If it's a first bike ride, for example, use a dead-end street or a school playground

where a fall will be less dangerous than on a busy street. Restrain yourself from giving unwanted advice; wait for your child to ask for your help, and when she does, you might say, 'You're doing fine.'

4. Praise your child for whatever she did right.
5. Tell your child how to improve her performance and have her practise again.

If you are teaching your child how to crack an egg and add it to biscuit batter, you would take these five steps:

1. Have your child wash his hands and put on an apron. Then explain that to break an egg successfully, you must tap the egg with enough force to crack the shell but not so much force that it shatters. Then you must gently pull apart the two halves of the shell while pouring the egg into the bowl.
2. Demonstrate the process.
3. Ask your child to try breaking the egg into an empty bowl. This establishes a risk-free situation; if he does drop bits of shell into the mixture, the other ingredients aren't ruined.
4. Praise whatever he did properly: 'That was great! The tap of the egg was perfect.'
5. Give instructions as to how the child can do the job better: 'Try not to squeeze so hard when you pull the egg apart.' Then ask him to try it again.

As you work, point out that adults make mistakes and show how an adult would salvage the batter if some pieces of eggshell dropped into it. (Use a spoon to fish out bits of shell.) Let your child become the resident egg-breaker for all recipes that you make. The continual practice will help him master the skill and having an official role in food preparation will instill pride.

AS YOUR CHILD gets older, remember that competence in life skills is as important as an A in maths. Children can gain competence and confidence by doing things on their own, so resist doing things for them. It's surprising how many young adults, on their own for the first time, don't know how to do laundry, iron clothes, or shop for groceries. Let your adolescents learn to do things for themselves. You may be surprised how handy those skills can be when your son or daughter can fix breakfast for a sibling or run to the shop to pick up a few things for you! What's more, it's good for your child, too.

Fostering Independence

(See also Encouraging Competence, p. 47; Nurturing Responsibility p. 49.)

Independence comes naturally to most children. It's generally the adults who have a difficult time accepting it. Some parents are overprotective and seem reluctant to let go. Others may send a child off to camp without consulting the child and then ignore letters about homesickness, saying 'She'll get over it.' Somewhere between these two extremes is a happy medium, and you can achieve it simply by listening to your child.

By listening, it's likely you'll pick up many cues as to when to let your child be more independent in certain areas. Most children are very vocal and make specific requests. For example, a three-year-old may want to use the bathroom alone, and a seven-year-old may want to walk alone to a friend's house. A sixteen-year-old will want to drive the car unaccompanied by his parents.

You know best when your youngster is ready to tackle a new situation. Try to be realistic and not over- or underestimate individual abilities. When your child is ready to take on a new task, be her coach and help her accomplish the goal. Let's say that your six-year-old has been invited to sleep over at a friend's house, but she's a little nervous about it. To prepare her for it, arrange for her to stay at Grandma's house to practise first. You might also suggest that the two girls simply spend the evening together. Your daughter can have dinner with the other family and you can pick her up at 9:00 P.M. The next time it's likely she'll be ready to stay the whole night. Like so many other things children must accomplish, this one task – sleeping at someone else's home – is a vital stepping-stone to independence.

Every child is different and you have to respect those differences. Pushing children to undertake tasks for which they aren't ready can cause problems. Consider a typical family stressor like schoolwork. You may believe that homework should be done in the child's bedroom, but your child would rather work in the kitchen, asking questions as needed. If you push your point, homework can become a battleground. Instead, compromise. She can work in the kitchen where you are, but she'll try to do as much as she can on her own. If you come up with a solution that provides a comfortable and secure atmosphere, your child will naturally come to need you less and less. Together you'll arrive at your mutual goal – her independence.

Nurturing Responsibility

(See also Encouraging Competence, p. 47; Fostering Independence, p 48; Making Chores a Matter of Routine, p. 70.)

As children grow older, they begin to do things on their own, which means taking on more responsibility. Toddlers want to be responsible for feeding themselves. Preschoolers want to get dressed alone. Primary school kids want to make their own meals or take care of a pet. Teenagers generally seek greater freedom – to stay out later, for instance – which also requires greater responsibility.

Parents generally welcome the responsibilities that give them more free time, such as being able to count on a four-year-old to get dressed by herself. However, it is sometimes difficult to feel comfortable with responsibilities that mean more freedom for a youngster, like walking to school alone or driving the family car.

As with so many other aspects of child-rearing, you and your child will both be better prepared for each new stage of responsibility if you come to it gradually. For example, if you've walked your child to school for the first two years, then you're in an excellent position to judge whether or not he's ready to be responsible for walking alone. If he's eager to walk with the neighbourhood kids and you feel he's ready, shadow them the first few times. That way, he'll be under your watchful eye while basically taking responsibility for himself. After this trial period, it's likely you'll both feel comfortable about his new achievement.

When children take on new responsibilities, you need to understand that the task won't go as smoothly as it would if an adult handled it. A child walking to school alone for the first time may run all the way instead, and a chore may be done sloppily at first. Over time, however, the child will be more careful and will handle various responsibilities more comfortably.

Be patient and encouraging during the learning phase. If you get upset and take over when something goes wrong, your youngster may lose interest in taking on responsibilities: 'If I'm just going to get yelled at when I do the washing up, why should I bother?' A child who is praised for a job well done will be more likely to want to improve. If the overall task isn't going very well, look for a specific part of the job to praise, or compliment her on her effort. Once you have praised your child and told her what she did well, you can then *briefly* tell her how she can improve.

When the responsibility in question is a chore, children often lose enthusiasm. Be firm and insist that the chores be done. Let a little one know that if she can't get dressed on time, she can no longer watch her favourite morning television programme – she needs to devote that time to getting ready. An older child will gain enthusiasm for taking out the rubbish when she realizes that if she isn't responsible enough to take out the rubbish, then she isn't responsible enough to go out with her friends on Friday night.

It's important for you to set a good example of taking on responsibilities. At times we hear from parents who call in sick when they aren't and who are then surprised when their children shirk their tasks. Take care to model responsible behaviour for your children.

Advocating Empathy

(See also Being a Positive Role Model, p. 39; Teaching Social Skills, p. 40; Saying You're Sorry, p. 85; Managing Tale-Telling, p. 114.)

Empathy involves having a genuine regard for the feelings of another person – being able to put yourself in that person's shoes, so to speak. It is a very valuable social skill, because an empathetic person understands the right and wrong things to say at crucial moments.

Children who are not empathetic have little patience with people and rarely consider anyone else's needs and feelings. The unempathetic child may talk in class about her birthday party, to which only eight of the twenty-four children are invited; she has no comprehension of the fact that this makes many of her classmates feel left out. These are the kids who are considered stuck-up or conceited, and some of them are bullies. In contrast, empathetic children are usually well liked and regarded as caring, conscientious and nice.

The ability to take the perspective of another person does not usually emerge until the primary school years. Preschoolers are still basically egocentric and see most things from their personal point of view. As empathy develops, kids become capable of understanding how it would feel, for example, to be the one who fell in the gym class. Later on, with additional maturity, they'll begin to feel empathy for the child who is last to be picked for the team.

Children who develop empathy gain greater tolerance and acceptance of others and are better prepared to be good friends. You can help your child by following these guidelines:

➤ **PRAISE YOUR CHILD WHEN SHE IS NICE TO OTHER PEOPLE.** For example, if she shares her toys with another child, tell her that you're proud of her and point out that her generosity made the other child happy.

➤ **EXPLAIN TO YOUR CHILD WHAT SOMEONE ELSE IS FEELING:** 'That little boy is *so* sad because he lost the money he wanted to spend on ice cream,' or 'Grandma was really happy with the tea towels you decorated for her! Did you see her big smile?'

➤ **CORRECT UNKIND BEHAVIOUR.** If your child says or does something unkind, calmly state how you feel. Use the format, 'I feel _____ when you _____.' After you have used this technique a few times and your child seems to understand, you might instead ask your child, 'How do you think I feel when you _____?'

➤ **BE FIRM ABOUT NOT ALLOWING YOUR CHILD TO BE CRUEL TO OTHERS.** If you hear your child being cruel or picking on someone, express your unhappiness and

point out how the other person wi[ll] 'Mary's feelings are hurt because yo[u] said you didn't want to play with he[r] can understand that you want to play with your cousin who is visiting, but you have to include Mary, too.'

LIFE IS FILLED with opportunities to teach empathy. Use daily experiences to help build empathy:

1. Clarify the situation and let your child explain what happened. Let's suppose your son, Timmy, calls his brother, Bobby, an idiot because Bobby wouldn't let him look at one of his football souvenirs. You might ask, 'Timmy, what did you say to Bobby?' Then ask, 'What happened that made you call him that name?' Don't be judgmental or punitive.

2. Help your child see the other child's point of view. You might ask, 'Timmy, how do you think Bobby felt when you called him that name?' Usually a child will admit that the other child probably felt bad. If not, press your child a little and ask, 'How would you feel if I called you an idiot?' When you make it more personal, most kids will then recognize that the other child must feel bad.

3. Get your child to work out a more suitable way to express his anger. If his brother won't let him look at one of his prized souvenirs, you might say, 'Timmy, how could you solve the problem without calling Bobby a name?' (In this case there may be no ideal solution. If Bobby doesn't want to share one of his special souvenirs with his little brother, Timmy may have to look at one of them while

Bobby holds it.) Be sure to give praise for an alternative solution. If you acknowledge that Timmy has come up with a good answer, he is more likely to use a problem-solving approach next time he is frustrated.

EMPATHETIC CHILDREN can understand the pain, sorrow, suffering and joy of other people. They are likely to be kind and generous in an attempt to make other people feel good. As a result, these children are usually successful in social situations and well liked by peers and teachers.

Preparing Your Child for Parenthood

(See also Being a Positive Role Model, p. 39.)

Preparing your child to be a parent is an exciting and important task, and don't think for a moment that it doesn't begin the moment you bring him or her home from the hospital. Your child will learn to be a good parent by seeing how you fulfill the role, right from the very beginning. Later on, the baby, child and teenager who has received enough care, attention and love in the earlier stages of life will be able to give these things to someone else – an excellent definition of good parenting.

Learning parenting by helping with the care of younger siblings is a great experience. Don't overburden him, however, or he may come to dislike the role. This experience may give him pause when he thinks of starting a family of his own.

Enlisting your child to work with you as a community volunteer – delivering meals to the needy, perhaps – is another useful way to teach him to care for others.

Having responsibilities early in life helps a person accept parental responsibilities. Have your child help with chores around the house and encourage him to help family members, friends and neighbours.

Since parenting also involves taking financial responsibility for another human being, encourage your teenager to find a job. Whether it's baby-sitting or working at a fast-food restaurant, a working teenager learns about financial responsibility.

It's also important occasionally to discuss with your child the types of financial considerations involved in parenting. Most children know about buying food and clothes, but they don't think about the cost of nappies, medical bills, education, baby-sitters, or buying a larger house or car. Being aware of this aspect of life helps children better understand what it means to become a parent.

In addition to discussing the responsibilities involved in being a parent, also talk about the pleasures. Children are a great source of pride and joy for most parents, and raising healthy and successful children is one of life's most satisfying tasks. Young people who enter into parenting with an awareness of these responsibilities are better prepared to be good parents.

chapter seven
DAY-TO-DAY ISSUES

We always expect that the major events of our lives will create the greatest difficulties, but often we find that it's actually what happens day-to-day that creates the most stress. Most families can cope with a household move more easily than they can manage some of the day-to-day irritants of family life: How do you find enough time to spend together? How do you feel about regulating television viewing? And now your child wants a dog? This section will help you with some of the day-to-day issues families face.

Finding Quality Time

Juggling family and job time is never easy, yet finding quality time to spend with your kids is crucial to raising happy children. Time spent with your child should be fun, pleasant, loving, happy and perhaps constructive. Remember, too, that quality time does not have to involve going out and spending money. For example,

Finding Quality Time

Managing Bedtime

Understanding the Importance of Play

Stressing Physical Activity

Monitoring Television Viewing

Supervising the Use of Computers, Video Games, and the Internet

Selecting Appropriate Movies

Answering the 'Why Can't We Get a Pet' Question

taking walks, riding bikes, having a pretend tea party, reading a story, or playing catch in the back garden are all great ways to spend time with your child.

Concentrate on doing what your child thinks is fun, not what you think would be a good learning experience. Although a trip to an art museum might teach your child a great deal, kids are easily bored and might prefer to go swimming with you. If you have a strong preference as to how the two of you spend time, you might suggest a basic activity, such as playing a game together and let your child choose the specific game. Don't be afraid to state your preference occasionally – quality time has to be something you find enjoyable, too.

Quality time isn't always something you can schedule; sometimes it just occurs because the two of you are together. For that reason, it's important to build family time into your daily schedule by routinely eating dinners together or by reading aloud to your children before bedtime; you can even create quality time out of something you need to get done, like running a couple of errands. Spend the time in the car talking and listening to your child and cap off the errands with a stop at the ice-cream shop.

During quality time keep the conversation uncritical and casual. Instead of talking about what your youngster did at school that day, solicit his opinions: What CDs are her favourites right now? What novel is she reading at bedtime this week?

Some people are critical of the concept of quality time because the term has been overused and abused. Some parents who spend little time with their children think that this is acceptable because they set aside a few hours a week of 'quality time'. You need to make an effort to find time for your children, but even a car ride to school can count as quality time if you use it as an opportunity for a chat about your favourite movies.

Managing Bedtime

(See also Setting Limits, p. 74; Speaking So Your Child Will Listen, p. 68; Overcoming Fears, p. 117; Setting Limits for Toddlers, p. 128.)

Some nights bedtime can be a wonderful time for you and your child, chatting together or reading a great story; other times it becomes stressful. Part of the problem is that everyone is tired. If two-year-old Mary took an extra-long nap and isn't sleepy at her usual bedtime, or if Mum gets a phone call during Benjamin's bedtime routine, everyone may become irritable.

The two keys to a successful bedtime are setting an appropriate time, which will vary by child and by age, and establishing a pleasant routine.

THE TIME

Children have different sleep cycles and needs. Some young children have no problem falling asleep at 7:00 P.M. while others will lie awake for a long time before drifting off. The sleep needs of children can range from nine to eleven hours.

Bedtime in your household will go more smoothly if you are aware of your child's sleep cycle and set the schedule accordingly.

If you have a few days with no morning engagements, note how late your child sleeps each morning. This will let you approximate the number of sleep hours he needs. If your unscheduled mornings are few and far between, then simply notice whether your child appears well rested based on his current sleep time. Remember, however, that children are traditionally untrustworthy when asked, 'Are you tired?' This question will almost certainly be met with a no, as it is the rare child who doesn't have one more thing to do before bed.

Sometimes parents base their children's bedtime on factors other than whether or not the child is sleepy. Some couples may work late and want to keep their children up so they can spend time with them (an afternoon nap can help little ones adjust to this schedule); others may want to be able to put the kids to bed at a decent hour so they'll have some time to themselves. Adjusting a young one's sleep cycle to one that works for the family is perfectly all right, so long as the child gets enough sleep.

As a youngster nears school age, it's important to establish a sleep schedule that is compatible with school hours. Like it or not, the world requires most of us to be up and functioning early in the morning.

If your children are close together in age, it may be easier to arrange one time for baths followed by a group story time. Then the kids can go to bed at roughly the same time. However, as your children get older, or if they are several years apart in age, then you'll need to set individual bedtimes. Although this situation may cause some envy, it is an important lesson of growing up. Younger children will observe that increasing age brings more freedom (staying up later) and more responsibility (more homework and chores).

Special occasions, sleepovers and summer bedtimes all call for a more flexible schedule.

If going to bed on time becomes a major problem, consider whether it's time to change bedtimes. Perhaps your child is growing older and doesn't need as much sleep. Or perhaps the usual bedtime can be preserved by eliminating an afternoon nap.

Also consider what else is going on in your child's life. Concerns frequently loom large at night, and an older child may have something on his mind that's keeping him awake. Anything you can do to comfort and reassure him will be likely to help, but remain consistent about bedtime. Otherwise your child will face his fears the next day without adequate rest.

THE ROUTINE

All of us sleep best when we've followed a predictable 'getting sleepy' routine, and we need to help kids develop specific sleep cues. Brushing teeth, taking a bath and getting into pyjamas can be followed by family bedtime rituals such as reading or telling a story, playing a quiet game together, or just chatting.

As your child grows older, as her days get busier and her bedtime routine becomes something she does alone, you may find that she needs some guidance in learning to quieten down. Limit her access to the television set and the telephone and encourage her to read or to listen to music in bed before she goes to sleep. Chances are she'll follow this routine for the rest of her life.

Understanding the Importance of Play

(See also Stressing Physical Activity, p. 58; Monitoring Television Viewing, p. 58.)

Play is the work of childhood and a vital part of a child's life. Through play, kids develop physically, learn to get along with others, hone specific skills and explore the world around them.

You can track the development of your children through the types of play they undertake. The very young start with solo play, where they amuse themselves with a toy such as a stuffed animal or blocks. By age three or four most move on to parallel play, in which two or more kids play side by side without truly interacting. They generally play with different toys but may discuss their play with each other. By around age five or six, mutual play begins, and because children now play actively with each other, cooperation becomes important.

Toys are important in play, but you needn't be overly concerned about the actual definition of 'toy'. The one-year-old who creates her own toy by banging a spoon on a pot while you fix dinner and the preschooler who creates a tent house out of some chairs and a blanket are both just as happy as the toddler who is playing with a busy box or a pull toy. Older kids may enjoy art or science kits but also take pleasure in inventing their own games.

THE BENEFITS OF PLAY

Play is vital to physical development. When children run, play tag, skip, or catch a ball, they are enjoying themselves while developing gross motor skills (control of the muscles used in moving around). Jacks, marbles, pickup sticks and art projects contribute to the development of fine motor skills (control of the muscles used in accomplishing small actions like picking things up). General coordination is improved by all types of play, and a game like hopscotch helps develop both gross and fine motor skills.

Play is also a great way for a child to develop her imagination. Playing dressing-up, running a make-believe shop and putting on a performance are wonderful opportunities for children to be creative.

Some children have imaginary playmates. This is quite normal, especially for three- and four-year-olds, and demonstrates that your child can think in an abstract manner.

Play is also one of the primary ways in which children learn about the world around them, and part of that learning is acquired through imaginative play. When the four-year-old plays fireman or several children play house, they are exploring different roles in life. You may even hear your preschooler scold her stuffed animal in a conversation reminiscent of one the two of you had recently ('I told you three times to stop playing with your juice. Now see what happened'.) This type of play helps a child work through various emotions and types of behaviour.

Learning to cooperate is another vital aspect of play. In order to make and maintain friendships, children must learn how to play with others, and that often means following the rules of the group. In fact, kids are often excluded from games if they cannot or will not follow the rules. Adults are often surprised by the intricacy of the rules for many of the games their children play, but developing their own rules can also help children feel independent.

Though play is generally pleasurable, children can become frustrated, when, for example, the block building your daughter is constructing falls down; your son's drawing of a cat looks more like a hippopotamus; two friends simply run out of games to play. By dealing with these annoyances, children learn to manage the problems of later life.

THE PARENTS' ROLE IN PLAY

When it comes to play, parents have three obligations:

1. To provide age-appropriate stimulation, starting at an early age. Even a newborn can be amused by a mobile, and as the baby develops, he will spend much time watching the mobile sway, often while kicking and 'talking' to it – and learning about the world around him. Later on, you need to provide safe, age-appropriate playthings. The toys needn't be elaborate, numerous, or expensive; they just need to keep your child actively exploring the world.

2. To provide opportunities for play. This may mean anything from not overscheduling your child to making sure the television set is turned off frequently. The child who frequently complains, 'I have nothing to do', just isn't accustomed to creating his own fun.

3. To play with your child. Play is one of the primary ways parents and children bond, and interaction between parent and child also helps children develop social competence. Must you get down on the floor and spend hours playing with your child while the dishes pile up? Not at all. Playing with an infant means tickling, cuddling, making faces and doing other simple, pleasurable activities. Even just smiling at your child is important and reinforces his social development. Later on, you can play peekaboo or roll a ball back and forth. As your child gets older, you can kick a ball around the backyard, play a board game, or go on a weekend adventure. You'll find that playtime can be wonderful for both of you.

No matter how busy you are, try to make time to spend with your child when he invites you to play. It doesn't usually take long to play a game of draughts or colour a picture with him, and by doing so, you show him that he is important to you.

Unfortunately some adults discourage what they regard as too much play. To them, play is what one does on holiday or during the weekend when other responsibilities have been fulfilled. They see play as fun but less important than working and striving to get ahead in the world. Unfortunately, they start pushing children to work hard at school or at a sport too soon.

Play is more than just an activity to keep kids busy. It's an essential part of their development. Your involvement is also necessary, so take advantage of play sessions and have a good time!

Stressing Physical Activity

(See also Being a Positive Role Model, p. 39; Understanding the Importance of Play, p. 56.)

A child who enjoys physical activity is likely to be an active and physically fit adult. By contrast, a child who prefers sedentary pastimes like reading and watching television is less likely to place a priority on physical activity later on. As has been well-documented, the consequences of being out of shape include weight problems, high blood pressure and heart disease. If you can instill in your child a love for a sport or another type of physical activity, it will serve him well in the future.

Unfortunately a simple suggestion, like 'Go outside and play', works only with some children. Most need additional motivation, and you will need to play a role in helping your child develop an active lifestyle.

The easiest thing in the world – and it's actually terrific for both parent and child – is simply to go outside and play with your kids. You can play catch or walk the dog; play tag football, tennis, or soccer; go swimming; or ride your bicycles. Taking time from your busy day to do these things with your children will show them that you feel exercise is important. Other family members, siblings and caregivers can also encourage physical activity.

Another good way to help your child be active is to encourage him to join a sports team. Most communities have cricket or soccer teams. (If your school or community isn't offering equal team opportunities to both boys and girls, it should be. Call and ask about this.) To emphasize how important this is to you, become involved to the extent that you can. If you have time, volunteer to help with practice or even coach a team. If you can't spare that many hours, help with carpooling and show up to cheer the team on as often as you can. Your participation shows your child that you value this activity.

Always stress that sports are for fun and that winning is nice but not always necessary. Children may shun physical activities and sports because they are self-conscious about their athletic abilities. In the right environment – perhaps a community team or a nurturing day camp – even the physically unskilled can have fun playing a game.

If you're an active person yourself, it's likely you've thought of our final advice: plan holidays that involve physical activity. Go walking, sign up for a bicycle tour, or stay at a place that has a swimming pool. Any of these activities can be fun for the whole family.

Monitoring Television Viewing

(See also Understanding the Importance of Play, p. 56; Stressing Physical Activity, p. 58; Supervising the Use of Computers, Video Games and the Internet, p. 61; Setting Limits, p. 74; Setting Limits for Toddlers, p. 128.)

American children spend an average of

between twenty-five to fifty-four hours a week watching television. This statistic is all the more alarming because unless the child is watching an intellectually stimulating programme or exercising along with an aerobics show, he simply sits and stares at the television set, doing nothing. National statistics show an increase in the number of overweight children, and experts attribute this to the fact that most children of today are much less physically active than children of earlier times. Part of this inactivity has to be attributed to time spent watching television.

THE BENEFITS OF TELEVISION

As we all know, television also offers incredible benefits. Shows such as *Sesame Street* and *Barney and Friends* teach young children about numbers, letters, body parts and language, and they expose kids to situations that can happen in their daily life. *Magic School Bus, Bill Nye, the Science Guy, Between the Lions,* and *Reading Rainbow* are instructive for children who are a little older. In fact, studies show that children who watch educational programming tend to perform better in school than kids who do not watch television.

Certain programmes also teach tolerance and appreciation of individual differences. Seeing a likeable TV character in a wheelchair is a good experience, and it's also beneficial when your child is oblivious to the racial background of the characters when selecting a situation comedy to watch.

Television also acts as social unifier by providing us with common information and experiences. We've all heard conversations that start, 'Hey, Fred! Did you see that great United game?' When children reach school age, this commonality of experience becomes important. Kids don't want to feel left out when those around them are talking about the latest popular Monday evening programme.

What's more, television is entertaining. We sometimes forget that kids need to have fun. It is not necessary for *everything* in their lives to be educational and serious.

THE DOWNSIDE OF TELEVISION VIEWING

That said, television has its downside. At it's worst it's a solitary activity that is socially isolating (unless family members watch together). And when kids are permitted to watch for long periods of time, they may become inactive and lose the ability to amuse themselves. Extended viewing may also stunt children's ability to imagine; teachers are concerned when children imitate TV show characters during play and seem unable to invent their own characters or plots.

Children who watch a great deal of television may also reduce their ability to concentrate for extended periods of time. In part, this may be attributed to the fast pace of television programming.

Television also provides a picture of the world that can influence children. As early as age two, toddlers may clamour for a toy they've seen on television, causing stress for parents who can't find or afford to buy the toy. And family values on programmes are often missing or hard to find. Few characters on television ever have to sacrifice; they do something only if they'll get something in return. They also cheat each other and argue constantly, cutting each other down with acerbic wit and hostility. Is this the message you want to give your children? We don't think so.

Television violence is also an issue. Despite concern from the public, mental health professionals and government leaders about the level of violence on television, the problem is not going to go away. In fact, a survey conducted between 1995 and 1996 (commissioned by the US National Cable Television Association) of broadcast and cable networks found that 61 per cent of cartoon-children's programmes show aggressive acts. (Amazingly, in 1972 an astounding 98 per cent of cartoons depicted violence!) While cartoon violence isn't realistic, one serious concern is that cartoons don't show the pain associated with violence. No matter how many times Road Runner is flattened, he still keeps popping up for the next encounter with Wile E. Coyote. This is very deceptive to children.

Repeated viewing of violent programming has been found to have varying effects. Some children may lack the mental development to recognize that the characters are played by actors and are not necessarily meant to set a good example. As a result, young children, particularly those with aggressive tendencies, may show increased aggression after watching television.

MONITORING YOUR CHILD'S EXPOSURE TO TV

Here are some ways to make TV viewing a positive experience for your child:

➤ Watch as a family.

➤ Designate a special hour, programme, or evening as 'television time'.

➤ Use a television-schedule magazine to select your programme, checking reviews and recommendations concerning appropriate family viewing.

➤ Watch the programme together and discuss it afterwards. Encourage your children to think about and express their reactions and feelings.

Your family's 'television time' can become a forum for discussing important issues and developing critical thinking.

And when you are watching television, remember that family members should come before programme content. Don't shush a child during a programme, telling her to wait until the commercial. While a nonstop talker who is interfering with the rest of the family's ability to understand a programme should be asked to wait, these requests should be very limited. People should not have to limit their comments to commercial breaks.

Television should not be used as a babysitter. Even if you can't watch with your children, you must be aware of what they are watching and for how long. Restrict all children to age-appropriate fare, and as you become more accustomed to the new rating system being used by the networks, you will find it easier to select appropriate programmes.

When you think your children have watched enough TV or should not watch a certain programme, turn off the TV and give them ideas for other activities, including things you can do together.

Should children have TV sets in their rooms? *No.* If they do, you won't be able to monitor how long they are watching or what types of programming they are viewing. It's also extremely isolating.

We're frequently asked whether children should be permitted to watch the news. Children can be frightened by media coverage of certain events. For example, a story of a murderer loose in a city can make some children fear that they are going to be murdered. Unfortunately, frightened children don't always discuss their worries with parents, so it's really better not to expose them to such stories.

By watching newscasts, children are exposed to trauma, war and constant bad news. In this sense, television may be less a reflection of the current world than a reflection of what is wrong or bad in the world.

TELEVISION is a powerful social force and is here to stay. If you monitor your child's viewing and talk about what you see, it's likely you'll find that television can be a positive influence in your child's development.

Supervising the Use of Computers, Video Games, and the Internet

(See also Setting Limits, p. 74.)

'Should we buy a computer for the children?' This is a concern of parents these days. The answer largely depends on the age of the children. While young children may enjoy the challenge of some computer games, for older children the computer is now an important tool for school. The child who has access to one at home will feel more comfortable with the one in the classroom.

LIMITING COMPUTER AND VIDEO GAME TIME

In moderation, computer and video games can be interesting and fun and can help a child develop eye-hand coordination. However, if you find that computer or video games are taking up an excessive amount of your child's time, set limits, just as you would with anything else that becomes excessive.

Parental discretion is also advisable in game selection. Many have very aggressive themes, and bullets, missiles and bombs are common weapons. Fortunately, some video games have pro-social or neutral themes, so shop around and see what alternatives there are.

Recently a number of games have been developed for girls; many of these are centered on topics such as beauty, shopping, or getting a date. While a game or two like this won't damage your daughter, look for other types of games for her as well. A complete library of 'girl games' like this certainly does little to break the stereotype of girls' focus on the superficial.

Remember that kids are basically inactive while they're playing video and computer games, so on a nice sunny day, or even a not so sunny day, be sure to get the kids outside for a while.

Should withholding the use of video or computer games be a form of punishment? When a child acts up, ignores the rules or limitations on the games, or fails to keep up with homework or chores, taking away his game privileges can be an effective form of punishment. If kids know that the cost of misbehaviour is losing access to a favourite activity, most will do what they can to be good. This is also a more rational approach than that of parents who fear bringing a computer or video game set into the home. Banning something enjoyable shouldn't be necessary. Just ask for – and enforce – moderation.

THE INTERNET

Many of the dangers of this new technology may be eliminated within a few years, but for now you should be aware of the hazards your child could encounter on the Internet.

One well-known danger, of course, lies in *exposure to inappropriate material.* Keep your computer in a main room of the house instead of in a bedroom. This will permit you to keep an eye on what your child is doing while she's on-line. Most systems now allow you to block access to certain areas, but because so much distasteful material is available, there's no guarantee that you will have all bases covered, so close adult supervision is recommended. If you have younger children, take time to go on-line with them.

Chat rooms are another source of potential trouble. You can block access to certain chat rooms, but you can't protect your child from adults who enter youth-oriented chat rooms, masquerading as kids.

Here are some protective measures you can take:

➤ Monitor your child's Internet use.

➤ Warn your child of the dangers that exist.

➤ Make it very clear that the child must *never* give your address or telephone number to anyone on-line.

➤ If your child makes a friend – real pen pals and relationships do develop on-line – you must be put in touch with that friend's parents before any additional information is exchanged.

Selecting Appropriate Movies

Your job as a parent involves sheltering your child from many things, including inappropriate movies. A child isn't mature enough to know that a certain movie, even an animated one, may give him nightmares, nor should children have to become numb to violence at a young age.

Until a child reaches preschool age, he doesn't have a long enough attention span to sit through a feature-length film. Preschoolers do enjoy films, but careful monitoring is necessary. Even feature-length cartoons – usually considered appropriate children's fare – may upset some children, so you really can't take anything for granted. If you have the opportunity, you may even want to preview the movie before your child sees it. If you don't have time, these resources can help you decide:

1. **The British Board of Film Classification's rating system (UC, U, PG, 12 and over, 15 and over, 18 and over, R) is helpful, but you still need to consider your child's**

maturity level and the film's subject. If your dog has just died, you may not want to take your child to a movie about a lost pet.

2. Most film reviews include a paragraph about whether the movie contains violence, bad language, nudity, sexual content, or other objectional material.

3. Some newspapers and magazines have columns for parents that review current films and particularly note whether the content would be upsetting to children of various ages.

4. Word of mouth is also helpful. Talk to a friend who has seen the movie. It may not be as bad as its rating would suggest. If you learn that a few bad words are the reason for the rating, you may decide to go and see the movie anyway.

With the very young, make sure that your child understands that movies are pretend. If a cartoon figure was real could it pop back into full form after being flattened into a pancake? If children understand that movies are make-believe, a big-screen animated storm or the fury of an animated god will seem less real.

You might also remind youngsters that people in movies don't really get hurt nor is real life accurately depicted. If a movie concerns a bank robber who gets away with the crime, ask, 'What would really happen if someone robbed a bank?' Most likely your child will know that in real life such a person would be punished.

A good way to start a discussion about a movie is to ask your child, 'What happened in the movie?' This way, you can see what the child thought about the movie before you condemn certain aspects of it.

If you and your child happen to see a movie that includes sex, violence, or other subject matter that makes you uncomfortable, discuss it. Explain what bothered you. You might explain, for example, that violence hurts people and that watching it makes you feel upset. Most kids will be satisfied with this simple explanation. You might also ask your child's opinion. Parents are often surprised by their children's awareness of right and wrong, and in general, children are influenced more by their family's value system than by the actions of fictional movie characters.

If your child loved the movie but you had some reservations about it, try to balance your critical comments by also discussing the good parts. Most movies have some redeeming qualities and pointing them out will make your child see that you are being fair and not dismissing it totally because of one thing.

GUIDING TEENAGERS

Preteens and adolescents often go to the movies with friends, so it's more difficult to control what they see. Try to be somewhat relaxed about making judgments. Just as most adults don't like to have materials censored for them, kids don't appreciate being told they can't handle certain subjects. While you certainly don't want your five-year-old seeing an R-rated movie, that same film might be acceptable for a young teenager. Respect your child and her ability to think for herself. Encourage her to discuss the movie with you.

Let her know you aren't going to criticize or become angry about her movie choices.

If, however, a movie is clearly inappropriate, then you should refuse to allow your child to attend, but be prepared to provide a replacement activity. Perhaps you could take your teen and a few friends bowling. By providing an alternative, you've shown lovingly that your concern is centered only on the movie, not on your child's friends or their desire for a social life.

Answering the 'Why Can't We Get a Pet?' Question

(See also Nurturing Responsibility, p. 49; Making Chores a Matter of Routine, p. 70; Negotiating with Your Child, p. 80.)

Pets can be a wonderful addition to a family. They are excellent companions and can provide children with the opportunity to learn about animals and about nurturing. Pets also offer children unconditional love. Having a pet can also teach children a great deal about death and loss. Unfortunately, most pets, particularly small animals such as hamsters and fish, don't have a long life expectancy. While the loss of a beloved pet is a painful thing, it is also a life experience that helps prepare a child to cope with other types of loss.

Pets are also a big responsibility, and several factors should be taken into account before you embark on what can be a rewarding, and challenging, undertaking.

ALLERGIES

First, if any family member is allergic to pets, you can spare the family the emotional distress of having to give up a pet by saying no from the outset. Although a few breeds of dogs are supposed to be hypoallergenic, the Kennel Club and your paediatrician will both tell you that if there are severe allergies in your family, you may have a problem.

Allergies don't have to mean 'never'. Instead, they can mean 'not *that* pet'. If you're not able to get a puppy or kitten, investigate whether some other pet – hamster, gerbil, fish, iguana, bird – will be satisfying.

Even if you have no reason to suspect allergies, try to have family members visit and spend time with the pet before you bring it home. If any of you experience allergic symptoms afterwards, you may want to investigate further before getting that pet.

FINANCIAL CONSIDERATIONS

Be sure that you will have the financial resources to feed the animal, get the required shots and licences and pay veterinarian bills that may be incurred. Don't buy a pet to please your children and then discover you can't afford to keep it. Having to give up a pet is very distressing for children and may even cause them to question your loyalty. 'If mum and dad can get rid of Fluffy so easily, maybe they'll get rid of me someday, too.'

If you feel that a pet will burden you unduly, then find other ways for your children to enjoy animals. Older children might start a neighbourhood pet-sitting or dog-walking business, for example. Younger children might want to bring the class pet home during school holidays.

SPACE AND TIME

Some pets require more space than others. Choose accordingly.

As for time, if all family members are out during the day, a pet may be wrong for your present lifestyle. Or choose a pet that won't mind being alone during the day. Hamsters, for example, are nocturnal, so they'll be happy to see you at dinnertime, and they need less attention than a cat or a dog.

SELECTING A PET

Decide carefully about the type of pet and be selective about the individual animal you bring home. (Remember, you're making a long-term commitment.) While it's fine to get a dog from an animal shelter, you don't have to bring one home from the first shelter you visit or on the first day. Listen carefully to what people tell you about any animal you're considering. A dog who 'loves to roam' could mean guaranteed stress for the family.

Be prepared to share the burden of pet ownership. No matter how responsible your child is, you're going to need to help. While children can and should carry an age-appropriate part of the burden of caring for the family pet, your pet is a living being. Ultimate responsibility will fall to you. Assign your child specific pet-related chores: feeding, cleaning up, filling the water bowl, grooming, cleaning the cage. But should Fido be forced to miss his dinner because Sam went on a sleepover? Of course not. Should Sam skip his sleepover in order to walk Fido? Of course not to that, too. Caring for a pet should be a shared family responsibility, and if you've chosen well, your pet will be a shared joy as well.

chapter eight

FAMILY COOPERATION, COMMUNICATION AND DISCIPLINE

The cornerstones of family life are communication and cooperation. Families who are happy enjoy talking together, being together and even doing chores together because they've created a strong family unit.

Anger, of course, occurs in all human relationships, and it isn't usually a problem – if it's expressed appropriately. Discipline is part of this section because it can be used, not punitively but to guide youngsters towards appropriate family behaviour.

This section of the book will guide you in creating this strong foundation for your family.

Speaking So Your Child Will Listen

Encouraging Bedroom Tidiness

Making Chores a Matter of Routine

Paying Allowances

Educating Children about Sex

Setting Limits

Using Time-Outs

Avoiding the Use of Guilt Trips

Spanking: The Current Thinking

Negotiating with Your Child

Anger in Daily Life

Getting Angry: Parental Anger

Saying You're Sorry

Speaking So Your Child Will Listen

(See also Being a Positive Role Model, p. 39; Teaching Social Skills, p. 40; Setting Limits, p. 74; Negotiating with Your Child, p. 80; Saying You're Sorry, p. 85.)

Listening is a complex process, and perhaps the single most common complaint we hear from parents is 'My kids never listen to me.'

Teresa M. McDevitt of the University of Northern Colorado breaks the process into four parts: paying attention, remembering what was said, feeling motivated to take action and finally, taking action. You can improve your child's listening skills by paying attention to how you make requests:

1. Get your child's attention before making a request. How often have you asked your child to perform a chore like taking out the rubbish when he's glued to the TV set? Your request about the rubbish doesn't have a chance of penetrating his consciousness! Eliminate distractions (turn off the TV or wait for a commercial), make eye contact and then state your request. You may want your child to repeat the demand back to you in his own words. Encourage him to ask questions if he doesn't understand.

2. Make requests or commands simple and specific. Too often parents give vague, nonspecific commands. What parent, for example, hasn't told a child, 'Be good!' What does this mean? Does it mean be quiet in church, or don't fiddle with Grandma's glasses? While a child may suspect your meaning, the command is so vague that he isn't inclined to follow it. In psychology, we often talk about alpha commands – clear instructions for a specific task with a deadline. Instead of saying to your child 'Clean your room', be specific: 'I need you to make your bed, put your games in the cupboard and put all your laundry in the hamper before we leave in thirty minutes.' These commands are precise, and everyone involved can agree on what is to be accomplished. With children under age eight you need to make the requests one at a time.

3. Remind your child of the task, if necessary. Kids have a funny way of 'forgetting' to do chores or fulfill commands, and it is sometimes difficult for them, as it is for adults, to become motivated to do something, like homework or a chore, that requires effort. Don't punish your kids if they occasionally need some prodding.

4. Praise your child for complying. In fact, you should praise your child even if you have to remind her to complete a task. As always, be specific. Say 'You folded your clothes so neatly!' rather than just 'Good job!'

ONE OF THE TRUE challenges of parenting comes when you have to respond to noncompliance. Sometimes parents take noncompliance as a personal slight and become extremely angry. If you understand that occasional noncompliance is part of human nature, you'll reduce your own stress and may find that your kids are actually more compliant because you're relaxed.

Like most parents, you realize that kids like to test limits and ignore commands, but that doesn't mean your kids should be allowed to walk all over you. Some household requirements and limits are obviously necessary. Decide which requests are most important and insist upon them: watching a sibling for a half hour while you go out is more important than unloading the dishwasher, for example. (Refer to 'Setting Limits', if you encounter resistance.)

If you are reasonable in your requests and make them at times when your child can pay attention to you, the odds are good that your youngster will comply more and more frequently.

Encouraging Bedroom Tidiness

Messy bedrooms often cause problems between parents and children. This difficulty frequently starts in preschool and continues for years, often worsening during adolescence.

Constantly having to nag a child to clean up her bedroom puts a strain on any parent-child relationship. So long as there is nothing unsafe or unhealthy about the state of your child's bedroom, try to remember that tidiness is simply not an important enough topic to argue about for the next eighteen years.

However, there are some strategies to help you maintain household sanity:

1. Make sure each child has a space (a room or part of a room) of her own, an area she feels is an extension of herself. Younger children should be allowed to suggest a colour scheme or a particular piece of furniture they like; older children can be permitted to decorate their own rooms. Be open-minded to the suggestions of young children and don't get into a power struggle with your teenager. If you truly dislike the way she has decorated her bedroom, just close the door so you won't have to look at it.

2. Provide your child with adequate storage space. Good space planning will make your child's life easier because there will be storage for clothing, toys and equipment. This, in turn, will make your life easier, because a certain level of order can be maintained. Evaluate your child's room every few years to make certain you're not still trying to stuff size 12 boys' sweaters into the drawer where the toddler-size sweaters used to go.

3. Set safety and health standards for bedrooms. Many parents don't allow children to take food to their bedrooms; if you do, make it a rule that the dishes must be brought back to the kitchen at the end of each day. Dirty dishes or garbage left in the bedroom can create a health hazard. Also be certain that there are no fire hazards in the room – piles of old newspapers near a radiator, for example.

4. Accentuate the positive. If your child's bedroom is neat, or if you can find one corner of the room where he has invested his time, compliment him: 'I really like the way you put your CDs in order. They look great, and I'll bet you've got a terrific system for finding what you want.'

5. Make special requests for special occasions. If you're planning to entertain, ask your child firmly to please clean his bedroom and explain why: 'Aunt Margaret is coming for a visit. Could you please put some things away in your bedroom so that she can see it when she's here?' Depending on your child's age, you might offer to help. Put on music or make a game out of the cleanup session so that picking up a room isn't seen as total drudgery.

IF YOUR CHILD'S bedroom is far from perfect, try not to focus on the dirty bedroom. Focus instead on his good points. If he's good at sports, gets good grades, is creative, or is kind to others, why should the condition of his bedroom be so important? Excessive parental criticism can lead to poor self-image, and thinking poorly of oneself isn't good for anyone, particularly a teenager. (You may be comforted to know that even a messy child may grow up to be a neat adult.)

If you allow your child to create a space he loves, you are likely to find that he will take pride in his room and take care of it.

Making Chores a Matter of Routine

(See also Building Self-Esteem, p. 42; Nurturing Responsibility, p.49; Speaking So Your Child Will Listen, p. 68; Paying Allowances, p. 71; Setting Limits, p. 74; Assigning Chores to Toddlers, p. 130.)

Chores are a necessary part of life, and it is important for all family members to participate. Though the chores themselves are often boring, they bring with them some surprising benefits. When family members accomplish tasks cooperatively, children learn specific life skills, develop a sense of responsibility and feel pride in being a contributing member of the family. Also, family stress is reduced when chores are shared by all.

What you expect from your child should be based on her age. A toddler or preschooler's first job around the house is learning to take care of his own needs – getting dressed, for instance, or preparing her own snack. Children will usually tell you when they are ready to do a task by themselves. If your child suggests it, let her give it a try before you help her.

Eventually, your child will be ready to help around the house. To begin, 'real' chores should consist of working with Mum or Dad to do a task together. Washing the lettuce for the salad while you're cooking, moving aside a footstool or the dining room chairs while you're vacuuming and helping to feed the dog are all tasks that most preschoolers relish doing with their parents.

School-age children are capable of more complex tasks like laying the table, dusting, feeding pets, taking out the rubbish, walking the dog and raking leaves or doing other garden work. By six or seven, a youngster is old enough to have specific chores assigned to her, and though you may need to remind her, you shouldn't need to stand over her while she does the task. You can stress responsibility during this period of development.

When assigning chores, try to take into account your child's preferences, talents and time commitments. A boy who loves the outdoors might be in charge of garden care whereas his younger sister, who loves animals, might be responsible for walking the dog. Kids may not like all the chores you need them to do – few enjoy taking out the rubbish, for example – but it's important for them to learn that some unpleasant tasks are simply part of life.

During adolescence, youngsters are capable of doing almost any chore and may even be physically stronger than you are. Chores are particularly important for teenagers because they involve them in everyday life and keep them tied to the family. However, because teenagers generally have very busy schedules, chores should be negotiated so that they are helpful to the family but also convenient for the teenager.

Having an older child baby-sit for the younger ones is a logical family chore and one most families require from time to time. Just be mindful that it can be overused. Kids at this age need to have time to pursue their own interests. If baby-sitting is keeping your teenager from playing on the netball team after school or from going out with friends on a Saturday night, look for alternatives; perhaps another neighbourhood teenager could help out some afternoons. Remember that your adolescent is not yet an adult and her responsibilities should not be overwhelming.

Occasionally, your child may not feel like doing a chore or may have pressing school commitments. As long as these occasions aren't too frequent, you might consider demonstrating your flexibility by letting your youngster skip the chore for a day or by offering to help. Working alongside your child is a good experience in teamwork and cooperation.

If chores become a constant battleground, the first step is to ask yourself if switching chores will solve the problem. If he now has to leave for school early to attend band practice, then walking the dog in the morning may indeed be more than he can handle. Suggest an afternoon chore he could do instead.

If your child refuses to do her chores or puts in little effort towards accomplishing them, start by reminding her and encouraging her to do them. If this is ineffective, consider taking away her television or telephone privileges for a period of time. Chores are a part of life, and children should not be exempt.

As with all other activities, find occasions to praise your child for a job well done and be specific about what you thought she did particularly well. Boast about her work to friends and relatives and thank her for helping you – something parents too often forget to do. Feeling valued by parents for the work she does will increase her self-esteem.

Paying Allowances

(See also Nurturing Responsibility, p. 49; Making Chores a Matter of Routine, p. 70; Negotiating with Your Child, p. 80.)

Having a regular allowance allows children to learn at an early age how to manage their money – a vital preparation for adulthood.

Money is generally meaningless to children under age five or six, so you may wish to wait until your child is in school to start an allowance. However, if older siblings are collecting an allowance, your four-year-old may want to participate, too.

The amount your child receives should be based on age and what the money is supposed to cover. Sit down with each child and make a list of expenses, including school lunch, after-school snacks and miscellany. (The younger the child, the more likely this list will include only miscellany.) Also decide whether a trip to the movies is a parent expense or a child expense.

Ask your friends how much they pay their children. In addition to learning what the proverbial Joneses are paying (something that is often important to kids), you may be reminded of some points you haven't thought of, such as who is responsible for buying family gifts.

Based on these discussions, ask your youngster to propose a realistic amount. After that, negotiate. This offers your child an opportunity to learn how to debate a position. As in any successful negotiation, both sides should feel they gained something; don't use parental power to negate totally what your child requests.

Once an amount is set, some families inflate it by a pound or two, explaining to the child that the extra money is to be dedicated to contributions. Then help your child find a local interest or a national cause – anything from your house of worship to the local animal shelter or a national organization that funds research for the cure for a disease – to which she'd like to donate her money. This is a tangible way to teach your child an important value.

Although children often squander their allowance on ice cream or junk food, try not to set rules or criticize. When she blows her entire allowance on sweets on Monday and then doesn't have money for something she wants on Friday, its likely she'll manage her allowance better the following week.

By the same token, you need to provide your child with some basic lessons in money management. For example, if your seven-year-old receives £2 each week, and he desperately wants to buy a detective kit that costs £12, you can point out that if he saves some of his allowance each week, he'll eventually have enough money to buy the kit.

Should allowances and chores be linked? No. Allowances should be paid with no strings attached. Chores are important to a family, and family members should do things for each other without expecting payment; they should feel responsible for each other's well-being.

Some parents balk at this advice and insist that their children will refuse to do chores if their allowance is no longer dependent on it. If your child resists doing the chores, you have other recourse besides withholding allowance. Try limiting the child's other privileges – like talking on the phone or going out with friends – to make your point.

Can you pay your child for extra household chores? Absolutely. If your child completes all of his regular tasks for the week and offers to mow the lawn, then it's fine to pay him. This actually is an important message about the work ethic. While there will be chaotic times when you'll need everyone to pitch in with no extra pay expected (the kids need to set the table and prepare dinner because Mum's busy bathing the family dog, rolled in a smelly mess), it's fine to reward children when they do above and beyond the expected. Also remember to thank them for their efforts.

Educating Children About Sex

(See also Being a Positive Role Model, p. 39; Nurturing Responsibility, p. 49; Dating, p. 151.)

Only about 15 per cent of college students report having received substantial sex education from their parents. Sex education in many families consists of girls learning about their menstrual cycle and boys being told about condoms – hardly an adequate education in human sexuality. Furthermore, one researcher, Dr. T. D. Fisher, has noted that the most obvious aspect of the father's role in sex education is his almost complete absence from the process!

Children who receive sex education from their parents are more likely to share their parents' values and beliefs about sexuality. If you and your child don't discuss sex, his only sources of information are his school, the media and his friends.

Sex education is perhaps the only area in which it is sometimes assumed that knowledge is harmful. However, ignorance and unresolved curiosity appear to be far more dangerous, and informed kids are more likely to make informed decisions. Some parents assume that talking with their children about sex is the same as encouraging them to have sex. This isn't true.

Effective sex education should include what kids want and need to know about the subject. Allow your kids to ask questions and don't shrink away from embarrassing details. There are ways to finesse so that you can provide the information your child needs without revealing intimate details about yourself. Most of the discomfort you feel when discussing sex with your children is probably due to the fact that your parents didn't talk with you about sex. It's time to break this cycle of noncommunication. If you do feel uncomfortable, try dealing with the subject honestly: 'I feel uncomfortable, but there are some important things I want to discuss with you.' Kids will appreciate your honesty, and it might ease their embarrassment.

When you talk to your children about sex, you should keep two primary goals in mind:

1. **To disseminate correct and factual information;**
2. **To make sure your kids feel comfortable talking with you about such issues.**

If your child feels comfortable discussing sex, he'll ask questions that will help you determine appropriate topics. (If your child has a question, this indicates he's ready for information about it.)

Begin talking about sexual issues when your child is a preschooler. At this age you might talk about boys and girls and the ways in which they are different, and you can also talk about body parts and their names (accurate ones). This will help your child understand sexual abuse. Tell your kids there are certain spots (any place covered by a bathing suit) where they shouldn't allow people to touch them. Encourage them to tell you if any kind of abuse occurs. Stress the fact that the adult is responsible, not the child.

Preschoolers are also curious about where babies come from. A brief but honest answer will suffice. For example, you might say, 'Babies come from inside a mummy.' This answer will probably satisfy kids until they are developmentally ready for a more detailed response.

Encourage your child to abstain from sexual intercourse until he is mature. While it is difficult to control the behaviour of teenagers, the values with which they are raised can help them make wise decisions.

Of course, no discussion of sex would be complete without talking about romance, love and commitment. One way for parents to broach these subjects is to tell their kids about their own past romances. Talk about when you were a youngster and had a crush on a certain person. Speak about meeting your spouse and falling in love.

A final important topic is sexually transmitted infections. The press has made us well aware of the danger of contracting AIDS through unprotected sex, but we must not forget the old dangers – venereal diseases. These can lead to pelvic inflammation and, eventually, infertility. An estimated 5 per cent of adults are infertile, and one definite cause of this sterility, particularly in women, is early sexual intercourse and the resulting infections.

Sex education is a lifelong process. Teach your kids as much as you can as soon as you can. Discussing these issues often will help desensitize you and your child, allowing a greater degree of comfort and trust. If your kids feel comfortable talking with you about sex, they will come to you when they have questions.

Setting Limits

(See also Advocating Empathy, p. 50; Speaking So Your Child Will Listen, p. 68; Avoiding the Use of Guilt Trips, p. 78; Anger in Daily Life, p. 82; Getting Angry: Parental Anger, p. 84; Reducing Sibling Rivalry, p. 109; Managing Tale-telling, p. 114.)

Every child needs to be given limits. The smart parent sets limits throughout the child-rearing process.

Young children need limits to keep them safe ('Don't run into the street') and to prevent them from hurting others ('You mustn't hit Johnny'). Very young children see themselves as the centre of the universe and have no idea what impact their behaviour has on others or on themselves. For that reason, they need an external control to stop them from behaving dangerously or aggressively. A preschooler who is stopped from using force to deal with a younger sibling will learn to avoid aggression with others.

As children grow older, they gradually develop empathy and can understand that mean or aggressive behaviour might hurt others, but they often lose this trait when they get angry. During an outburst, a child might hurt other people through verbal aggression, such as name-calling, or through physical aggression, by hitting or kicking. If no control is put on this behaviour, this child may continue to be aggressive.

During preadolescence and adolescence, a child becomes more independent, and there may be some parent-child conflict. Your adolescent still needs external control to learn to be fair, considerate and non-aggressive. As long as the limit-setting is not associated with anger, you can be assured that even though adolescents may resist or struggle against limits, most teenagers appreciate and respect you for setting guidelines and understand that you do so out of love.

Needless to say, setting limits is one of the more challenging parts of parenting. Here are some of the techniques we have found to be extremely effective for parents:

1. Make it easy for your child to live within the limits.

➤ *Establish schedules and routines.* They make a child feel secure and supported. If your youngster gets into the habit of doing his homework before turning on the television, the likelihood of finding him watching TV without having done his homework is greatly reduced.

➤ *Write out family rules and post them where everyone can see them.*

➤ *Be consistent and firm.* Once you establish a rule, stick with it and don't give in. If your child begs for flexibility, be firm, but don't get angry.

➤ *Have realistic expectations.* Even the best-behaved children sometimes misbehave and disobey. If things aren't

going well, consider your child's age and abilities as well as what you're expecting of him. Adjust the limits as necessary and change the rules as the child gets older.

➤ *Offer only a limited number of choices.* By saying 'Would you like to wear the blue shirt or the red one?' you establish a feeling of control.

2. Encourage good behaviour.

➤ *Give your child praise and attention.* Instead of punishing him for misbehaving, offer praise and attention when he behaves well. The praise and attention should *immediately* follow the good behaviour. If your child takes out the rubbish without being reminded, praise him right afterwards for remembering. If you withhold or delay the praise, the connection between the praise and good behaviour will be weakened, especially in younger children.

➤ *Offer rewards and privileges for desirable behaviour.* A reward might involve an enjoyable activity such as playing a game with you. Special privileges could include extending curfew or watching a certain television programme. If a child knows something enjoyable will come out of being good, you increase the likelihood of his being good.

3. Teach problem-solving.

➤ *Encourage a child who misbehaves to think of alternate solutions or types of behaviour* (see Part One for our five-step approach to problem-solving). This technique will help the child develop a sense of responsibility for and control over his behaviour. Instead of striking out at the classmate who took a block from the pile with which your nursery school child was building, your son could have asked the child to return the block or told the teacher so she could intervene.

4. Use time-outs.

Time-outs are so useful and effective that we have devoted an entry to this topic. See 'Using Time-Outs as a Method of Discipline' for full details.

5. Redirect your child.

➤ *Suggest an alternative activity for a child who is about to misbehave.* If your four-year-old whines on car trips, take with you activities to keep her busy, or sing or talk with her while you drive.

6. Ignore unacceptable behaviour.

➤ *Withhold your attention following poor behaviour.* Sometimes children will do something annoying simply to gain their parents' attention. (Indeed, children who misbehave sometimes receive the most parental attention.) If you ignore the annoying behaviour, then it no longer serves the child's purpose. Don't tell your child you are ignoring the behaviour, as this will defeat the purpose.

➤ *This method should not be used with bad behaviour requiring immediate correction, such as hurting oneself or others.*

7. Withdraw privileges.

➤ *Take away privileges when your child behaves badly.* Make sure that you withdraw the privilege immediately following the misbehaviour. If your teenager forgets to feed the dog in the morning for two or three days running, leaving you to perform that task, tell her she has lost her telephone privileges for the remainder of the week.

REGARDLESS OF your youngster's age, you need to be firm when you reprimand or set limits on her. However, it is critical to avoid anger, blame and a harsh tone. Instead, a brief and succinct expression of dissatisfaction with her behaviour will suffice.

When adolescents resist limit-setting, you can explain your logic and reach a compromise on minor points. Again, if you remain calm, firm and persistent, gradually you will see a decline of the unwanted behaviour.

Using physical punishment, such as spanking, as a method of limit-setting has generally fallen out of favour, as parents have come to recognize its destructiveness and search for more effective techniques.

Parents can use a wide variety of techniques to help improve the behaviour of their children. Your task is to find the method that works best for your family.

Using Time-Outs

A time-out occurs when you interrupt inappropriate behaviour and have your child sit quietly in a certain place for a specified period of time.

Time-outs represent a reasonable and relatively simple way to make your point, and they are generally quite effective with children under the age of twelve. They should not be a punishment but rather a form of discipline that helps decrease an undesirable behaviour. Consistency is important in using the method effectively.

By removing the child from the scene, you deprive him of the opportunity to get attention for his misbehaviour, and this gives him a chance to quieten down on his own. The time-out offers the added benefit of laying the groundwork for learning emotional self-reliance and self-control. In addition, it permits you to solve the problem without becoming angry.

Used properly, time-outs should eliminate your need to scold or be upset with your child about what has happened.

HOW A TIME-OUT WORKS

If your four-year-old hits your two-year-old, you state calmly: 'Leslie, you know you're not allowed to hit your brother. That's a time-out. Please sit in the orange chair and think about what you've done. We'll talk about it when your time-out is over.'

Afterwards restate the reason for the time-out: 'Okay, Leslie. Your time-out is over. Remember that you went into time-out for hitting your brother. I don't want to see it happen again.' This will help Leslie remember exactly why she had to sit in the orange chair, and she should find it easier to remember not to hit her brother in the future.

If your child is in time-out because he refused to obey a command – 'Put your shoes in the bedroom, for instance' – he must agree to comply with the request before being permitted to leave the time-out area.

HOW TO SET UP A TIME-OUT SYSTEM FOR YOUR FAMILY

Decide how and when time-outs will be used for your family. An eight-year-old who is rude to a visiting relative might be given a time-out, but a three-year-old who spills her juice accidentally should simply be asked to help you clean it up.

Select a time-out area. It should be a spot in the house where you can still see the child. That way you can be certain of compliance and you can monitor the child's safety. Consider using a corner of a room, a specific chair, or the stairs. Because there should be no toys or other form of entertainment in the time-out area, using the child's bedroom is generally not a good idea.

Explain to your child why he is being placed in a time-out. You could explain that if he screams and kicks when he doesn't get what he wants, you have no choice but to put him in a quiet place for a few minutes.

During the time-out, the youngster should sit quietly, and you should not talk to him – even about the incident. He should not be able to follow you around the house or bargain for an end to the time-out.

Some kids may refuse to go into a time-out or may leave before the time is up. If that happens, guide your child back to the designated area, talking with him as little as possible.

How long should a time-out last? A good rule of thumb is to give one minute of time-out for each year of the child's age: a four-year-old would spend four minutes in a time-out, and a ten-year-old would be asked to remove herself for ten minutes. Though you should never exceed the minute-per-year guidelines, you may want to vary the time depending on the severity of the infraction. A nine-year-old who smacked his little brother, for example, might get a longer time-out than a nine-year-old who played ball in the house. You'll be surprised at how long four or five minutes will seem to both you and your child under these circumstances.

Use an egg timer, a kitchen timer, or some other form of alarm to keep track of the time. By doing so, you avoid the little voice calling, 'Is my six-minute time-out over yet?' When the time-out begins, you simply say, 'Your time-out will last until you hear the buzzer.'

Don't hold a grudge against your child after the incident. Remember that you have already disciplined your child, and you don't need to keep bringing it up.

As the time-out method begins to diminish the poor behaviour, start using praise to reinforce good behaviour. As your child feels encouraged, he will try to elicit that same excited and pleased response from you again and again by repeating the behaviour you praised. When used appropriately and consistently, a time-out system can result in permanent, positive change.

CHANGING BEHAVIOUR THROUGH TIME-OUTS FOR TOYS

Sometimes a time-out for an inanimate object can result in behaviour changes in children. If a certain toy is the source of constant disagreement, you might put the object itself in a time-out. For example, if your kids are constantly battling over a specific video game, you might tell them that no one is allowed to play that video game for one hour, and at the end of that time they need to have developed a new strategy for sharing. If they don't, the toy will go back into a time-out.

You can use the same technique with the television set. If your kids are bickering over what programme to watch, you can place the set itself in time-out until they come up with an equitable way to decide what show to watch.

Avoiding the Use of Guilt Trips

(See also Building Self-Esteem, p. 42; Setting Limits, p. 74; Getting Angry: Parental Anger, p. 84; Saying You're Sorry, p. 85; Avoiding Power Struggles, p. 144.)

Guilt is a powerful weapon that most people consciously or unconsciously use occasionally. Though it works in many cases, you should refrain from using it. Guilt might help correct certain types of behaviour, but it usually causes self-blame and resentment in children because it implies that they are blameworthy and do not deserve to be treated with respect.

The purpose of discipline is to teach *constructively* so that children behave well because they want to, not because they fear being made to feel guilty. In parenting, your ultimate goal is not just to improve behaviour but to build a strong bond in the parent-child relationship.

Instead of using guilt, set firm limits and make sure that your child knows ahead of time what is expected of him. Then there should be no confusion about whether he misbehaved. If he does misbehave, correct the behaviour in a gentle but firm manner. Don't keep bringing it up, especially if it doesn't recur.

Instead of constantly making a child feel bad about misbehaviour, make him feel good about when he behaves well. This will help build self-esteem.

Spanking: The Current Thinking

(See also Being a Positive Role Model, p. 39; Setting Limits, p. 74; Using Time-Outs, p. 76; Getting Angry: Parental Anger, p. 84; Saying You're Sorry, p. 85; When Parents Disagree about Parenting, p. 93; Handling Aggressiveness, p. 113.)

Spanking is a controversial method of discipline, and one that we do not advocate. Physical punishment does not teach your child how to resolve conflicts, and it carries no message concerning proper behaviour. It's also confusing. Kids who are spanked assume *they* are bad, not that their *behaviour* is bad. In addition, you are your child's most important role model, and by spanking your child, you send the message that hitting someone is okay. When you then tell your child that he isn't to hit his little sister, your credibility is undermined by your own actions.

Another important reason to avoid spanking is that it's all too easy to lose your temper. The only way to guarantee that you will never physically abuse or hurt your child is if you never hit her. Many cases of child abuse begin when parents start to dole out some type of punishment and their anger escalates beyond their control. A bad day at work or a smart-aleck remark from the child being punished may push a parent beyond normal limits, and the child is hurt.

Spanking can also damage the parent-child relationship. A child who is spanked learns to fear her parent, particularly if the parent does not clearly explain why the spanking occurs. Few parents want their children to associate them with pain or violence.

Parents of toddlers frequently argue that spanking is acceptable because toddlers are too young to be reasoned with effectively. Thus, spanking or a slap on the hand appears to be the only solution. For example, a parent with a toddler who constantly wants to rummage through a kitchen cabinet that contains cleaning products may argue that the child should be spanked 'for his own good'. However, toddlers may not necessarily learn, based on that punishment, that they must not go into this cabinet. A more logical solution is to make your child's environment safe for exploration. Cabinets or cupboards that need to be off-limits should be fastened with child-proof safety catches so that the child cannot gain access to the dangerous chemicals. When you can prevent temptation or misbehaviour, you should do so. Leaving your toddler at home with a sitter when you take your nursery school child to a play, taking activities along for the children on a long car ride, and other preventive measures will reduce the likelihood of misbehaviour and therefore cut down on the need for discipline.

While we strongly urge parents to refrain from spanking, our daily clinical practice makes us well aware that some parents believe strongly in their right to spank their children. For this reason, we share with you guidelines developed by Dr. Barton Schmitt, a paediatrician and professor at the University of Colorado School of Medicine:

1. SPANK CHILDREN ONLY when they have engaged in dangerous behaviour that could result in serious injury – for example, when Jane impulsively runs into the street without looking for cars, when Tommy turns on the rubbish disposer even though he has been repeatedly told to stay away from it, or when Michael continues to try to stick his finger into an electrical outlet.

2. SPANK ONLY with your open hand. Never use a fist or an object. Using an open hand allows you to control the amount of pressure because you can feel the force of the blow. The intent of spanking isn't to hurt the child, but simply to gain her attention so that you can explain why her behaviour was dangerous.

3. NEVER SPANK using more than one swat. You're not trying to cause pain, you're simply relaying the message that the behaviour was unacceptable.

4. SPANK YOUR CHILD ONLY on her buttocks or her hand. Slapping your child in the face can be extremely humiliating and very painful.

5. DO NOT SPANK your child every day or more than once a day. Spanking your child frequently will make her feel that she lives in a violent atmosphere. If she continuously engages in behaviour that you think merits spanking, then more rigorous limit-setting is in order.

6. DO NOT USE SPANKING as a consequence for a child's aggression. Think about how illogical it is to hit your child because she hit someone else. The only message this sends your child is that hitting is acceptable as long as the victim is smaller or more vulnerable than the aggressor.

7. NEVER SHAKE YOUR CHILD. Shaking a child, even minor shaking, can be exceedingly dangerous and can result in severe injury. Children under age five are particularly susceptible to injury from shaking; blindness, mental retardation and even death can result.

In our clinical work, we have observed that children are more frequently psychologically damaged by frequent yelling than by occasional spanking.

Negotiating With Your Child

(See also Being a Positive Role Model, p. 39; Building Self-Esteem, p. 42; Speaking So Your Child Will Listen, p. 68; Setting Limits, p. 74.)

A compromise is a settlement in which each side gives up some demands or makes some concessions. Some parents worry that negotiating means simply caving in after your child wears you down. If adults always stuck rigidly with their thoughts and did not remain somewhat flexible, there would be constant disagreements. It is only through flexibility and compromise that both parties in a disagreement can feel satisfied with the outcome and feel that they have won.

When you negotiate an issue with your youngster, make it clear that each of you should have an opportunity to present your side. You must listen carefully to your child ('My friends get to stay out a half hour later than I do, and I'd like to get the same curfew they have') and point out that your child also must listen to your point of view ('I worry about you when you're out late'). The less emotional you both are in expressing your views, the better the negotiation is likely to go, and you will probably arrive at a reasonable compromise. In this example, you might extend the curfew but ask your teenager to phone in at a certain time during the evening.

If you show that you can be flexible, will your kids become manipulative, always trying to get their way? Not at all. While children do feel good about themselves after winning a point such as the later curfew, you actually bank some goodwill. You may find that your son or daughter is particularly cooperative the next time you make a request.

THE BENEFITS OF COMPROMISE

Compromise is a good life skill to teach.

1. It builds a child's self-esteem. A compromise is often called for when a child wants to change a rule or request. Since she has asked for this change, any concession, no matter how slight, can make her feel as if she has won her case, thereby empowering her to think for herself and discuss things with you another time.

2. It teaches a skill. The ability to compromise is a skill that is needed later in life, and practising it with you is a great way for your child to begin. Let him state his needs and make a case for his point of view. This practice encourages younger children to use words rather than have a temper tantrum. The skill will be useful throughout life.

3. It demonstrates to your child that you are flexible. Rigidity is not an admirable trait, and by being flexible, you demonstrate to your child that, if you're given a good reason, you will change your mind.

4. It shows your child that you are considerate. Eventually your child will see that part of the reason that you have compromised is that you want to make her happy. This is a good lesson for your child and you will be a good model to your child.

5. It teaches appropriate assertiveness. Through negotiation and compromise, your child will learn to state her requests and stand up for her beliefs. This assertiveness can have a powerful and far-reaching impact on your child's life.

WHEN NOT TO COMPROMISE

Compromising on certain points doesn't mean you have to compromise all the time.

, you compromised with your
 he wanted to eat for dinner,
 tarts protesting his nine o'clock
 u should listen to his arguments
but firm. You might say, 'I hear what
you're saying, but it is important that you get
plenty of sleep. It's time to go to bed now.' Say
this pleasantly. Your child may go to bed but
then come out to ask for some water. Be firm
and let him know that he can get some water
but has to go back to bed immediately.

In addition, don't negotiate anything that
concerns safety or goes against your values
or standards. You need not, for example,
negotiate with the seven-year-old who wants
to see an R-rated movie, the twelve-year-old
who wants to get her belly button pierced, or
the preadolescent who wants to stay out until
midnight with what you consider a bad
group.

Be firm but kind and respectful, explaining the reasoning behind your position.
Unfortunately some adults associate 'no'
with 'anger'. In reality, they needn't be related.
Your child may get angry if she doesn't get her
way, but if you remain consistent, gradually
the child will see that you mean business and
accept your decision without resentment. If
anything, she may have more respect for you
because you are firm but also often willing to
compromise.

Anger In Daily Life

(See also Teaching Social Skills, p. 40; Ad-
vocating Empathy, p. 50; Setting Limits, p. 74;
Using Time-Outs, p. 76; Avoiding the Use of
Guilt Trips, p. 78; Negotiating with your
Child, p. 80; Getting Angry: Parental Anger,
p. 84; Saying You're Sorry, p. 85.)

Anger is a normal emotion that most
people experience almost every day. It
springs from our natural instinct to fight for
what we want and to protect ourselves
when we feel we have been treated unfairly.
When we are tired, overwhelmed, or under
personal stress, small things can make us
angry more easily than when we are calm
and well rested.

Anger is part of the human experience,
and if it finds a ready – and safe – outlet, it
will generally dissipate quickly. However,
anger is insidious and even dangerous when
people use inappropriate outlets for their
anger, or when anger is suppressed or becomes so prevalent that a hostile or violent
manner becomes a way of life.

In children, anger can range from the
two-year-old's tantrum over the cat's refusal
to play with her to the eleven-year-old's frustration over a teammate's dropping the cricket ball and causing the team to lose the game.

As a parent, being upset with your child
occasionally is part of the parenting experience. Sometimes anger actually serves as a
teaching tool: if your little one runs into the
street without looking, it is appropriate for
you to raise your voice and use a stern, angry
tone, because you need to communicate how
upset you are at the possibility of the child's
being hurt.

Other times you may be frustrated by
your child's behaviour. If you come home
after a very long day and discover that your
school-age child is watching television and
has evidently ignored his promise to do a few

chores before starting his homework, you may feel irritated. While your disappointment at his behaviour should be communicated calmly, the anger you feel is human.

Forgiveness is also important, and everyone needs to understand that holding a grudge can be destructive. Parents act as powerful role models for children, and the way you express your anger will greatly influence how your child's anger is communicated. Both parents and children need to recognize when they are angry, so that they can direct it appropriately.

While declaring that you are upset about something is one way of expressing anger, people show anger in many other ways: by being impatient, arguing, yelling, or, in the extreme, turning to violence. Many people suppress their anger until they become so overwhelmed that their emotions explode and they scream at someone or storm out of a room slamming a door behind them. Other people show their anger in indirect ways – by withdrawing, feeling depressed, or becoming manipulative.

Dizziness, racing heart, sweating and a fear of losing control are physical symptoms that sometimes accompany anger, particularly when we feel we have no outlet. The long-term effects of continued anger can include high blood pressure, digestive difficulties and many other physical problems.

Mild anger can usually be diffused or controlled by directly expressing displeasure with the situation. The nursery school child who learns to use words to express her frustration when a classmate takes some of the blocks she was playing with will see that words can bring about solutions. The classmate may not have realized he was taking something she was about to use, and he may give the blocks back once she explains they were part of her game. Or if a child-to-child solution isn't working, the little girl can tell the teacher what has happened. Though she may still feel anger over the disruption of her game, that feeling will diminish as she uses words to work out the difficulty.

More severe anger may be diffused by taking a time-out – removing yourself or asking a child to remove herself from a situation before the angry feelings get out of control. For example, a parent who is quite angry at her child over a mishap may take a time-out by going to the next room for a few seconds to calm down. Though this seems simplistic, it works. Stepping away from the problem, even for a few minutes, permits your fury to subside and allows your 'let's get this solved' mechanism to take over. Of course, in any situation where you want to take a breather, you need to make sure that your child is safe before you leave the room. You might put a toddler into a playpen or ask an older sibling to watch her for a minute.

If your child has angered you by doing something wrong, you can still discipline her. Just do it when you are calm and can control what you say and do.

Sometimes anger can be controlled by taking a new look at a situation. For example, Mary may be upset with her four-year-old son because he ate sloppily in front of his grandmother. Mary may be very sensitive to what her mother-in-law thinks of her and may fear that the woman will view Mary as a

mother for not yet having created a
_ fect son.

Instead of focusing on proving something to her mother-in-law, Mary might look at the situation in a new way: Her child eats sloppily because he is only four. If the mother-in-law comments on his manners or eating habits, Mary might respond unapologetically, 'He's doing the best he can for a four-year-old. We're working on table manners, and he'll get better as he gets older.'

HELPING YOUR CHILD DEAL WITH ANGER

Anger has to come out in some way, and it's important for children to have safe outlets for their unpleasant emotions. This may sometimes be difficult for you as a parent because your child's distress may make you feel guilty or angry. Nonetheless, helping your child learn to manage anger is one of the most loving things you can do.

There are two important methods of managing anger. The first involves thinking calmly before you act; the second entails verbalizing your emotions. If your child recognizes when he is angry and then learns to talk it through, more than likely he will come up with a solution.

One technique we use to help both adults and children learn to express how they are feeling is the 'I feel _____ when _____ because _____' method. If your daughter is angry with her sister, she might say, 'I feel angry when you use my hair dryer without asking my permission because you never remember to put it away, and then I have to

search for it when I want to use it.' This technique is simple and straightforward, and most people understand its use.

Start using it yourself – you'll find that it works.

Getting Angry: Parental Anger

(See also Being a Positive Role Model, p. 39; Making Chores a Matter of Routine, p. 70; Setting Limits, p. 74; Avoiding the Use of Guilt Trips, p. 78; Anger in Daily Life, p. 82; Saying You're Sorry, p. 85; What to Do When You're Overwhelmed by Your Own Problems, p. 96; Taking a Holiday from Parenting, p. 97.)

Inevitably, there will be times when you blow up at your child. When this happens, apologize as soon as you realize what has happened. Explain that you were tired, had a bad day, or were just fed up with the situation and made a mistake. Blaming your child for causing the anger is inappropriate. Don't say, 'I'm sorry that I yelled at you, but you made me mad.' Instead, say something that shows that you take responsibility, like 'I'm sorry that I yelled at you. I had a really bad day and took it out on you. I was wrong.' Give your child a hug to show that you still love him.

WHAT HAPPENS TO CHILDREN WHO FACE FREQUENT PARENTAL ANGER

Being exposed to frequent bursts of extreme parental anger is one of the most destructive things that can happen to a child, because encountering a parent's fury makes the environment frightening and unpredictable.

Within a household, most parent-child interactions should be calm and pleasant.

Serious problems arise when more than half the conversations end up in unpleasantness. Children who live in households where parents are angry most of the time undergo changes in behaviour:

➤ They become afraid to express their opinions because they fear retaliation from their parents. In these homes children sometimes determine that it is better to protect themselves by not talking than it is to say what they feel and have someone verbally or physically attack them.

➤ Some children may become overly sensitive to criticism, even if it is expressed gently, and they will react with anger to any reprimand.

➤ Using anger becomes a pattern for how they interact with other people. They may be lonely children because they strike out at those around them, and in the future they will have problems in intimate relationships, dealing with co-workers and bosses and in having good relationships with their own children.

➤ They may develop psychiatric disorders such as depression, they may become highly anxious and fearful and feel hopeless about their lives, or they may take a different route by displaying antisocial behaviour.

➤ These children often grow up with health problems. Having headaches or backaches and being accident-prone can result from being exposed to extreme anger, and the impact of anger on the development of high blood pressure, heart disease and gastrointestinal problems such as ulcers is well known.

HOW TO REDUCE YOUR ANGER

Parents often 'lose it' because they are so overwhelmed by working, child-rearing, family errands and all of life's other demands. If you feel this is the cause of your distress, try finding ways to reduce your obligations or ask for help from your spouse or friends. Many people find that exercise or carving out special time to spend on something they enjoy has a generally calming effect, and physical labour, even scrubbing the kitchen floor, when you're upset really does help diffuse some of the stress you're feeling over being angry. (Refer also to Chapter 5 on managing stress.)

Saying You're Sorry

(See also Being a Positive Role Model, p. 39; Teaching Social Skills, p. 40; Advocating Empathy, p. 50; Avoiding the Use of Guilt Trips, p. 78; Anger in Daily Life p. 82; Getting Angry: Parental Anger, p. 85.)

Apologizing is frequently one of the first interpersonal skills children are taught. Yet ironically adults often have a hard time admitting that they have done something wrong. It is natural to want to present oneself as perfect to one's children. After all, kids tend to idealize their parents and expect them to be the ultimate authority figures. However, parents make mistakes sometimes (having to break a promise, yelling at a child, or hurting her feelings), and the manner in which a parent's misdeed is corrected is usually more important than the mistake itself. This correction process should usually include an apology.

When parents make a mistake or can't fulfill a promise, children customarily respond with anger, sadness, or fear. However, parents usually focus on their own reaction to the situation (feeling guilty, being upset with their boss and so forth) instead of considering how the child feels. Remember that the purpose of an apology is to make your child feel better. It is your way of indicating that you are sorry to have injured, insulted, or wronged your child.

Given the long-term nature of the parent-child relationship, it becomes even more important that apologies are offered naturally and frequently.

HOW TO APOLOGIZE TO A CHILD

The primary goals of an apology are to acknowledge responsibility for a misdeed, to express remorse, to begin to rebuild the parent-child bond, to make the child feel better and to alleviate your own guilt.

According to Christina E. Mitchell, director of counselling and testing at the University of Texas at Tyler, when you apologize to your child you should:

1. EXAMINE your reasons for apologizing. Sometimes parents say a quick 'I'm sorry' to their children before they have had time to actually think about their actions. Kids are quite good at ascertaining other people's emotions and can often recognize insincerity. Taking the time to empathize with your child will make your apology strike the right note.

2. FOCUS on your own behaviour during the apology. Don't bring up your child's behaviour, although you may discuss that at a later point. For example, if you called your child an idiot because he broke your favourite dish, simply apologize for the name-calling: 'Tom, I'm really sorry I called you an idiot. I know it was an accident, and I shouldn't have blown up at you.' Don't blame the mistake on your child's behaviour: 'I wouldn't have got angry if you hadn't broken the dish.'

3. AVOID begging for forgiveness, which could lead your child to assume that an unpardonable wrong was committed. Make the apology simple and direct: 'I'm sorry I can't take you to the zoo as we planned. I have to work on Saturday. Believe me, I'd much rather be with you.'

4. DON'T EXPECT your child to accept the apology immediately. Remember that your child has a right to be angry, so give him time to cool off. Don't assume that you automatically merit forgiveness just because you are his parent. If your child refuses to forgive you, patiently explain that you understand and you aren't angry. Briefly repeat that you are sorry and note that you will be around to discuss the situation later if needed.

5. REALIZE that an apology consists of more than a simple 'I'm sorry.' As the cliché indicates, actions speak louder than words. Your later actions will determine whether your apology was sincere. If you immediately make the same mistake, your child will not believe that you were actually sorry. Additionally, you need to make some restitution. If you missed an event with your child, plan another one at a time when you know you can make it. Too often parents make imprudent promises to their children and consistently disappoint them.

6. MAKE SURE that your child understands what has occurred. For instance, ask your child, 'Do you understand what I'm saying to you?' to make sure that she grasped the apology.

If you learn to follow these simple steps, apologizing to your child will become second nature. You and your child will both feel better about the situation after an apology.

chapter nine
PARENTAL ISSUES

FEW PARENTING BOOKS place priority on talking about marital and parental issues, but the issues that affect you as parents are vital to discuss. What should you do if you and your spouse get into a fight in front of the children? And what about those days when you're just sick to death of parenting? As for divorce and remarriage, the way they are handled is vital to the well-being of the children.

You'll find this section to be a very helpful part of the book.

Deciding on the Size of Your Family

How many children should you have? You and your spouse should discuss this issue carefully, weighing the benefits and drawbacks objectively.

Most people have a vague

Deciding on the Size of Your Family

Telling Children that They Were Adopted

Parental Disagreements

When Parents Disagree about Parenting

Taking Special Joy in Parenting

What to Do When You Dislike Your Child

What to Do When You're Overwhelmed by Your Own Problems

Taking a Holiday from Parenting

The Effects of a Parent's Affair

When Divorce Is Inevitable

Remarriage

Successful Single Parenting

idea of what size family they want. Some want to have two, three, or even more children so that the kids can keep each other company and have the support of siblings. Others think one child is enough. Sometimes couples want to have a child of a particular gender and they keep having children until they produce one of that sex.

For some parents, financial considerations are of primary importance. We have tried to de-emphasize the significance of money in raising children, because it's not necessary to be wealthy in order to raise a well-cared-for and well-adjusted child. Obviously, however, enough money is necessary to meet a child's need for shelter, clothing, food and an education. If you then take into account long-term considerations, including college and possible financial sacrifice if one of you cuts back on your work hours during the child-rearing years, the financial picture changes considerably. While most parents don't begrudge money spent on raising a family, you do need to consider the cost of raising a family.

Another primary consideration concerns your energy and psychological strength – for example, the stability of your relationship and your commitment to taking care of the children. It takes stamina to be on call twenty-four hours a day for years and years, with very little time off.

If you weigh the pros and cons and opt for a large family, remember that it's still important to be a one-to-one parent. You need to bring out each child's individuality and make each child feel special. This means finding the time to take an interest in each child's

school activities, address any special needs and guard their privacy in what may be a crowded house. A large family can be wonderfully rewarding, but don't stumble into it blindly!

Telling Children That They Were Adopted

(See also Fulfilling the Basic Needs of Children, p. 38; Speaking So Your Child Will Listen, p. 68.)

Adoption is a topic that is hard to keep secret. Your child will eventually find out that he's adopted, and this important information should come from you. Nondisclosure of adoption gives your child the message that adoption is bad or shameful.

Years ago children sometimes weren't told they were adopted and learned about it later – sometimes as late as adulthood – from others or by discovering legal documents, birth certificates, or photos. These deceived kids almost always react poorly and feel anger towards their adoptive parents for keeping such a secret.

Today most experts agree that revealing the adoption is the best option. It establishes honest communication between parent and child and avoids deception. In addition, knowing about their origins is important to most children. After all, one of the first difficult questions children ask is 'Where did I come from?' If your child asks you if he is adopted, don't lie about it.

Ideally, you should begin presenting your child with this information before he asks. The manner in which you tell your child about his adoption is crucial and will determine his reaction and adjustment. Learning of their adoption is likely to be upsetting rather than traumatizing for most kids.

For your part, you will almost certainly worry about your child feeling that his biological parents abandoned him. Reassure him that his birth parents had a hard decision to make and made it only for his benefit. Point out how happy you are that you have him, how full he has made your life and how happy he makes you.

You may also worry that your child will reject you and want to go back to her biological parents. If you talk openly and honestly about adoption with your child from an early age, this is unlikely. In addition, adoptive parents fear being told, 'You can't tell me what to do, you aren't my real parents!' If you have a good relationship with your child, you may discuss your fear with her: 'Sometimes I'm afraid that you'll want to leave me and go and live with your other parents.' This disclosure will help your child see that you really love her and that you have fears, too, an honesty that will likely bring you and your child closer.

THE THREE STAGES OF ADOPTION REVELATION

1. BEING TOLD. Discussions about adoption should begin when your child is between ages two and four. Start with very basic information. For a very young child, you might say, 'Mummy and Daddy couldn't have a baby together, so we got you from another mummy.' Similarly, you may explain, 'Your mummy and daddy couldn't take care of you,

so they wanted you to come and live with us because they knew that we would love you and take good care of you.' Obviously, you should avoid telling your child any unpleasant details about the biological parents (drug use, for example), and you must not imply abandonment. Also avoid making excuses for the birth parents. Don't feel compelled to say that the biological parents really loved your child. This can be confusing and cause 'love' and 'abandonment' to merge in your little one's mind. Your child may then fear that you, too, will abandon her.

At this age, the legal aspects of adoption are irrelevant and shouldn't be mentioned. However, at all ages, you need to assure your child that nobody can take her away from you. Children today see frightening news stories of biological parents taking back their children from adoptive parents, so you have to make it very clear to your child that this will never happen to her. Point out to your child that the birth parents gave permission for the adoption and wouldn't want to disrupt the child's life.

2. UNDERSTANDING. After you have told the child about her adoption, your next step is to help her understand what this means. Encourage her to ask questions and talk about her worries.

3. ADJUSTMENT. The final step is for the child to adjust to the news of her adoption. Sometimes this involves a sort of mourning period for the loss of her birth parents. Be patient. Allow her to talk about the birth parents; in the process, you'll learn what may be bothering her.

AS YOUR CHILD gets older, he will probably ask questions about adoption, and these questions will tell you what you need to discuss. Don't assume your child will share with you all of his questions or fears. Periodically ask what he knows about adoption and what it means to him. That way your child will perceive adoption in his own way and talk about it in a way that can serve as your guide in deciding what to discuss.

Sometimes after an adoption is revealed, a child may test her limits by misbehaving or breaking rules to see how the adoptive parents will respond. Be firm and tell your child that you disapprove of her behaviour but that you love her and would never abandon her.

Some children may want to meet their biological parents. Usually this desire stems not from a rejection of the adoptive parents but from the child's curiosity about his birth parents and about whether or not he has brothers and sisters. You need to use your own judgment on this. Some biological parents are willing and even eager to meet their children, and the visit may be a pleasant experience. If the birth parents are alcoholics or drug users, however, your child probably shouldn't be in contact with them. Again, you should be honest and tell your child why you don't think a reunion is a good idea: 'Your real mummy couldn't take care of you because she has a lot of problems.' Present distressing information gently. Also be certain that your child really wants to meet his birth parents and is ready to do so. Having two mothers and fathers is confusing and some kids simply aren't ready for it.

Parental Disagreements

(See also: Being a Positive Role Model, p. 39; Anger in Daily Life, p. 82; Getting Angry: Parental Anger, p. 84; When Parents Disagree about Parenting, p. 93; When Divorce Is Inevitable, p. 99.)

Kids learn how to get along with others by watching their parents and seeing what they do. Frequent arguments between you and your spouse may give your children the notion that the way to solve problems is to yell, shriek and generally try to outscream the other person.

One of the most common causes of parental arguments is money, because people often have dramatically different ideas about how to spend it. Couples rarely discuss finances before they are married, even though starting a family is a tremendous financial responsibility that frequently causes stress. Arguing about money can make your child assume that there is not enough to pay for basic needs, such as shelter, clothes, and food.

Arguing about relatives is also common. For instance, your spouse might not want your mother to come for a visit. This type of argument can be damaging because the child may fear being separated from a particular relative.

It is wholly inappropriate to quarrel about sexual matters in the presence of your children. Unquestionably, this situation can be extremely humiliating for the partner being attacked, and hearing about sex can make a child exceedingly embarrassed and insecure. Such arguments border on child abuse and should be avoided at all costs. If your spouse starts such an argument, immediately remove yourself and your children from the situation.

Arguments about child-rearing should also be avoided when children can hear. These arguments, sometimes innocuous in content, can be internalized by the child to mean 'Mum and Dad are arguing about me', Such a situation leads the child to feel guilty, thinking that he is the cause of the trouble, or assuming that his parents are angry at him. Similarly, a disagreement about discipline or rules might lead a child to manipulate the situation. If you assert that your child cannot have friends over when he is home alone and your spouse disagrees, your child will probably ask your spouse for permission knowing that a yes response is more likely. You and your spouse must provide a united front in regard to the care of your child.

WHEN AN ARGUMENT CAN'T BE AVOIDED

Although you should always try to avoid fighting in front of the children, sometimes you just can't. For example, your spouse may start an argument when the entire family is in the car. Thus, R. Taffel offers the following pointers to help ease the difficulty of these situations:

1. KEEP THE TONE of your voice and the argument as light as possible.

2. DON'T DISPARAGE your spouse. Stick to the issue being discussed and don't criticize your spouse's personal characteristics. Above all, don't call your spouse names or curse. Focus on the problem, not on your spouse.

3. FINISH THE SPAT quickly. Don't prolong the quarrel by bringing up old or irrelevant issues. Discuss one problem and briskly reach a compromise.

4. MAKE UP WITH YOUR SPOUSE. Preferably, you and your spouse should show your affection for each other by hugging or kissing. Even if you are still tense or upset, be sure to apologize and signify that the argument is settled. Your kids are likely to duplicate your argument style with their friends, family and future spouses. Hence, the manner in which you conduct yourself affects your child in many ways.

5. AFTER THE ARGUMENT, talk about it with your child. Ask what she thought was going on during the fight. Explain that sometimes people argue in order to solve problems. Comfort and reassure your child. He may fear that a divorce or abandonment by one parent is imminent. Confirm to your child that he is loved by both parents and that you and your spouse love each other.

4. IF YOUR SPOUSE will not relent and the argument becomes abusive, end it quickly and leave the situation with your child. This may be hard to do, but you must attempt to do it.

IF YOU MAKE A HABIT OF following these guidelines, your kids will be spared any ill effects of parental arguments.

When Parents Disagree about Parenting

(See also Getting Angry: Parental Anger, p. 84; Parental Disagreements, p. 92; Taking a Holiday from Parenting, p. 97.)

Since each parent comes from a different background, variations in child-rearing styles are only natural. When you and your partner are trying to decide how to handle everything from curfews and allowances to dating and schoolwork, you're bound to disagree on a number of points.

When you encounter these differences, don't immediately jump to defend your viewpoint. Ask your spouse the reasoning behind his view and tell him why you believe in your view. This way, perhaps the two of you can decide what is best for your child.

Forget about trying to win the argument or put down your spouse. Often, your spouse will have valuable information and may be right about a topic. For example, your spouse might say, 'I think that instead of spanking Johnny for lying, we should put him in a time-out.' You may feel this is less effective, but ask nicely why he thinks a time-out will work best in this case. He may provide a sound, well-reasoned argument. Be open to learning something from your spouse.

When you and your spouse disagree on an issue, try to maintain a united front when the children are around. Children often sense when parents disagree and may try to play one parent against another.

Always remember that, in parenting, there is more than one right way to do things. If you both are vehement about a particular issue, try to work out a compromise. You'll need to negotiate, with both of you giving in a little. Just keep focusing on what would be best for your child.

Of course, sometimes a spouse may not give you any reason for his views and may not listen to the reasons for your view. In this case, there isn't much you can do, and a compromise cannot be reached. (If this pattern is common in your relationship, you should consider counselling.)

Unfortunately, the parent who is more in control of the relationship will probably try to control how the children will be raised. This is unfortunate, since the need to control becomes a serious problem for the well-being of the child and the entire family. The dominant spouse may use all types of manipulation to make the other spouse do things her way. This disagreement can lead to resentment between the spouses. Sometimes the submissive parent may go along with the dominant parent in the spouse's presence, but will talk against the parent behind her back. This is destructive for the marriage and also devastating and confusing for the children.

If you and your spouse argue constantly about various issues concerning the children, consider whether something else is going on. Sometimes these arguments are caused by an underlying problem in the marriage. For example, a parent may feel closer to her child than to her spouse and may display this favouritism by not allowing the spouse to punish the child. Similarly, a parent may find it easier to disagree with his spouse over a child-rearing issue than to confront a deeper marital problem. Look closely at your motivation before you press an issue or start an argument about parenting. If you are having other problems, try to talk them out or seek outside counselling.

Taking Special Joy in Parenting

(See also Developing Creativity, p. 45; Finding Quality Time, p. 53; Stressing Physical Activity, p. 58.)

Can you be a parent and have fun at the same time? Absolutely! With any luck, being a parent will be a great source of pleasure for you. After all, what could be more enjoyable than watching your child grow and mature? Ideally, you should do something pleasurable with your child every day. Take him out, read to him, take walks, play sports and board games together. You can be silly and let your child be silly, too.

Here's another great way to enjoy being with your child: include your child in the activity you love most in the world. If you're an avid gardener, let your toddler help you when you're working outside. Or set up a window garden together. Chances are that your enthusiasm will be contagious, and over the years, you'll have company as you work in the garden. What could be more delightful?

Having fun doesn't have to be expensive. Visit the library, do a craft project, work on a puzzle, or just talk.

You are the most important person in your children's lives, and you need to teach them that life is enjoyable and fun.

What to Do When You Dislike Your Child

(See also Finding Quality Time, p. 53; Getting Angry: Parental Anger, p. 84; What to Do When You're Overwhelmed by Your Own Problems, p. 96; Taking a Holiday from Parenting, p. 97; Successful Single Parenting, p. 102.)

It is not uncommon for parents to dislike their children when they feel overwhelmed, resent their lack of privacy, or get bored being at home tending to kids all the time. Unfortunately these feelings can result in parents being angry or irritated with their children frequently. If this has happened to you, it doesn't mean that you aren't a good parent. You're only human, and anyone can have these feelings. They tend to occur more often in single parents because of the increased responsibility and lack of social support available to them.

Although these feelings are normal, it's an uncomfortable way to feel. In order to maintain a healthy parent-child relationship, it's important to improve your outlook. You can do this in a variety of ways, most of which will give you time to focus on yourself for a while:

1. **ACKNOWLEDGE** when you need a break from parenting and don't feel guilty about taking one.
2. **SET ASIDE** time to socialize with friends.
3. **IF YOU'RE MARRIED,** spend time alone with your spouse.
4. **HAVE YOUR SPOUSE** take the kids out now and then so that you can have an evening to yourself to relax.
5. **HAVE RELATIVES** or a trusted baby-sitter take the kids so that you and your spouse can spend time alone at home.
6. **FIND SOMEONE** with whom to talk about your feelings. This could be a

spouse, a trusted friend, a relative, or a co-worker. Or if you're concerned about your feelings, seek out a counsellor or religious leader who can help you sort out your feelings.

GENERALLY, feelings of dislike arise when parents are under stress, but there are other reasons for not liking a child. Some parents may find their child an embarrassment because of a character weakness, an unattractive appearance, or a physical disability. Other parents may resent the amount of money and energy children require. Or a child may remind his parent of someone the parent dislikes. Because of this association, a parent may be unconsciously biased against the child.

If any of these thoughts sound familiar, consider joining a parents' support group or undergoing counselling. An outsider can almost certainly help you focus on what's good about your child so that you can fall in love with your kid again.

Spending a lot of time with anyone can cause you to get tired of him. The important thing is to find an outlet and not feel guilty about your emotions.

What to Do When You're Overwhelmed by Your Own Problems

(See also Negotiating with Your Child, p. 80; Anger in Daily Life, p. 82; Getting Angry: Parental Anger, p. 84; Taking a Holiday from Parenting, p. 97.)

Like everyone else, it's likely you have problems of your own. Depression, anxiety and substance abuse are common problems that plague adults. And coping with a difficult situation in your own life makes it more difficult to fulfill your role as a parent. Therefore, it's important to take your own situation seriously and do what you can to feel better. By doing so, you'll be helping your entire family.

HOW TO COPE WITH PROBLEMS OF YOUR OWN

Here are a few steps to take when you're feeling overwhelmed:

1. USE THE FIVE-STEP METHOD of coping with stress, outlined in Chapter 5. Examine your own role in contributing to your problems, and learn from your mistakes. Remember your job is not to become impatient or angry at yourself but to solve the problem.

2. DISCUSS YOUR PROBLEMS with a trusted individual such as your spouse, a parent, a friend, or a relative, and be open to suggestions. At some point, professional help may be in order. You will have a wide variety of mental health professionals to choose from – social workers, psychiatrists, psychologists and counsellors. Find someone you trust and with whom you feel comfortable.

3. TRY NOT TO blow up at your kids. Often when people have problems, they tend to get angry easily. If you do lose your temper with your child, you will feel bad later, and your anger is difficult for your child to handle. If this does happen, make sure that you apologize later. Let your child know that you are a human being and at times you will get angry, but you are trying your best to feel better.

IF IT IS YOUR SPOUSE who is having difficulty, reach out to offer your support. Try to gently help her see the problem, and don't attack, blame, or criticize her. With your help, she may be willing to seek professional help. One warning: If you see that she is out of line with the children, don't sit by quietly. If you think the situation could become dangerous for the children, get help immediately or remove yourself and the children from the home for a time.

In extreme circumstances a parent may be so overwhelmed that he just can't function. In this case, your first and most important task is to place your children in a safe and stable environment while you seek help. Perhaps you can turn to a family member or a friend. If absolutely necessary, Social Services can temporarily place your children in a foster home. This is a painful step, but if you can no longer take care of your children's basic needs and ensure their safety, the best thing for them is to be cared for until you can get your own life in order.

Taking a Holiday from Parenting

(See also Chapter 2, The Basic Needs and Feelings of Parents, p. 7; Chapter 5, The Family Guide Method for Coping with Stress, p. 29; Fostering Independence, p. 48; Nurturing Responsibility, p. 49; What to Do When You Dislike Your Child, p. 95.)

Sometimes you need a rest from parenting, just as you would from any full-time job. Don't feel bad – everyone needs some time off now and then. If you can't get away for a real vacation, be creative:

➤ **ASK FOR HELP.** Ask your mate, parents, relatives and children to help you redistribute the chores. Maybe a reduction of your burdens will give you the relief you need.

➤ **DO SOMETHING INTERESTING.** Perhaps you need the stimulation of something new. Consider taking a class or finding a hobby. Having new things to think about is invigorating.

➤ **CARVE OUT AN HOUR EVERY DAY, OR EVERY OTHER DAY, THAT IS ALL YOUR OWN.** Find time to slip away to the beach or wander in the park on your own.

➤ **TAKE A REAL HOLIDAY, EVEN IF IT'S JUST FOR A DAY OR TWO.** Do you have a willing relative who would take care of the kids? Or could you hire a sitter for the weekend? If your children are old enough, leave them with friends for a few days, with the promise that you'll repay this gesture by taking their kids for a time.

LOOK FOR EVERYDAY opportunities to relax and let off steam. Doing so will help you have more energy and tolerance, and it will give your child a chance to spend time with other people, including your spouse, who may have fresh energy for the task. After your brief holiday, you can approach your job with renewed vigour and commitment.

The Effects of a Parent's Affair

(See also Being a Positive Role Model, p. 39; Saying You're Sorry, p. 85; What to Do When You're Overwhelmed by Your Own Problems, p. 96; When Divorce Is Inevitable, p. 100.)

Marital infidelity is common in our society, and the impact of an affair on the couple's relationship, and consequently the whole family, is almost always very significant. The offending spouse may have low self-esteem and suffer from an extreme desire to be wanted. While the desire to be wanted is generally normal, having affairs can only lead to destruction in families. Even if the couple agrees to forgive and forget, the wronged spouse may still feel hurt and may use the affair as ammunition in marital arguments. Some choose to exact revenge, usually by having an affair themselves. This can quickly escalate and become exceedingly destructive to everyone involved. In many cases, a separation or divorce occurs.

Kids become aware of their parents' affairs in a variety of ways. Sometimes one parent confides in the child or uses the information as a way to turn the child against the offending parent. Children are usually savvy enough to ascertain when there is a problem in their family.

In our own clinical work we've found that children react to a parental affair in one or more of the following ways:

➤ Denial and refusal to believe that the parent could do something so contemptible.

➤ Anger at the parent for causing so much pain for the family or ruining the family's happiness or reputation. Usually, this anger emerges slowly as the child comes to terms with what has happened and what it may do to the family.

➤ Worry about the parent's actions.

Children often feel confused or perplexed and question *why* a parent would do such a damaging thing.

➤ Open rejection of and hostility towards the offending parent. The child may refuse to talk with or even to see the parent. This situation can be exceedingly disruptive for the entire family, and things are unlikely to improve if there is a communication breakdown.

➤ Feeling insulted and humiliated. A child may feel that the parent's actions show that he or she is displeased with the family. It is not uncommon for the child to take much of the blame for this displeasure, feeling that if he had been good, this never would have happened.

➤ Anxiety. Children may become anxious about the possibility of a divorce.

IT IS NOT UNUSUAL for children in this situation to run away, destroy property, steal, lie, have problems at school, or abuse substances. They may do this simply because they're angry with the parent, or they may believe that the parents will become so concerned about the misbehaviour that they will focus on trying to solve these problems, and the marital fight will go away.

Regardless of the outcome or how the parents resolve, or fail to resolve, the problem, the simple fact remains that a child in this situation has lost trust in her parents. This loss of trust will have major repercussions in the way she handles her relationships with other people. Although many children will be completely repulsed by the affair, unfortunately some will make the same mistake when they become adults.

Remember that as a parent you act as the primary role model for your child. We highly recommend that you and your spouse receive marital counselling to help eradicate some of the consequences of the affair for the entire family. Your children may need counseling as well.

When Divorce Is Inevitable

(See also Chapter 5, The Family Guide Method for Coping with Stress, p. 29; Building Self-Esteem, p. 42; Speaking So Your Child Will Listen, p. 68; Getting Angry: Parental Anger, p. 84; Parental Disagreements, p. 92; Remarriage, p. 100; Successful Single Parenting, p. 102.)

Divorce is one of the biggest stresses a child can face, because it represents a major loss. The child 'loses' the parent who leaves the house and 'loses' the other parent who, because of the divorce, might have to deal with stress, a lower income, a poorer neighborhood and other problems. What's more, emotional upset combined with the stress of legal hassles often leaves parents feeling angry, depressed, or distant from their children. As a result, the child also loses a major portion of a parent's energy, which is now spent on issues surrounding the divorce. The outcome of this ugly battle is that the children inevitably suffer tremendously.

It is hard for most children to understand why the two most important people in their lives, who once loved each other, are now bitter enemies. Children often assume that they are to blame for a divorce, feeling that if they had behaved better, the divorce wouldn't have happened. In this case, a child is likely to suffer from self-doubt and will need constant reassurance from both parents.

According to research conducted in 1993 by Janet Walker of the University of Newcastle, the most difficult aspect of divorce for children is not the separation from one parent, but the continuing conflict between the parents. Some parents ally themselves with their children against their ex-spouse so that the child feels torn in terms of loyalty. The child wants to please both parents, but the parents are making it impossible. Thus, it is imperative that you and your ex-spouse reach a truce and end your arguing as much as possible.

Keep in mind that children who adjust best to their parents' divorce are those who are able to maintain regular and meaningful contact with both parents with limited dissension.

Marian H. Mowatt, a clinical psychologist, has identified typical reactions for certain ages: Toddlers and preschoolers may react with confusion and feel abandoned; they may be clingy and whiney with the remaining parent. Secondary school children may blame themselves for the breakup and show a great deal of grief. Adolescents may seem indifferent to the divorce, but they often hide their feelings and are at high risk for depression.

HELPING YOUR CHILD THROUGH DIVORCE

After the divorce, there are ways to make life easier for your child.

1. PERMIT your children to express their feelings. It is common for children to experience grief following a parental divorce, and they should be able to express it. Some children are afraid to talk about the divorce because they aren't sure how the parents feel. If the parents are glad about the divorce, children may be reluctant to discuss their sadness that one parent is gone. Thus, you have to reassure your children that their feelings are legitimate and you want to hear about them.

2. ENCOURAGE your children to verbalize their worries. They might worry about finances or such things as in which house the bike will be kept in the case of joint custody. If your spouse always drove them to school, they may worry about who will do that after the divorce. Other times, the child will worry that he will never see the parent who is moving. Even though you may have a great deal of animosity toward your ex-spouse, encourage visits as often as is feasible. Often you will be able to soothe the children's worries by coming up with practical solutions.

3. ALLOW your child to ask questions. Be prepared to answer tough ones, like 'Don't you love Mummy anymore?' and 'Why is Daddy moving out?'

4. BE PREPARED for your children's anger. Divorce is a dissolution of the family, and children often feel angry. Let your children vent their frustrations and try not to take it personally.

5. ACCEPT HELP from relatives, friends and neighbours. Let them baby-sit or help you around the house. This will reduce your stress and allow you to be a better parent. In addition, your child will probably benefit from having other adults around.

6. ACKNOWLEDGE that having a two-parent family is not as important to your child's welfare as is the time and energy you devote to creating a stable and supportive environment. A single parent can provide a great home, so don't spend your time and energy beating yourself up for your divorce or worrying about your child.

7. UTILIZE community resources. Kids can join a local club or a similar organization that will give them a place to hang out and interact with responsible adults. Also, many communities have some type of 'children of divorce' support group. This may be especially helpful during the early months, when divorce first becomes obvious or imminent.

8. CONSIDER family therapy. Sometimes the problems surrounding divorce will be more than you can handle. Fortunately, there are trained professionals who can help you and your child adapt to the changes that have arisen.

Remarriage

(See also Chapter 3, Marital Happiness Leads to Family Happiness, p. 15; Chapter 4, The Benefits of an Extended Family, p. 25; Teaching Social Skills, p. 40; Setting Limits, p. 74; When Parents Disagree About Parenting, p. 93.)

A few decades ago divorce and remarriage were relatively rare. Because few couples got divorced, people didn't have to worry about blending families. Today about one in three marriages is a remarriage.

While the pressure to succeed in a second marriage is intense, these marriages are often stronger because people have learned from their previous marital experience. In addition, people are older and generally more mature when they remarry.

Certainly a major problem with remarriage is that a stepfamily comes into existence, and creating harmony among new family members can be challenging. A child often enters into this situation in a fragile state, suffering from the breakup of the original family due to death or divorce. As a result, some kids are hostile to their stepparent or stepsiblings and feel that their territory is being invaded. Sometimes the mythical image of the evil stepmother or the cruel stepfather frightens children.

To help prevent these problems, plan activities to enable your child to get to know your future spouse long before the wedding. In addition, these steps will help your child feel more comfortable with the new situation:

1. NEVER DISCOURAGE your children from talking about or keeping pictures of the other parent and encourage contact by phone and in person, if possible.

2. TALK TO YOUR CHILDREN about the new stepparent. The children may feel that the stepparent is an outsider, or they may fear that they will receive less love from you because you have to share your love with this new person. If your children feel threatened by your remarriage, it is doubly important to discuss their emotions without becoming angry. (Watch their body language. Some kids may hesitate to talk about their feelings because they fear another marital breakup and the loss of yet another parental figure.) Listen carefully to their fears and concerns; don't dismiss them.

3. REMEMBER that it may take time for your children to feel fully comfortable with and affectionate towards this new person. If they seem to dislike the stepparent, accept their feelings for now and set up some basic rules of conduct. Insist, for example, that your children show respect to the stepparent. Discourage angry or irrational arguments with the stepparent and treat this behaviour as disobedience. Also, be certain that your children make an effort to get along with your new spouse. With patience and thoughtful effort on the part of your new spouse, chances are this relationship will improve.

4. PROVIDE a united front with your new spouse. The two of you need to discuss child-rearing issues before the marriage. Consistency is important, and kids need to know that if they misbehave, the biological parent and the stepparent will respond in the same way. You also need to make it clear to your children that you and the stepparent have discussed discipline and that the stepparent has the right to set limits. Make it clear that you and your spouse agree on these issues, so that the child will not fear that the stepparent will be unduly harsh. Often kids say, 'Bob is not my father. He can't tell me what to do!' Be up front with your child and say that the stepparent is an authority figure who must be respected. After all, the whole family has to share the home and try to get along together.

5. POINT OUT to your child the advantages of your remarriage. The children now have a new parent to help take care of them and maybe even new siblings to play with. Stepparents can be wonderful caregivers who are willing to do just about anything for their new children, so encourage your children to express their gratitude to the stepparent.

6. IF AN ARGUMENT between your child and new spouse erupts, don't automatically support one side or the other. You might feel protective of your child and instinctively assume that he is right, or you might be thinking about preserving the marriage and blindly support your spouse. Your best course of action is to listen to both sides and try to guide them towards a fair agreement. The more objective you can remain, the more successful you'll be at calming heightened emotions. Also keep in mind that sometimes kids start fights with stepparents to test the loyalty of their biological parent, and this is certainly a trap you want to avoid.

OVERALL, remarriage can have many benefits for you and your children. However, you must respect your children and understand that this new situation may create tremendous stress for them. Ultimately, however, your own comfort and happiness will almost certainly make things easier for your child.

Successful Single Parenting

The demands of raising children are enormous, and there is little doubt that parenting can be done more thoroughly by two involved people than by one parent alone. However, although it may be harder, a single parent can definitely raise happy, well-adjusted children. What's more, though most people expect the single parent to be female, there are many single fathers who are successfully raising their children. If there is at least one person who cares about a child's welfare, the likelihood that the child will turn out well increases dramatically.

One key to successful parenting is a support network. Talk to friends and relatives who might be willing to help you occasionally on a regular basis and hire outside help when you need it. Neighbourhood teenagers are usually affordable and are lots of fun for children. In addition, make the school aware of your situation. The school counsellor who realizes your child has only one parent may keep a more watchful eye on your son or daughter. Don't be afraid to ask for help. Having more people around who care will help your children feel well-cared-for.

Be available to your child as much as possible and try to keep communication flowing. Your child should understand that you will make time to hear about her problems, concerns, or successes. Schedule a time every night to be with your kids. Make sure that this time is sacred and you aren't trying to do several things at once.

A major concern of single mothers is

whether a male role model is needed for their sons. Most children manage to find male role models outside the home. Many children have a grandfather or uncle whom they can look up to and respect. Some children may find a male neighbour, family friend, or teacher whom they admire. Although it can be helpful to children to have a same-sex role model in the home, it is not necessary. Letting your child develop relationships with relatives and friends will suffice.

chapter ten

OVERCOMING FAMILY DIFFICULTIES

FAMILY LIFE ISN'T always easy. Tensions among siblings, a fearful child, a death in the family . . . Many situations are very difficult for families to handle. Let's examine some of the problems that parents encounter frequently.

The Spoiled Child

(See also Finding Quality Time, p. 53; Setting Limits, p. 74; Negotiating with Your Child, p. 80; Can Babies Be Spoiled? p. 125.)

Although the adage 'Spare the rod and spoil the child' has become antiquated, parents today still seem to be afraid of spoiling their children. Part of this fear comes from confusion over what constitutes spoiling.

No child will be spoiled by being given what she needs and some of what she wants.

Providing a comfortable and giving environment will not spoil children. If anything, it's healthy and will help a child learn to trust others.

Children do become spoiled, however, when money and material objects are substituted for love, time and affection. Even though they may have a playroom filled with toys, they *still* don't have what they need – attention from their parents. Needless to say, it's far better for you to spend time with your children than to spend money on them.

Another important part of not spoiling a child is being willing to say no and mean it. Children need guidance, and if you firmly and kindly direct your child, chances are that he will grow up to be a nice, unspoiled adult. If, for example, your nine-year-old constantly plays video games instead of doing his homework, you will have to pack up the video game set and put it up in a cupboard for a time. And when the grandparents offer to buy your seventeen-year-old a car for his birthday and he says he wants it to be a convertible, you're going to have to exercise better judgment than he is – new drivers need safe cars, not ones that carry a higher degree of risk. Whining, wheedling and tantrums should fall on deaf ears once you've made what you feel is a sound decision.

This isn't to say you shouldn't negotiate. If your child brings up a good point about an issue under discussion, you should consider it. For example, you might initially reject your teenager's request for a mobile phone. But if your teenager points out that she has to drive ten miles to work and might need to call for help in case of car trouble, you might reconsider. In this case, the parent has to be reasonable, and giving the teenager the mobile phone won't constitute spoiling.

Avoiding Favouritism

(See also Finding Quality Time, p. 55; Putting an End to Scapegoating, p. 108; Reducing Sibling Rivalry, p. 109; Managing Tale-telling, p. 114.)

Favouritism is exceedingly common, simply because we all have personal preferences even when it comes to our children. Most parents recognize the importance of fairness and of being equitable to all of their children. Unfortunately, some parents report that they adore one child and don't really like another very much.

Several circumstances can contribute to favouritism.

➤ **POSITIVE TRAITS.** Parents may prefer the children they feel most proud of – children who are intelligent, hardworking, dedicated to schoolwork, helpful around the house and eager to please.

➤ **'PROJECTIVE IDENTIFICATION',** A child may display characteristics that a parent has always aspired to have. Thus, a parent who is obese and unhappy about it may favour the child who is thin and treat the overweight offspring with dislike and disdain. Another child may be favoured because he reminds a parent of his own good qualities. A father who loves tennis may simply adore spending time with his child who seems to show the promise of professional aspirations in tennis.

> **REMINISCENT QUALITIES.** A child may remind her parent of a favoured sister or a hated uncle, and this resemblance can have an impact on the way the child is treated.

> **WHETHER THE CHILD WAS WANTED AND THE QUALITY OF THE PREGNANCY.** A child who was conceived accidentally may be less well treated than one who was conceived through a planned pregnancy. Similarly, the ease or difficulty of birth can make a difference in how parents feel.

> **GENDER.** The sex of the child may also result in favouritism. Many parents prefer to have boys. Indeed, in a study of school students conducted by Irving Harris and Kenneth Howard, boys more often reported being a favoured child than did girls. A preference for males may be particularly true for the first-born.

> **BIRTH ORDER.** Parents are usually anxious when handling their first child. They are uncertain about their parenting skills and nervous about hurting the child or making mistakes. In contrast, parents are more relaxed in dealing with later children as their confidence in their parenting skills increases. As a result, parents may feel more relaxed around younger children and generally like them better. Similarly, some parents may become very close to their youngest child to combat the empty nest syndrome, when the last child leaves home.

PARENTAL favouritism can be expressed in a variety of ways. Sometimes it's subtle; other times it's quite obvious. A parent may be more involved in the activities of the favoured child – helping with homework, talking more, attending more of that child's special events, or providing more encouragement or support. The parent may also burden the less-favoured child with more, or more difficult, household chores. Favoured children are also less likely to be punished and more likely to receive a lighter sentence than a non-favoured child.

Comparison, which is related to favouritism, is very destructive. Human beings love to compare things or people. As you grow to love one person more than another, however, you may devalue the less favoured family members. Devaluing a child can lead to lower self-esteem and cause the parent-child relationship to deteriorate or become combative. What's more, comparing a ten-year-old's great ability at maths to an eight-year-old's lesser talent basically dooms the younger child to never succeeding at maths. In addition, being compared unfairly to an older sibling has now established a major psychological barrier that the younger will have to overcome.

Favouritism is a major contributor to everything from sibling rivalry to depression and other psychological problems. In order to avoid the potentially devastating effects of favouritism, we recommend that you take the following measures:

1. Discipline your children fairly. Make sure that the same rules apply to everyone and are enforced equally. Don't let one child break a rule without punishment while another child is severely punished for breaking the same rule. Of course, when making rules you should take into account the ages of your children. It is fair, for example, for older children to have later bedtimes because the younger ones know they will eventually be granted this privilege.

2. Assign chores fairly based on the age and ability of each child. Allow the kids to discuss the distribution of tasks so that they feel that it's fair.

3. Attend children's activities equally. If necessary, make a chart that shows when each child has activities and divide your time among all of your children. Spend time with each child and do things that each one enjoys.

4. Identify what you like about each of your children and build your relationship upon these qualities. For example, if you and your child both like football, you can improve your relationship by playing touch football in your back garden or attending football games together.

WHEN YOUR CHILD asks if you have a favourite, what's the best reply? Most parents respond by denying it outright, which usually doesn't convince the child. Instead, confirm that you love all of your children but you like different things in each of them: 'I love you because you are generous and you make me laugh. I love your brother because he is kind and tries to help around the house.' Further, try to cite somewhat equal qualities. You don't want to comment on one child's intelligence while praising the other for keeping a neat room.

While you can't control your basic emotions, you can control the way you treat your children. By working at liking a child who is going through a difficult stage, you may find that your child surprises you and reveals many lovable qualities when given the chance.

Putting an End to Scapegoating

(See also Being a Positive Role Model, p. 39; Building Self-Esteem, p. 42; Avoiding the Use of Guilt Trips, p. 78; Anger in Daily Life, p. 82; Saying You're Sorry, p. 85; Avoiding Favouritism, p. 106.)

Unfortunately, some people need to have a target for blame. By blaming other people, we can temporarily feel better about ourselves and feel that we belong to a group. This tendency irrationally to blame others is called scapegoating. It is a way in which people get reassurance that they are acceptable, and regrettably, this reassurance is gained at the expense of others.

Scapegoating occurs within a family when two or more people stick together and blame a third person – either a child or a parent. If they have someone to blame then the family members can feel better about themselves. The family will, *temporarily*, function better if the members have someone to call 'bad' and can consider themselves 'good'.

Scapegoating can take on many forms. However, when the scapegoat is a child, the process usually follows the following pattern:

1. THE COMPLAINTS about the child's behavior exceed the severity of the child's offences.

2. COMPLAINTS about the child often start at birth: 'You were such a fussy baby. You cried all the time.'

3. THE CHILD is described as a Jekyll and Hyde – good one moment and terrible the next.

4. THE CHILD'S good behaviour is seen as manipulative and deceitful: 'You're just being good so that you'll get dessert.'

5. THE FAMILY claims that other people don't know what the child is really like.

6. THE SIBLINGS join in pointing out the child's weaknesses.

7. NO ONE takes into account the circumstances. For example, the child may have been practising the piano when everyone planned Mum's birthday surprise, and *that's* why he wasn't in on it; not because he didn't want to cooperate.

8. THE SCAPEGOAT is not 'part of the family'.

9. THE SCAPEGOAT may be unattractive or less intelligent.

10. IF ONE of the parents is no longer in the family unit, the scapegoated child is described as being 'just like' the absent parent.

11. THE SCAPEGOAT may be physically abused.

12. IF TREATMENT eliminates the child as a scapegoat, another child will often be scapegoated.

If you see that a family member has become a scapegoat in your household, here are some steps you can take to improve the situation:

➤ **BE REALISTIC.** If a problem exists in your family, acknowledge it and do what you can to solve it. Temporary stress, not just long-term relationship problems, can sometimes result in undeserved anger at a family member. For example, if you've just lost your job, you may be taking out some of your anger on one of your kids. If you're puzzled or over-whelmed about what's going on within the family, therapy may be the best solution.

➤ **DON'T FOCUS ON THE FAULTS OF A CHILD.** Try to be fair to all of your children. Everyone has likeable characteristics, and as soon as you determine what you like best about your more difficult children, focus on that quality – particularly when things get bad.

➤ **IF YOUR CHILD MISBEHAVES, LOOK FOR PATTERNS.** Sometimes parents will note that a child acts up when a particular person is around. Perhaps your son is a good kid, but when he's around his sister, he hits her and picks on her. Your son is obviously not evil or bad; he just has a problem getting along with his sister. Another kid may act up in church or at the supermarket. If you can see that your child is not *always* bad, you will be less likely to use her as a scapegoat.

Reducing Sibling Rivalry

(See also Advocating Empathy, p. 50; Setting Limits, p. 74; Avoiding Favouritism, p. 106;

Managing Tale-telling, p. 114; Setting Limits for Toddlers, p. 128.)

Ties with siblings are often the longest life relationships people have. Because siblings have shared so many experiences, they can offer each other enormous support and comfort and can share pleasant family memories throughout their lives. Adults frequently feel that a brother or sister will be more likely to understand a problem than would a friend.

There is little doubt, however, that most siblings spend a certain amount of time bickering and fighting. In a survey conducted by Janice M. Prochaska and James O. Prochaska, nine- and ten-year-olds reported having an average of approximately five fights a day with their siblings! Their reasons for fighting included the following:

1. One of them was in a bad mood.
2. One wanted to get even.
3. One was protecting her room or toys.
4. One sibling wanted to prove he was number one.
5. One or both were bored.

As you can see, children don't even need a good reason to fight! Contrary to popular belief, children claimed they rarely fought to get parental attention. Further, kids reported having a good time with their siblings an average of nine times a day – in other words, kids have fun more often than they fight. Yet few parents remember the good parts because the fights are so much more noticeable!

Some theorists argue that the root of sibling rivalry is children's reluctance to share their parents; on a symbolic level, each child is trying to eliminate the one with whom he competes for the parents' attention. Because of this, one of the biggest threats to sibling compatibility is parental favouritism. Children frequently develop a deep resentment of the favoured sibling. Therefore, parents need to work particularly hard at treating all children fairly.

AGE AND TEMPERAMENT CAN AFFECT RIVALRY

During the preschool and early primary years, it's common for siblings to show little affection for each other and to squabble frequently. As children enter middle childhood (six to eleven years old), the amount of warmth and companionship between siblings may increase, but the conflicts may continue. During adolescence, teenagers increasingly turn away from the family and towards peers for support and companionship. Thus it's common for adolescent siblings to have little to do with each other.

The age differences between your kids will also affect their relationships. Kids who are very close in age may strongly identify with each other. Those who are far apart in age may have less interest in each other, and older kids may feel burdened by having to spend time with much younger kids.

Finally, temperament can influence sibling relationships, and drastic differences in character can lead to problems. One child might be quiet and withdrawn, for example, whereas the other is loud and enjoys playing practical jokes. Clearly, these two kids may not get along well. In contrast, a close match between temperaments can sometimes result in a wonderful friendship between siblings.

HOW YOUR PARENTING STYLE AFFECTS RIVALRY

Your parenting style will have a great effect on how your children relate to each other. Two parenting styles – laissez-faire and autocratic – have been associated with poor child adjustment and more severe sibling rivalry.

The laissez-faire parent offers little direction or supervision. The children are basically in charge of the household and frequently experience conflict with each other as each struggles to gain control.

The autocratic parent has complete control over the children and their actions. The children are in direct competition with each other for parental attention and approval.

The healthiest parenting style is one whereby children participate in the decision-making process for issues related to them, but where the parents make the ultimate decision. In these families, the kids feel as though they have guidance and some control over their lives.

CREATING THE RIGHT ATMOSPHERE

One simple way to help children get along is to institute a hierarchy. Give special status to the oldest child, explaining that greater responsibility comes with increasing age. From the beginning, teach your little ones to respect their older siblings. In return, older siblings should be encouraged to support and look out for their younger siblings. In

this way, all your kids will feel responsible for the well-being of their brothers and sisters.

By recognizing each child as a unique individual, you'll also help create family harmony. Instead of comparing your children or their skills, find out what each child does that is special. Emphasize these qualities. Also spend time with each child alone. Help each one with homework, if necessary, and spend a few minutes every night tucking each child in and saying good night. This is a good opportunity for each one to talk to you for a few minutes for whatever comfort or guidance he or she may need.

Minimizing the need for territory and possession disputes is also helpful. Make it clear who has permission to do homework in what room and which clothes, games and toys belong to each child. Hand-me-downs are used in almost all families, but make sure that each child – even the youngest – has some new things that belong only to her. Rivalry is often intensified if everything must be shared and the younger siblings never have anything that is new or belongs solely to them.

Sacrifice as a family value (as discussed in Part One) also increases sibling compatibility. If your children are occasionally willing to sacrifice their rights for the good of their siblings, your children will get along with each other. Collaboration and cooperation are important in a family, and if these qualities exist between siblings, your entire family will function more smoothly.

Don't tolerate verbal abuse, name-calling, or violence between siblings. If a physical fight erupts, separate the kids, preferably in different rooms, and allow them to calm down before you talk to them.

Invite your children to discuss family-related decisions and take their ideas into account when making final judgments.

Be sure to praise your kids when they are getting along well. It's more natural to pay attention to bad behaviour, but praising appropriate behaviour is one of the best ways to ensure that it will continue.

SIBLING PROBLEM-SOLVING

Children must learn to work out their problems with siblings. One aspect of this is learning to forgive. Encourage your children to apologize and make some sort of restitution when they have hurt each other. Be a good role model by apologizing to your children when you make mistakes. Persuade your children to work out their problems on their own and reach a compromise. Of course, you want to oversee this process, especially at the beginning. If a serious injustice has occurred, you will want to discuss the situation with your kids.

If you need to intervene in a fight, don't yell or scream, just get the children's attention and stop the action. Being angry only reinforces the connection between problems and fighting for your kids.

TEACH EMPATHY THROUGH ROLE-PLAYING

If you point out the effects of unacceptable behaviour, you begin to encourage empathy and compassion. If one child calls the other a derogatory name, have the kids switch roles and re-enact the scene. Then ask the child who did the name-calling how she felt about being the victim. Usually kids will admit that they felt bad, and you can point out that they certainly wouldn't want to make others feel bad. Role-playing works best with children age eight and over.

DRAW UP SIBLING CONTRACTS AS NEEDED

If your kids have many conflicts, you may want to implement a contract between them. Contracts can be used for many different issues, and we have found that most kids, particularly adolescents, will honour them.

Once your children are calm, help them take the following steps:

➤ Clearly define the problem. A contract should address only one problem and works best when it concerns a specific type of behaviour.

➤ Let each child present his or her side.

➤ Help them agree on a compromise.

➤ Put their agreement in writing. Include the date on the contract and agree upon a term for the contract – in other words, decide how soon a new contract should be written. Include the consequences of violating the term of the contract – doing the other person's chores for a week, for example.

➤ Have the contract signed by those involved.

IF YOU CREATE an environment that permits your children to be friends most or all of the time, your immediate reward will be a harmonious household. Your long-term reward will be kids who are friends.

Handling Aggressiveness

(See also Teaching Social Skills, p. 40; Spanking: The Current Thinking, p. 79; Anger in Daily Life, p. 82; Reducing Sibling Rivalry, p. 109; Stealing, p. 115; Acting Out, p. 167.)

Aggressive kids often engage in bullying, fighting, threatening or intimidating people, or using weapons. They may also destroy property – slashing car tires or intentionally breaking windows – steal property, or set fires. These kids get into trouble at school, at home and in the community. Even mild aggressiveness in a child is very frustrating for parents.

Try taking these measures to reduce any type of aggression in your child:

1. BE A GOOD ROLE MODEL. Don't tell your child: 'Don't ever hit anyone,' and then yell and scream at your spouse when you're angry. (You might see the difference between yelling and hitting, but your child probably will not.) When you're frustrated or angry, take a moment before you say or do anything. Obviously, this means that you should refrain from hitting your child or spanking him for a misdeed. Brainstorm about alternatives and use a nonviolent solution.

2. TEACH YOUR CHILD how to solve problems (see the five-step model in Chapter 5). This skill is crucial for children who are aggressive. Briefly, have the child examine what is bothering him, consider the worst possible consequence, admit what part he played in causing the problem, make a list of possible solutions and decide upon an action and stick to it. It's best to write this process down so that each step is carefully undertaken. Children who can take partial responsibility for the problem and come up with a solution to a frustration will be less likely to behave aggressively.

3. PRAISE YOUR CHILD when he solves a problem without becoming aggressive. For example, suppose your son wants to take a turn at a video game and his brother won't let him. The aggressive solution would be to hit his brother. Instead, your son tells his brother that he just wants to play for five minutes and then he'll swap. (They can use a kitchen timer to time each turn.) Praise your son for coming up with a good solution and tell him how smart he is. Children who are aggressive particularly need encouragement.

4. SET FIRM LIMITS on aggressiveness. Make it clear to your child that you don't approve of aggressive behaviour and if necessary put your child into a time-out. (Refer also to the techniques recommended in Setting Limits, page 74.)

5. USE OUR SUGGESTIONS for helping make a child more empathetic (see Advocating Empathy, page 50). Some kids who are aggressive are not good at guessing what another person is thinking. If someone accidentally pushes him, a child who is aggressive might assume that the push was hostile and will respond by pushing back. Empathetic children are better at understanding other children's feelings.

IF YOU HEAR your child was involved in a fight, reserve judgment until you have heard his side of the story. Even a child who is aggressive should be allowed to defend himself.

If a child has been labelled a troublemaker at school and is now trying to gain control of her aggressiveness, she may still be viewed with suspicion by some people. Schedule a meeting with her teacher or counsellor and explain what you've been doing to help change this behaviour. If the school personnel are aware of the situation, they may be able to encourage an improvement in your child's behaviour.

Managing Tale-telling

(See also Teaching Social Skills, p. 40; Building Self-Esteem, p. 42; Setting Limits, p. 74; Anger in Daily Life, p. 82; Getting Angry: Parental Anger, p. 84; Putting an End to Scapegoating, p. 108; Reducing Sibling Rivalry, p. 109.)

Children tend to go through a period when they are very rule-oriented. This stage normally begins in preschool when children learn about rules and the consequences of breaking them. Preschoolers are very careful to abide by the rules in order to avoid getting into trouble. During the primary school years, children move into a stage in which they put emphasis on social rules.

In a certain way, telling tales combines these two phases. By telling tales, older children are attempting to please and be good. The tell-tale wants everyone to obey the rules. In addition, she thinks that telling tales is good behaviour that will please adults. A child who tells tales may not specifically want to get others in trouble; he may simply be outraged that other kids are breaking the rules. He may also hope to be seen as good by acting as the house police officer.

Telling tales is one of the primary ways that sibling rivalry is shown in families. Jealous children love to get their sibling into trouble. A child may think that if her sibling is in trouble, she will be seen as good and be more loved by the parents.

Telling tales also causes problems outside the home. Few things irritate other children more than being told on at school. Friendships can be ruined, and a tell-tale is likely to be very unpopular, because no one likes a snitch.

Your response to a tell-tale is important. The child's motive may make a difference in how you handle the situation. Is she just gossiping? Is she being a troublemaker? Or is she really worried about the behaviour about which she is telling tales?

Strategies for Managing Tell-tales

➤ Don't punish the other child in front of the tell-tale. Do it privately and emphasize to the tell-tale that you have taken care of the problem – she doesn't need to worry about it anymore.

➤ Don't praise the tell-tale unless the other child was engaging in dangerous behaviour such as crossing the street without looking for oncoming cars. In this case, you should be grateful your tell-tale was there.

➤ Ask the child how she could solve the problem herself or deal with it in another way, if the behaviour about which the child tells tales is not dangerous.

➤ Encourage the tell-tale to be upfront about what is bothering her. If the tell-tale says, 'Nelson is cheating at Monopoly,' tell her to discuss this directly with her brother, not to tell tales just to get him in trouble.

➤ Ignore the tale-telling if the behaviour is not particularly serious.

IF TALE-TELLING persists, consider whether your tell-tale is putting others down to feel better. If so, you may want to look for ways to increase his self-esteem. Children who feel good about themselves do not need to make others look bad.

Stealing

(See also Being a Positive Role Model, p. 39; Teaching Social Skills, p. 40; Stressing Physical Activity, p. 58; Setting Limits, p. 74; Getting Angry: Parental Anger, p. 84.)

If your child is caught stealing, don't blow up. Undoubtedly, you'll be extremely angry. It can be embarrassing and upsetting to think that your child has become a thief. However, in order to help your child, you need to handle the situation calmly. Don't try to make

him feel guilty or ashamed; that would be counterproductive.

The first thing to do is to let your child tell his side of the story. Say, 'I want to know why you stole something.' Your child might resist and say, 'I don't know. I didn't think about it.' Don't accept that answer; push a little harder. The child's reasons for stealing are important in helping you determine whether this is an isolated occurrence or an established pattern of behaviour.

WHY KIDS STEAL

1. Peer pressure. When kids go to the shops together, they'll sometimes dare one member of the group to steal something. Because the theft is not well thought out, kids are frequently caught. Kids in this category usually show remorse and don't repeat their mistake.

2. Desire for material possessions. Our society places great value on owning material things, and to a teenager having just the right jacket or sneakers can seem overwhelmingly important. As a result, some kids turn to stealing. (Remember though that stealing may happen no matter how many possessions your child owns so the answer doesn't lie in trying to answer every material need.) Some kids will continue to steal; others in this category will be frightened enough by being caught that they will stop.

3. For the thrill. These kids tend to brag about their exploits, particularly to peers. Kids in this category often continue stealing, and the behaviour can be hard to stop.

HOW TO DEAL WITH STEALING

Regardless of your child's reason for stealing, don't protect him. If the shop owner decides to press charges, don't beg him to drop the case. If you take care of the problem, as parents often do, you'll send the message that you'll always cover for him and he can get away with anything.

Resist the impulse to punish your child and brand him a crook or a thief. Avoid drastic measures, including name-calling.

Here are some of the ways you can put a stop to stealing:

1. Clearly define 'stealing'. A good definition is 'being wrongfully in possession of something that doesn't belong to you'. Defining it may seem ridiculous, but when you're trying to correct a behaviour the child needs to define it explicitly. If your child is caught with stolen property given to him by a friend, then it's still stealing. Once you discover that stealing has occurred, don't let your child argue about it.

2. Set up clear consequences. Let your child know exactly what will happen if he is caught stealing again. Make sure that the consequences fit the crime. Ideally, have the child return the stolen item and apologize. Don't shame your child or call him names.

3. Have your child replace the stolen item. Have him pay for the item by working. Younger children can do extra chores around the house; older adolescents might get a part-time job.

4. Don't put unfair temptation in your child's way. For example, don't leave your purse or wallet sitting on the table while your child is home alone. Some parents will complain that they should not have to worry about stealing in their own homes, but if your child is having a problem with stealing, it's not fair to tempt him.

5. Don't try to trap your child. Some parents set up a video camera to film their children stealing in the home. Other parents search the child's room looking for contraband. Although these methods might be effective in documenting stealing, they will critically undermine the parent-child relationship.

6. Get your child busy in a school or community activity such as a sport, a play, or a volunteer project. A child busy with constructive pursuits has less time to steal. Also, keep an eye on your child. Make him check in with you and tell you where he's going. Children who are left unattended and can go wherever they please are more likely to steal because they aren't under close scrutiny.

7. Be a good role model. If a shop assistant gives you back extra change, be sure to return the money. Similarly, if you find a ring in a carpark, take it to the shop's lost-property department. These things are important at any time, but they are even more important when your child is with you. Buying items you know were stolen can also encourage children to steal, as they see someone profiting from it and they see you condoning theft.

Stealing creates great stress in the family. For most first-time offenders, just being caught will be frightening enough to stop the behaviour. But if the problem is more than you can manage, consider counselling. Your local police department may have a programme that can help you.

Overcoming Fears

(See also Building Self-Esteem, p. 42; Helping the Shy Child, p. 44; Anxiety, p. 173.)

Fear is an intense reaction to some object or situation. (This is in contrast to anxiety, which is a more general feeling of concern or worry.) Fear can be useful, however, in warning people that they may be in danger.

Fear differs from a phobia in that almost everyone experiences fear occasionally, but a phobia is much more severe in nature. Children with a phobia react with *extreme* distress when they are around a feared object. Some children may run away, scream, or faint, and the fear usually doesn't subside.

Four-year-old Roger fears loud noises and runs to his parents' bedroom during late-night thunderstorms. He also fears large animals, snakes and the bogeyman – all of which are common fears of young children. Twelve-year-old Cindy has a phobia about bridges and screams in terror whenever her parents drive the car over a bridge of any kind. Roger will almost surely outgrow his fears, but Cindy's parents should look for professional help in dealing with her phobia.

According to the American Psychiatric Association, mental health professionals have identified four general categories of fear:

1. **Animal (dogs, snakes, bugs)**
2. **Natural environment (storms, heights, water)**
3. **Blood-injection-injury (having injections, seeing blood, getting hurt)**
4. **Situational (flying, riding in an elevator)**

Most kids become progressively less afraid as they grow older and begin to gain more control over their environment. However, if your child is currently very fearful of something, these guidelines should help:

➤ **NEVER MAKE FUN OF A FEARFUL CHILD.** Remember that your child would not be afraid of something unless he thought that he might get hurt. When adults are fearful about something – say, insects – they generally realize that it doesn't make sense; kids, however, rarely realize that their fears are irrational or excessive.

➤ **OFFER TO HELP.** Ask your child how you can make it better. Your child may know exactly what will help. For example, if your child is afraid of the dark, a night-light or a stuffed toy to sleep with may solve the problem. In other situations, you may have to be a little more creative. For a child who is afraid of snakes, you might try putting rock salt or lime as 'snake poison' around the foundation of your house. Or if your child is afraid of ghosts you might hold an 'exorcism'. With young children, conducting some type of ritual is almost always better than simply trying to talk about it.

➤ **DON'T ASSUME THAT YOUR CHILD CAN BE TALKED OUT OF HIS FEAR.** Reasoning with a child who thinks the dog is scary-looking is very difficult. To a child, it makes sense to be afraid of something that looks scary, so it's difficult to change his mind.

IF YOUR CHILD'S fears are interfering with his life, seek help from a mental health professional. Fortunately, professionals have had a great deal of success in addressing childhood fears.

While many different methods are used, one that is currently popular is relaxation training. With this technique, kids are taught to tense and relax their muscles so that they can see the difference between 'tense' and 'relaxed'. Then when they are confronted with the feared object, they can be more relaxed.

Another technique helps people become less afraid by gradually exposing them to thoughts of the feared object. Once they are comfortable with that, they approach the feared object, such as a dog, under the supervision of a professional.

Explaining the Concept of Death

Death in a family is a crippling event. Too often, however, death is not talked about, and this lack of communication can lead to problems later on.

It's best if the concept of death can be introduced casually, rather than when a family member or close friend has just died. These discussions should start when a child is young, perhaps as early as four years old. The talk doesn't need to be formal; it can be introduced when the opportunity occurs. If your pet or a friend's pet dies, this offers an occasion to talk about the end of life. Or when you're looking at old family photographs, you might point out family members who have died. You can talk about these people, mentioning that they are no longer alive and discuss what they meant to you.

In discussing death with your child, be prepared to talk about your beliefs regarding an afterlife. Children like to have things spelled out in detail for them, and one question they frequently ask is 'What happens to people after they die?' The answer to this question depends on your religious beliefs and those of your mate, and it's important for the two of you to agree about the message you are going to convey. Keep in mind that children are greatly comforted by the thought that they will see their loved ones again someday, so if that falls in line with your beliefs, then be sure to share it.

Other questions you might prepare for include 'What makes things die?' 'Can dead things come back to life?' 'When will I die?' and 'When will you die?' What you tell your child will depend on your personal beliefs, but be as honest as you can and answer all of the child's questions. You must follow your comfort level in deciding how to tell your child about these things.

WHEN A LOVED ONE DIES

When someone you love dies, your children will need extra support. These suggestions might be particularly important following the death of a close relative, especially a parent.

1. Be honest. Some parents keep the death of an extended family member a secret from the children. 'The kids don't have to be upset by this,' they may reason. However, remember that the child will eventually find out, which could lead to bitterness and anger and a distrust of you for not being straight.

2. Pay close attention to your child. Children don't know how to grieve. Instead of sadness they may feel anger or guilt and isolate themselves. Don't expect a child to look sad or cry. In fact, some children might seem totally unaffected by the whole thing. This lack of sadness does not mean that the child doesn't miss the person who died. Instead, the child may not know how to express her sadness without feeling overwhelmed. Similarly, she may fear her own death, and this fear may be intense if the person has died of a disease, which the child may fear she has as well.

3. Children eight and older should be asked if they want to be involved in the formal grieving process. Children are often not allowed to attend the viewing, the funeral and other death-related functions. However, these rituals can provide closure for children just as

they do for adults. Of course, attending these functions will be difficult, but it may be helpful in the grief process, and most children will choose to participate in these activities. Keeping your child away can lead to later resentment from the child, who may feel alienated and isolated.

4. Talk about the person who has died. In some families, after someone dies, the person is rarely mentioned again. This silence is not helpful for kids, who assume that everyone else is coping easily with the loss. Also, kids might be afraid that if they die, everyone will just forget about them.

5. Understand that grieving is a personal process. Everyone copes in a different way. Normal grieving will not hurt a child. However, if the child makes no progress towards feeling better and especially if he stops going to school or starts using drugs, seek assistance from a mental health professional.

REGARDLESS of how it is handled, the death of a loved one is devastating. Be sure to encourage your child to talk about the death and the person who has passed away. Only by talking about it can you see how your child is reacting and what help he may need.

chapter eleven
BRINGING UP BABY

THERE ARE FEW more joyful moments than learning that you and your spouse are expecting a baby. You're just embarking on a very long, interesting, challenging and rewarding journey. In the following pages we will discuss some of the concerns we hear from new parents.

Choosing Your Baby's Name

Selecting a name for your baby is an important decision that can affect your child for the rest of her life. Names become a part of a person's personality, and kids sometimes feel that they are different from everyone else if their names are unconventional.

Consider selecting a name for your child that is not overly uncommon. Sometimes parents think they are doing their child a big favour when they create a new name in order to ensure that their child's name will be unique. Although the new name might be perfectly charming, children have often told us that they hate having these 'weird' and 'new' names.

Choosing Your Baby's Name

Siblings and the New Baby

Teaching Trust

Can Babies Be Spoiled?

Keeping the Baby in Your Room

They feel more comfortable knowing that others have the same name they have. Sometimes they are teased or have to pronounce the name several times whenever they meet new people. And even if this teasing is not a problem, the name is bound to be mispronounced and mangled for a lifetime.

Talk to your spouse and try to come up with a name that you both find pleasing. Be sure to test how it sounds with the last name the child will have and consider logical nicknames. You may select the most beautiful name in the world, but if the child is likely to be known by her nickname, it should be one you like. Also, check out what his or her initials will be. Many a school child has been teased because of initials. If possible, try to make those work for the child as well.

Siblings and the New Baby

(See also Building Self-Esteem, p. 42; Fostering Independence, p. 48; Setting Limits, p. 74; Avoiding Favouritism, p. 106; Handling Aggressiveness, p. 113; Setting Limits for Toddlers, p. 128.)

Acceptance of a new baby in the family can be very difficult for older children, who may worry about having to share their parents' attention. However, there are many steps you can take to ease the transition into becoming a larger family.

1. Tell your older children about the baby as early as is reasonable. Some couples don't like to talk about a pregnancy until after the first trimester, during which there is a greater risk of miscarriage, but certainly by the time the pregnancy becomes apparent, you'll want to have told your child.

2. Stress each older child's new role as a big brother or big sister. Point out that eventually the child will have a new playmate. You can also hint rather strongly that the new baby is going to be the older child's greatest fan. From a very early age, your new baby is sure to think that the older sibling is just about the most interesting thing that's ever been seen on two feet.

3. Avoid major changes that could be directly linked to the baby. If you need to move, try to do so early so that the move seems separate from the baby who arrives three months later (three months seems like an eternity to most kids).

If your youngest child still sleeps in a cot and you feel it's time to move her to a big bed, do so well in advance of the baby's arrival and put the cot away for a few months. Toddlers can be very possessive of their cribs, and they may feel resentful and insecure: 'The baby has my bed and all of the attention. Maybe the baby will take all of Mummy and Daddy's love, too.'

4. Give your older child appropriate tasks to do. You can help him feel like a part of the family by letting him select the mobile for the cot, by asking him to help you place his hand-me-down clothes in the baby's drawers, or by allowing him to make or build something for the baby.

5. Prepare your child for the big day. 'When it's time for the baby to come, Nana will come and take care of you so that I can go to the hospital. After the baby is born, you'll come and visit us just as soon as the doctor says it's okay.'

6. Ask a favourite relative or friend to take your older children on a special outing. Perhaps they can go out for lunch or to the park or anywhere away from the baby. This visit will help make the children feel special and less ignored.

7. Teach your older children safe ways to hold the baby. Just as children need to be taught how to hold a kitten or puppy, they need to be shown what they can and can't do with a newborn baby. With supervision, even your three-year-old could hold the baby in her lap when she's sitting on a sofa, for example. Monitoring their time together will be important until your older child proves that he's trustworthy. Older children sometimes verbally or physically attack a baby, and this obviously cannot be tolerated. (See 'Setting Limits' and 'Handling Aggressiveness'.)

8. Calmly correct your child if she misbehaves, but don't scream at her for a minor transgression just because you're tired from being up all night with the baby. Be gentle with your older child and don't punish her for things that wouldn't have elicited the same reaction before the baby's birth. Discipline should remain constant. Throughout these early months, consistency is also crucial. If you always read a bedtime story to your daughter before the baby arrived, then it's very important that you continue to do so now.

9. Coordinate with your spouse so that your older child can have attention during critical times. For example, if you really want peace during the baby's evening feeding, perhaps your spouse could invite your older child to help fix dinner.

How a child reacts after the initial flurry dies down will largely depend on his age. Children older than five are often very excited and eager to help with the baby – sometimes to your great dismay. Try to harness their energy so that they are able to do helpful things while still keeping the baby safe. For example, at bath time, perhaps your five-year-old can be in charge of drying the baby while you do the actual washing. Similarly, you might ask your child to bring a nappy or toy for the baby.

Jealousy may be most severe when the child is under age five and when a small age gap exists between children. (Many clinicians recommend planning to have children at least two or three years apart as this helps minimize sibling rivalry.) Because a new baby inevitably gets lots of attention, some older children revert to childlike behaviour to try to increase their share of attention. An older child might begin to suck her thumb, wet the bed, ask to be fed from a bottle, or speak baby talk. Parents should discourage this behaviour while simultaneously making the child feel good about herself. For example, if your child requests a bottle, you might say, 'Sweetie, bottles are for little kids. You've worked hard and now you know how to use a glass, clever girl.'

Children older than eight generally feel less threatened by a newborn because they understand their place in the family unit.

Teaching Trust

(See also Fulfilling the Basic Needs of Children, p. 38.)

Trust is vital in every successful relationship.

Whether a child learns to trust or distrust others depends largely on the early parent-infant relationship. Though a child may have many people in her life who look after her, including grandparents, teachers and friends, those first formative years with the parents are vital to moulding her capacity to trust others. Though we don't use the word 'always' very often in this book, trust must *always* exist in a good parent-child relationship.

To help your baby become a trusting individual you need to be a responsive caregiver right from the beginning. The infant's perception of the world focuses on whether or not his fundamental needs are met: being fed, changed and bathed. Your physical presence, attention to his needs and consistent comfort will lead towards a healthy attachment and trust in you. If your child is with a caregiver during the day, make sure this person is responsible and understands the importance of meeting the infant's needs warmly and reliably.

If you answer an infant's needs again and again, he'll begin to learn that you'll always be there. As he gets a little older, this basic trust will help him be patient and wait when you can't change or feed him the second he wails. Later on, it will make him confident that although you're a little late picking him up at school one day, you will eventually come for him. He'll assume that you're stuck in traffic; otherwise you'd be there, as always.

As your child gets older, you can enhance her trust in you by keeping your promises. For example, if your three-year-old is broken-hearted because she's ill and has to miss out when the family goes to the circus, you might promise her something to make up for her disappointment. Be sure you keep that promise. Children remember what they are promised.

Children learn quickly who can be depended upon and who can't. False promises can lead them to believe that what the parent says isn't necessarily true. Though you will not be able to keep 100 per cent of your promises, do your best to help your child see that you intend to.

When a child begins to see that her needs – both simple and complex – are met, she will come to view the world as a safe and responsive place. Thus, in later years, she will be more likely to trust teachers, principals and other authority figures, because she started life with someone who taught her that those around her could be trusted.

If parents ignore their children's needs, get annoyed by their demands, or aren't there for them, the children learn that no one can be trusted. As a result, they may have difficulties trusting, relating to and bonding with other people.

TRUST IS VITAL to young ones as they begin to make friends, choose a partner and work with others. Those who can risk relying on someone else will almost always have an easier time in life. There will be people who disappoint them, but for the most part people who trust tend to maintain a basically positive outlook on life because they were instilled with trust initially.

Can Babies Be Spoiled?

(See also Fulfilling the Basic Needs of Children, p. 38; The Spoiled Child, p. 105.)

'Will I spoil her if I pick her up?' 'Will I spoil him if I hold him for a long time?' Some new parents worry about spoiling the new baby by simply doing what the baby seems to need. Fortunately, there's good news: it's almost impossible to spoil an infant. Your two-month-old may go through stages where she constantly wants to be held, even though you've changed her nappy, fed her and cuddled her. By crying, your baby is not trying to tell you that you are a bad parent. She may have wind or simply need to release her emotions. We have heard some parents say, 'Oh, she just wants to be held all of the time.' Well, who can blame her? What a great place to be, all snug and warm in her parent's arms. Don't let others make you feel you are overindulging your child when you are actually being a supportive and caring parent.

Of course, constant crying when you need to prepare dinner or help another child can be very frustrating indeed, so investigate various remedies such as an infant seat or an automatic swing where she can sit right with you while you help her sibling with homework. When you can, hold your baby without worrying about spoiling. Then keep her safe

and as happy as possible when you simply must do something else. That won't hurt her either.

Keeping the Baby in Your Room

(See also Overcoming Fears, p. 117.)

Parents often want infants to sleep in a crib in their room for a very practical reason: the baby often needs extra attention at night. If he sleeps in your room, you can manage his night feedings in a relaxing environment without disturbing the rest of the household. This makes perfect sense. What's more, sensing that his parents are nearby makes the infant feel secure and sleep more soundly. It also promotes close attachment between parents and child.

When the baby begins to sleep through the night, usually at about six months of age, you can move him into his own bedroom, a bedroom shared with a sibling, or a partitioned area of the family room or dining room.

This transition should begin by the time the child is nine months old. Your baby may cry the first few nights in the new environment, but you need to be strong. Ignoring a child's cries is hard for any parent, but if you maintain your resolve, the problem will solve itself relatively quickly. When your child cries, you should go in for a safety check. Offer comfort and reassurance, but don't relent. This not only implies you may change your mind about things, but also reinforces his fear that there's something unsafe about this new environment.

As your child gets older, he may appear at your bedside now and then, asking to be taken in. If he's had a nightmare, isn't feeling well, or just generally needs reassurance, he may want to join you for a little while. Three- to six-year-olds often creep in, as this is a classic age for being afraid of monsters, the dark, or the bogeyman. Be sensitive to your child's fears about being alone. Being flexible occasionally and letting your child join you won't do any harm. If he seems to need to stay for more than a few minutes, consider rolling out a sleeping bag on the floor by your bed.

Needless to say, if your child is in the room with you, you must refrain from sexual activity or find another place to be intimate.

If an primary school–age child is afraid to stay alone in her bedroom, consider possible sources of anxiety in other areas of the child's life. For example, a child who is having peer problems may want that extra closeness with the parents to help soothe her. To help her remain in her own bedroom where she'll likely be more comfortable, tuck her in and sit with her for a while, even until she falls asleep. Doing so will not spoil her; you are just taking care of your child.

chapter twelve

THE TODDLER AND PRESCHOOL YEARS

THE YEARS BEFORE your child starts nursery school are a time of incredible growth and change. During this period, your child will learn to sit up, babble, crawl, walk, feed herself, talk and socialize. She will move from playpen to school in an amazingly short time, so it's important to treasure these times with your child. Before you know it, your child will be an adult, conquering the world on her own.

During this time parents worry about making mistakes: If I send him to school too early, will it damage him? What happens if I can't get him toilet trained by a certain age? Should I put her in day care or hire someone to care for her at home? We understand your concern about making mistakes, but don't worry: as long as you are supportive of your child and not overly harsh, it is difficult to make any single decision that will seriously harm your child. Just relax and enjoy this time with your funny, curious young explorer.

Setting Limits for Toddlers

Potty Training

Assigning Chores to Toddlers

Here you'll read about toddler issues including:

Setting Limits for Toddlers

You may not know it, but your toddler has a job – that of explorer. The challenge for parents is to make certain that as their toddlers curiously touch, taste and chase after all the things they see, they still remain safe.

The problem with toddlers is that they are virtually incapable of obeying your rules – even those that are meant to ensure their safety. Consider the nature of the being: Toddlers are just beginning to speak and comprehend language, and as a result, most of them cannot be reasoned with, nor do they understand the concept of time-out. In fact, many don't yet understand the word 'no'. They also have no way to determine that an object or a situation is dangerous. Even though they're told repeatedly not to plug in the vacuum cleaner, it doesn't occur to them not to try to plug in the toaster.

Therefore, creating a safe environment is an important step in not having to set limits all the time.

Begin by making your living area as safe as possible so that you won't constantly have to tell your toddler not to touch things or to be careful:

1. Clear all surfaces. Remove small or breakable objects that are within the reach of a curious toddler. You might find it helpful to remove the coffee table entirely, particularly if it's glass, until your child's coordination improves and he is less likely to fall or bump his head against it.

2. Secure any items that your child could pull down. Be sure that bookcases are bolted to the wall (toddlers have been known to try to scale them); place the cords on curtains or blinds out of reach or cut them so that your child cannot use them as a noose.

3. Lock up small breakables, medicines and all cleaning chemicals. Safety latches on cabinets are not foolproof, so if your toddler seems precocious at getting through impenetrable barriers, store toxic and dangerous items far out of her reach.

4. Follow industry guidelines. If a toy manufacturer says a toy is not for children under three, don't bring it home. Many toys for older children have small parts that a younger child could swallow. If you have more than one child, sort through your older child's things and put away certain toys. Those that are dangerous for a younger sibling should be saved for times when you can supervise play or for when your toddler is napping.

VISITING

Visits to non-toddler territory can be stressful. If your mother-in-law collects glass figurines that are displayed throughout her home, you might offer to help her move them out of harm's way for the duration of your visit and then help put them back later. Even then, one adult needs to supervise the child at all times. It only takes a moment for a toddler to find an aunt's open bag with medication in it or an unlocked kitchen cupboard containing cleaning supplies.

During the toddler years, attentive supervision (by you) and cheerful distraction (for your toddler) must become as much a part of your life as eating and sleeping.

If your toddler does break objects, try not to get angry. At this age, most destruction is accidental.

Potty Training

Some people think it's important to start potty training by eighteen months. Others say you should wait until your child is three. What will happen if you train too early or too late? These are hotly debated issues as they so directly affect the day-to-day life of the parent and child.

Toilet training cannot be forced. If you take a relaxed approach, even if it means delaying the start of preschool for a few months, your child is likely to train earlier because your tension is gone. Pressuring a child on critical issues generally doesn't work, and it can cause other, more difficult problems.

Exactly when should you train? There's no right or wrong answer to that question. Every child is different, so pay close attention to your own child to determine when he is ready.

In toilet training, as with any issue, don't ever compare your child unfavourably to other children. Resist the urge to say, 'Johnny is the same age as you, and he already knows how to use the potty. Don't you want to be a big boy like Johnny?'

Your child won't go to college in nappies. We promise you.

GETTING STARTED

Awareness is the first step in the potty training process. Most toddlers soon realize that older kids and adults don't wear nappies. Since children love to imitate those older than they are, they will begin to move towards spotty training on their own but at their own pace. Some will be determined to master the skill as soon as possible; others may be quite reluctant fully to relinquish babyhood.

The process will be more successful if you don't even consider starting until your child is able to tell you he has to go to the lavatory. If he does not yet have a word like 'pee-pee' or 'potty', then he should at least use a gesture, such as pointing to his pants, to tell you he needs to go to the lavatory.

Most families use a potty chair rather than expecting a child to learn to use an adult-size toilet. The chair-like attachment that fits directly on the toilet works fine for the child, but it's a nuisance to remove it for everyone else.

You may want to buy a potty chair several months before you plan on using it. Then start familiarizing your child with it gradually. For example, you may simply take the child into the lavatory several times and show him the potty seat. Ask him to pull up the lid to look inside and then put it down again. Praise him for completing small tasks. Even if you plan to use a potty chair, introduce your child to toilet flushing so that nothing about the process will startle him.

Your child will tell you in very subtle ways when he's ready for the next step. He may ask you questions about the lavatory or the toilet, or he may question why other children don't wear nappies. Ask him if he wants to learn to use the toilet, but don't persist if the answer is no. He may eventually tell you he wants to start using the toilet.

Stay in the lavatory with your child when he's expressed interest in using the potty. Your child may be nervous or even scared, so you should be there to make it easier for him. If he's successful, compliment him on what a good job he's doing.

Do what you can to make the process fun. If your child seems at all fearful, have him give the toilet a silly name so that the toilet will seem more approachable. You can make up a bedtime story about a little boy or girl who learns how to use the toilet and has all kinds of wonderful things happen to him. There are also some excellent storybooks on the topic, and most children will want to hear them again and again.

Toilet training is often not a speedy process and setbacks are common. Your child may use the toilet regularly for several weeks and then suddenly start having accidents. Be patient. She needs to complete the training at her own pace. And no matter what you do, don't punish her for having accidents. If you do, she may associate the lavatory with punishment and will become afraid to use the toilet at all.

If the nursery school date is nearing and you're not quite sure your child will make the deadline, discuss it with your child. Many children crave the company of other kids, and learning that they have to be in underwear before they can go to school may make them work a little harder at mastering the task. If, however, your child is dreading nursery school, keep quiet. He or she might figure out that continuing reliance on nappies is the perfect excuse to stay at home.

If your child is starting nursery school, inform the staff of the words your child uses to describe going to the lavatory. This will help the teachers prevent accidents.

THE FINAL TRANSITION

Once your child is using the potty chair regularly, you're likely to be eager to help him make the transition to the toilet. Encouragement and praise are generally the best ways to move on to this new behaviour. Most children are quite proud to be called a big girl or big boy. Thus you can use these phrases as a reward for using the toilet.

If you don't push the process, your child will let you know when he's ready. At that point you'll find that he or she will learn quickly and your nappy bag will be a thing of the past.

Assigning Chores to Toddlers

(See also Encouraging Competence, p. 47; Making Chores a Matter of Routine, p. 70.)

When it comes to doing household chores, you will have no more eager helper than your toddler. A two-year-old will exhibit great pride at successfully carrying her dinner plate from the dining room to the kitchen! And sweeping? Wow! What a great way to spend the morning!

Unfortunately, of course, toddlers are longer on enthusiasm than they are on ability. Developmentally, they aren't capable of doing any chores on a regular basis. Toddlers aren't yet reliably dexterous, nor do they have the mental ability to focus on the fact that one chore consists of many different tasks. (Think how many things you do when you tidy up a room.)

Nonetheless, your toddler will be disappointed if he isn't invited to help. Next time you're doing a chore, ask him to help. If you are vacuuming, ask your toddler to pick up toys off the floor and put them in the toy box. When you're folding clothes, have him help by folding the smaller items such as underwear, flannels and socks. (Having a helper with the patience to sort and match the socks is a real blessing!) You can even teach your two-year-old to tear up and wash the lettuce for the salad. As you work together, find ways to make the drudgery fun. Clean up to music, or chat as you work.

Toddlers are not yet experts, and some chores, such as sweeping, will actually take longer when done toddler-style. Try to be patient, or if you simply don't have time to do a chore slowly, explain that you're in a terrible rush and simply have to do it yourself; you'll let her do it the next time. It's more demoralizing to the child if you let her start and then impatiently tell her you must finish it quickly.

When your toddler helps you with chores, your primary goal is to encourage the helpful behaviour. For that reason, no allowance or other material reward should be given. If your child knows firsthand that you appreciate her help, she will be more likely to enjoy doing chores without expecting a reward. This is also the first step in teaching her that eventually she must do tasks for her own gratification: 'I cleaned my room because I feel better when it's neat.'

Offer specific encouragement. Praise is likely to be more effective in young children than financial rewards. Instead of saying, 'You did a nice job,' be precise and praise one particular aspect of the child's performance. You could say, 'You did a great job of stacking the books on the shelf.' Thank the child for helping you and let her know that the task went more smoothly, was easier and was more enjoyable because she helped.

Prepare yourself for the fact that help from a child this age can actually amount to significantly more work for you. However, allowing your child to help can help foster self-confidence, encourage joint activities and teach responsibility. It also introduces the concept of chores. In a few years your child will mature into someone who really is a big help!

chapter thirteen

THE PRIMARY SCHOOL YEARS

The primary school years are sometimes thought of as the easy parenting period – if there is such a thing! During this time children are generally old enough and capable enough to manage their physical needs, but they continue to be responsive to their parents.

The biggest task at this age is beginning the formal learning process. The child's life is now structured, as he has a schedule of classwork, homework and special lessons.

The preadolescent years, between eight and twelve, are fun for most kids. The development of long-lasting relationships becomes important during these years when peer acceptance becomes vital. Children who are not accepted by their classmates often find school difficult and may be susceptible to depression or other problems.

Preadolescent children are still largely dependent on their families. Take advantage of these years and enjoy them!

Overseeing Homework

What to Do When Your Child Balks at Going to School

When Children Curse

Public Lavatories: Deciding When Your Child Can Go Alone

Can Your Child Stay Home Alone?

Overseeing Homework

(See also Developing Creativity, p. 45; Encouraging Competence, p. 47; Attention Deficit/Hyperactivity Disorder, p. 175; Learning Disorders, p. 195; Speech Problems (Communication Disorders), p. 223.)

Homework often creates stress between parents and children: Kids complain that parents are frequently unavailable, unwilling, or even unable to help them. Parents, for their part, may resent the fact that after working a long day themselves, they have to nag their children to do homework.

These strategies can help do away with homework stress:

1. Allow your child some time to wind down after school before tackling assignments. Adults need time to relax after they come home from work and before they cook dinner or take care of other responsibilities. Kids deserve a similar break. They should be allowed time to relax by watching television, napping, or listening to music. A healthy child does many different things every day and should be allowed to spend his leisure time according to his personal tastes: reading, making models, painting, playing outdoors, taking care of a pet, or practising a musical instrument. Encourage your child to participate in these activities. Kids don't learn from homework alone.

2. Provide a quiet space for homework. Younger children may need you nearby while they complete an assignment, so the kitchen might become a quiet zone if you need it to be. Turn off the television and set rules about how long your other children need to respect that homework time. Some older children may prefer having a desk in their room. If your child has to share a room, set rules about interruptions. The sibling who shares the room can do homework at the same time or find something to do elsewhere in the house. Explain that with fewer distractions, homework gets done more quickly.

3. Set a specific time for homework. Allowing your child to select a time period to do homework will encourage independence and self-motivation. If you stand over your children every day and say, 'It's time to do your homework,' they will get the work done on time but will learn little about initiative or responsibility. In addition, kids learn more from homework if it is self-initiated. While most families prefer that homework be completed before dinner or before a certain TV show, it's ideal if you can let the child select the exact time for getting it done.

4. Be available for guidance. Even though you are probably tired after a long day of work, help with homework if you're needed. Your participation communicates your support and illustrates that your child's work is important to you.

5. Praise your child's work. Ask to see homework assignments when they are returned by the teacher, and praise your child. Even if he did not receive a particularly high grade, point out what he did correctly. Teachers are busy and cannot always provide as much praise as each child needs.

6. Integrate your family activities with school activities. If your child is studying a list of vocabulary words, encourage him to use the words around the house and praise him when he does so. Similarly, if your child is learning measurements, have her help you with a recipe. Such practice will show your child a practical use for the abstract skills learned in school. You might also go on special outings that correspond to homework assignments. A trip to a park, for instance, may be in order when your child has an assignment involving different types of trees. The outing needn't be extravagant or even cost money to be a great learning experience and an enjoyable family occasion. This kind of enrichment takes a lot of time and commitment, but the payoff for the whole family is worth it.

Parents need to be involved in all areas of their children's lives and this includes school. Your children will benefit if you demonstrate that what they do all day is important to you.

What to Do When Your Child Balks at Going to School

(See also Teaching Social Skills, p; 40; Building Self-Esteem, p. 42; Helping the Shy Child, p. 44; Fostering Independence, p. 48; Overcoming Fears, p. 117.)

No one is surprised when a three-year-old would rather be with mummy than go to nursery school, but when an older child consistently resists going to school, parents begin to worry.

There are many different reasons why children don't want to go to school, and your child's reason may point the way towards a solution to the problem.

1. FEAR. Some kids are afraid of something at school. A bell, for example, might frighten a timid child. Another kid might be so afraid of school buses, classrooms, or tests that he avoids school. Discuss the problem with your child's teacher. If the two of you can identify the source of the child's fear, chances are that you can then explain to your child why there's nothing to be afraid of.

2. SOCIAL REASONS. Some children fear being picked on. Others feel that their teacher is mean and embarrasses them in class. Social situations are hard for some children, and they tend to avoid new people. More training in social skills or help in overcoming shyness can make these children feel more comfortable being around people. Alerting a teacher can also help. She may be able to arrange for one or two kids in the class to make a special effort with the child who is having a difficult time settling into the classroom.

3. ATTENTION. Some kids refuse to attend school because by not attending they finally get the parental attention they crave. These children may feel ignored in the family. They realize that skipping school is a great way to get attention, even if it's negative.

When a child misbehaves to gain attention, you need to do two things: First, ignore the misbehaviour; overreacting will just prolong it. Second, reward good behaviour; praise your child whenever he does something good.

It's distressing to hear wails of 'I don't want to go to school' every morning. However, be patient with your child and include the school in the process. Most schools will work closely with you to help your child feel that she can come to class again without anxiety.

When Children Curse

(See also Being a Positive Role Model, p. 39; Setting Limits, p. 74; Negotiating with Your Child, p. 80.)

The use of mild curse words such as 'hell' and 'damn' is not as great a problem as some parents think. While no one wants a four-year-old using swear words, many teenagers curse as a matter of course; it is one of the ways they try to fit in to a particular social group.

Curse words should not be a part of every conversation, but if your child curses occasionally when he's upset or when he's talking with friends, you might do well to overlook it. However, some family rules may help you keep cursing at an appropriate level in your home. (You need to start discussing this topic while your child is in primary school, because by adolescence, you'll have less opportunity to influence relatively minor issues such as language.)

1. When your child begins to use curse words, sit down with him and make a list of the words that are unacceptable in your home. Consult all of your kids. They may have very different ideas from you about what words are offensive.

2. Some words, which kids use as curse words, are demeaning in a sexist or racist way, or they are insulting to various religions.

Your child should be aware that these words are not acceptable. If he uses them, stop the conversation and ask for a definition. Being forced to focus on the meaning will help him realize the inappropriateness of the word, and he may be less likely to use it again.

3. Name-calling should be forbidden.

4. Insist that there be no swearing in front of younger siblings, even if they are simply listening in on a conversation or hearing one side of a telephone conversation.

5. Cursing should be limited to the home or when with their friends. Point out the risk of using poor language at school. Teachers and principals frown on the behaviour, and a large percentage of school suspensions are because of cursing.

6. Praise your child for using good language.

IF YOU DON'T want your child to curse at all or to use certain words on the list, set up consequences. Taking away video game, telephone, or car privileges can be effective, as can setting an earlier curfew. Be consistent and always administer the consequences. If you're serious about modifying the behaviour, your child will learn to comply with the rules.

Public Lavatories: Deciding When Your Child Can Go Alone

(See also Encouraging Competence, p. 47; Fostering Independence, p. 48.)

If you and your child are of a different sex,

life becomes complicated when it comes to using public lavatories. Children quickly reach an age where they want to use the appropriate lavatory. Your job is to balance your child's very real desire for independence and correct sexual identity with issues of safety.

Good news is coming: some shopping malls, airports and museums are building family lavatories. For now, however, you'll have to keep your child with you – and in the stall with you – as long as he or she needs help going to the toilet.

This is the time to start training your child for an eventual solo experience. Let him be in charge of the lock so that he has plenty of experience at working various types of attachments and let her wrestle with the toilet paper dispenser herself. Show how various toilets flush and explain about the ones that do so automatically. If you are a single mother of a boy, ask a male friend to take your son into a men's lavatory to show him a urinal.

Once extra help is unnecessary, let him use a separate stall with an agreement that you'll wait for each other at the basin.

Fathers of daughters will often need to make spur-of-the-moment decisions: Once you enter the men's lavatory, take your daughter directly into a stall. Leave the lavatory right away if she can't stand at the basin without seeing the urinals. Use a moist disposable towel or a damp paper towel to wash her hands.

When the time comes to let your child go into a public lavatory alone, perhaps when the child is a mature age six, station yourself outside the door and tell him you'll meet him right there. Tell your child that he shouldn't talk to anyone in the lavatory and if he needs help or is approached by someone he doesn't know, he should come back out and tell you. Wait outside the door until your child is finished.

If your child stays in the lavatory too long, ignore the sign on the door and walk right into the lavatory to ensure that he is all right. You may be tempted to ask someone entering the lavatory to check on your child, but remember that you told your child not to talk to anyone. Having a stranger approach your child to check on him sends an incorrect message.

When your child comes out, praise him by saying how brave he was and how grown-up he has become.

If you feel your child is too young, or if you're uncomfortable about the public building where you're using the lavatory, tell your child you're keeping him with you because it makes *you* feel more comfortable. Tell him this has nothing to do with him; it has only to do with your own worries.

Can Your Child Stay At Home Alone?

(See also Fostering Independence, p. 48; Nurturing Responsibility, p. 49.)

When is your child old enough to stay alone? For most kids, this is about age ten. However, you know your child best and can usually determine when she is ready to be left alone. A six-year-old who begs to stay at home alone shouldn't be allowed to do so, simply because no six-year-old should be left with the burden of possibly having to handle an emergency. By the same token, the reluctant ten-year-old should not be forced to stay alone.

There is no set legal age in the UK at which children can be left alone although the NSPCC recommends that no child should be left under the age of 16. It is therefore up to the parent to decide a child's readiness.

THE FIRST HOME-ALONE EXPERIENCE

Regardless of your child's age, make certain that your child's first periods of being at home alone are brief. Any child will be somewhat anxious and worried the first few times, so you don't want to be gone too long. A ten- or fifteen-minute visit with a neighbour is ideal; you won't be gone long, and you'll be nearby if your child needs you. Your next trip might be a short one to the supermarket.

Whenever you leave a child alone, take these precautions:

➤ If possible, provide a number where you can be reached.

➤ Always leave a list of emergency phone numbers: plumber, doctor and so on. Stress that 999 is the number to call in a real emergency.

➤ Scout out a support team – perhaps a neighbour and a grandparent – whom the child can call if he's lonely or scared.

➤ Discuss emergencies. Stress that if he feels something is an emergency, he should definitely make that important telephone call. However, if he's simply a little nervous or lonely, encourage him to call his support team and make sure that one of them will be at home while you're out.

➤ If your child is left alone for a prolonged period of time, such as when you are at work, set a time when you'll check in with each other.

➤ Establish rules for the kitchen. Unless your child is an old hand at cooking, he shouldn't be allowed to use the stove, oven, or grill. Use of the microwave should depend on his skill and level of responsibility. It's best to leave a snack for him that does not require cooking – for example, pudding, fruit, or a sandwich.

➤ Discuss how to handle telephone calls. 'Mum's not available right now,' or 'Dad's in the shower' are good replies.

➤ Stress the importance of not opening the door to strangers. Consider installing a security peephole in your exterior doors, and if necessary, place a small step stool at the door so your child can see through it. You may also tell your child not to play outside or have friends over when he's alone.

➤ Every family should have a fire escape procedure, and it should be reviewed regularly. All family members should know how to escape from every room in the house, and there should be a designated meeting spot away from the house so that family members can be accounted for. Have fire drills when everyone is home.

➤ Give your child a scheduled time for your return, and then stick with that schedule. Sometimes children assume that the worst possible catastrophe will occur. If you're running late, be sure to call and let your child know you're on the way.

IF YOU WERE to read anyone the above list of rules, he would almost certainly be intimidated! Most of these rules are general family safety rules that you should present over a period of time in preparation for the day when your child will stay at home alone.

LEAVING SIBLINGS AND TEENAGERS HOME ALONE

Leaving siblings at home together for an afternoon or evening is generally a perfectly good plan. Indeed, baby-sitting can be a good opportunity for an older child to develop nurturing skills and to increase her sense of responsibility. However, if your children don't get along, or if they fight when you're gone, you may need to wait another year or so. You want to be absolutely certain that neither child is at risk of being physically hurt or mentally tortured while you're away. And if you do have children who get along well and the system works well for the family, don't abuse it. Your fourteen- or fifteen-year-old will resent not being allowed to go out with her friends on Saturday night.

One would like to think that adolescents are better prepared than younger children to be at home alone, but this isn't always so. While they are perfectly capable of caring for their own needs, some teenagers may find that an empty house offers great temptation. Their friends may pressure them into sexual activity or other risky behaviour. If you suspect your home is being used for activities of which you don't approve, you can arrange to be at home more, or you can establish some new rules for your teenager, such as no guests when you're not home.

chapter fourteen
THE TEENAGE YEARS

ADOLESCENCE is a time of dramatic change. Your teenager will shoot up, fill out and reach out to new friends of both sexes. Many parents have a hard time during these years, but those who maintain open communication with their teenagers find that the parent-child bond is quite durable. Even though some adolescents act as if they reject parental contact and values, it is still important for them to feel supported and loved.

Adolescents are faced with the task of establishing who they are, what they believe and what they want in the future. They try on new roles, which may be reflected through changes in clothing, hairstyle and language.

Adolescence can be a challenging time for parents as their youngsters continue to explore the world in new and potentially dangerous ways. Some teenagers begin smoking, undertake sexual activity, or experiment with illegal drugs.

The Importance of Peer Relationships

Setting Phone Limits

Avoiding Power Struggles

Hair and Clothing Styles

Music

Dating

Cutting Class and Skipping School

How to Handle a Brush with the Law

There are pleasant developments as well. You're likely to find that you now share some interests with your teenager, and it's exciting to get a glimpse of who and what she is to become.

The Importance of Peer Relationships

Friends are important to children of all ages, but they are particularly important during adolescence. Wanting independence from the family and turning to outside people for support is a natural part of development.

During the teenage years conformity is crucial and being different is generally discouraged. Kids want to be like, act like and dress like their friends. They want to be accepted by a clique and feel approved of by peers. It isn't surprising that teenagers rate friendships as their number one source of enjoyment and support.

Don't be threatened by your child's new-found friendships. Although she will probably spend less time with you as she gets older, this doesn't have to result in diminished closeness between the two of you, nor is it a long-term rejection of family values. She's simply growing up. Realizing how very important these relationships are in navigating through the adolescent years will help you understand the wisdom of encouraging your child to make good friends.

Here are some ways to help adolescents make and keep friends:

1. Serve as a role model. Invite your own friends to your home for social occasions. If you have friends whose kids are close to the ages of your own, that's all the better.

2. Encourage your teenager to invite friends over. Even if they get loud, don't discourage their presence; if your child can't have friends over, it will be more difficult for her to socialize outside of school. What's more, as long as the kids are at your house, you know what they're up to.

3. Get to know your teenager's friends and mention things you like about them to your teenager.

4. Include your teenager's friends on family outings occasionally. For example, you might go to a football game, the movies, a picnic, or a theme park. Having friends along generally increases the fun, so be open to it.

5. Be willing and available to provide transport when you can. You can facilitate friendships by making sure teenagers can get together now and then. As they get older, they may want to go to a movie or town together, and you should drive them there, too, if possible. Few things are more frustrating for adolescents than to be invited to meet friends somewhere and then be unable to get a lift. Although you needn't be at your child's beck and call at the expense of everything else, do try to be accommodating. For example, you and your teenager might agree on which days you'll be their chauffeur and which nights you'll have off, though if you're not overburdened, you might even offer to help on your nights off if the kids are stuck without a lift.

6. Encourage your child to get involved in clubs, sports, church activities, or volunteer projects in order to be in contact with other kids his age. By bringing together people who share similar interests, these activities facilitate friendships, even for shy kids, and provide them with a worthwhile pastime that helps stem any tendency to look for trouble.

MANY TEENAGE friendships result from a desire to avoid isolation rather than from genuine affection for others. This becomes clear when teenagers spend a great deal of time with friends but engage in relatively little genuine caring behaviour. It's important to remind kids that it takes effort and sacrifice to build a strong relationship. For example, if the clique turns against your daughter's friend, encourage her to stick up for her friend, even if it means possibly angering the rest of the group.

These are emotionally turbulent years for teenagers, and you need to be there to remind your children that no matter what the ethics of the group, love, loyalty and sacrifice are still the ingredients of true friendship.

Setting Phone Limits

(See also Setting Limits, p. 74; The Importance of Peer Relationships, p. 142; Avoiding Power Struggles, p. 144.)

Being in touch with their friends is the staff of life to a teenager, and the telephone is a favourite mode of communication. If you want to feel more kindly towards the telephone, keep in mind that when your daughter is home and on the phone, you know exactly where she is and you didn't have to drive her anywhere. Family management of the telephone, however, can be difficult. Here are some guidelines:

➤ Set a time on school nights after which no more phone calls will be permitted. Discuss this with your teenager and set a time you think is reasonable. On weekends, you might extend phone privileges to a later hour.

➤ If phone availability (for you to call out or for receiving incoming calls) becomes a problem, you may want to get Call Waiting or add a second phone line.

➤ Limit phone time if your teenager has no time for the family or for completing homework or chores. Gauge your time limit by how much time he was spending on the phone before you decided to create a new system. For example, two hours might seem like a reasonable compromise if he was on the phone nonstop from 4:00 P.M. until 9:00 P.M. Be sure to explain that this rule is necessary because you feel it's important to have uninterrupted homework time and time to spend with the family. Then be consistent and reasonable. If your teenager has done his homework and you have to attend a meeting, give phone privileges for the night.

➤ If your teenager has friends who live far away, there's nothing wrong with calling them occasionally, but establish limits – after fifteen minutes of long-distance calls per month, for example, you will deduct additional charges from the next week's allowance.

➤ Some teenagers discover 0890 or 0891 numbers, which are very expensive. The telephone company can arrange it so that these calls can't be made from your phones. Phone companies have been dealing with disgruntled parents for years and may, in fact, have a solution for any number of your telephone problems. Consult them and see.

WITH A LITTLE management, the telephone can again become a useful communication tool in your household as well as one that your teen can continue to enjoy.

Avoiding Power Struggles

(See also Being a Positive Role Model, p. 39; Speaking So Your Child Will Listen, p. 68; Negotiating with Your Child, p. 80.)

Sometimes we hear a parent say to a child, 'That's the way it is because I say so! You have to do it my way!' This type of statement, which is usually screamed or said through clenched teeth, is not very effective with adolescents.

One of the tasks of adolescence is identity formation, which by its very nature involves separation from parents. As a result, some struggles between child and parents are bound to occur. The child feels compelled to challenge adult authority and establish greater control in his life. However, some parents exert power over their children simply to show that they are in charge. Parents need to understand that an adolescent's refusal to respond to adult authority is part of a natural growth process. You should not take it personally or use it as a source of constant arguments with your child.

If you have a heated argument with your child, don't force him to do what you want by simply saying, 'Do this because I say so!' Provide him with rational reasons, just as you would an adult. Respect should be given to all people, regardless of their age.

By being cooperative and open with your child, you serve as a good model of adult behaviour. Children who observe their parents being flexible will get along better with other people, because they will be more open to negotiation. A disagreement can then become a win-win situation for everyone.

MAKING YOUR REQUESTS CLEAR

If your child's radio is blasting, you have several choices. You can yell and scream, and he will probably turn the volume down. The next time you yell and scream, however, he may become frustrated and refuse to do so. To avoid a power struggle, follow these steps:

1. CLEARLY STATE the problem without blaming your child: 'Eric, your radio is too loud.'

2. EXPLAIN WHAT action is necessary and make the request in a respectful manner: 'Please turn the music down.'

3. EXPLAIN *WHY* the action is needed: 'I'm trying to read, and the music is bothering me.'

4. THANK YOUR CHILD for being compliant and considerate: 'Thank you for turning down the volume.'

5. AT THIS TIME, it would also be beneficial to praise your child for an unrelated matter: 'By the way, I noticed that you finished mowing the lawn. It looks really great. I can tell that you worked hard on the job.' This compliment will build self-esteem and encourage further cooperation.

YOU WILL HAVE greater success with your teenager by using this method than by getting upset.

If your child becomes increasingly combative about a multitude of issues, look to see what else is going on. Discuss the problem with him, noting that you don't want to have an uncomfortable relationship. Ask for his suggestions about how the two of you can solve the problem and enjoy each other. Be flexible in discussing his suggestions and willing to accept part of what he proposes.

If he's unreasonable, smile and say, 'You know that's not going to work. . . . Come on, be serious. What can we do about this?' At this time you might want to suggest something and ask his opinion about your suggestion. The two of you may be able to come to an agreement that way.

If all of these approaches fail and you find you're in continuous conflict, consider consulting a mental health professional.

Hair and Clothing Styles

Because fitting in with their peers is so important to adolescents, they want to wear the clothing and hairstyles that are considered fashionable in their social group. These styles aren't likely to be to your taste. In fact, kids tend to pick clothes or hairstyles that they know adults would never choose, largely because they are busy trying to establish their own unique identities.

When your child appears wearing a hairstyle or clothing you don't like, you'll be well advised not to overreact. While you may want to comment, avoid nagging or making a big deal about it. Remember how you feel when someone says something unkind. You may want to keep silent unless you can comment in a well-meaning way – for instance, 'I liked your hair brown better than blue.' Your child doesn't choose a new style specifically to upset you or rebel against you; he wears it because it's the latest fad, and he's trying to find a unique identity. However, if you're overly unpleasant or officious about it, chances are good that your teenager will continue to wear similar styles just to test you again.

Remember, too, that most hair and clothing styles aren't permanent. Tattoos and body piercing, on the other hand, are more worrisome because health issues come into play: these teenage fads can transmit disease. Save your 'no' power for permanent changes and possible health hazards.

Demands for the most expensive jeans or sneakers often add stress to the family. Sometimes for financial reasons, you simply have to say no. Communicate your values by explaining that it doesn't make sense to spend so much money on an item that will be used only briefly. However, only your teenager can judge how very vital an item is to her happiness. You can then tell her that she's free to buy the coveted item with her own allowance, or you might suggest you'll buy it if she pays half of the cost of the item. This way, if all of her friends really are wearing a particular style, you've given her a way to evaluate whether or not fitting in is that important to her.

Be patient with your teenager during this time of experimentation. Most kids find their own sense of self and then begin to wear perfectly acceptable clothes that they like and find comfortable. It just might take a while for this to happen.

Music

Parents frequently voice concern over the music their kids listen to. Some lyrics are said to promote or glamorize violence, drug use, sexual activity and suicide. These concerns have been fuelled in recent years by the attempt to censor music with questionable lyrics.

As a result of these outcries, most music with explicit content is now labelled with warning stickers. However, policing the music your teenager purchases or regulating what he hears on the radio isn't an easy task. Instead, try following these guidelines:

1. LISTEN to your child's favourite radio station for a few days, even though it's not to your taste, or ask your teenager to recommend a few of her CDs for you to play.

2. IF YOU HEAR songs that are objectionable, talk with your teenager about your objections. Explain your viewpoint and elicit his opinion. A song you find objectionable may also be objectionable to your child.

3. IF THE MUSIC clearly contradicts the beliefs endorsed by your family and you feel you need to take the CD away, explain your objections to him and ask him to throw it away himself. Describe in detail why the music upsets you, and establish what the family beliefs are and why those beliefs are important. For instance, if a certain song glorifies violence against women, explain how these violent acts make a woman feel. As always, elicit your child's opinion and make it clear that you value his feelings.

4. RESPECT YOUR CHILD. Music is important to every generation, and most kids today enjoy a specific type of music. Furthermore, music is usually an important component of kids' lives; one survey revealed that 95 per cent of secondary school students listen to music for at least one hour a day. Telling your child that the music he prefers is 'worthless' or 'bad' needlessly distances the two of you.

5. JUDGE THE MUSIC on its own merits. Sometimes genres that are targeted as objectionable, such as rap, advocate environmental responsibility, discourage drug use and encourage the use of condoms. Don't dismiss an entire genre because some kids who listen to it dress or act a certain way.

DESPITE THE MEDIA stories that stress the relationship, there is little support for the claim that kids who listen to explicit music display more behaviour problems. Generally you don't have as much to worry about as you might believe.

Remember, too, that every generation's music has come under attack by some adults.

Parents who grew up in the fifties may remember critics of rock music claiming that it fostered problematic teenage behaviour.

It is natural to be protective of your child; however, you can't shield him from everything and you must teach him to think on his own. What's more, selecting for himself the type of music he listens to is one important step towards independence and critical thinking.

Dating

(See also Educating Children about Sex, p. 73.)

Most youngsters begin to date during adolescence, which typically begins between ten and fourteen years old. However, the preparation for this process may have begun much earlier. Junior school children may commit to being boyfriend and girlfriend, eat lunch together one day and break up the next. Parents find this process very mysterious, but the children are simply inching towards adolescence.

Parents who have always encouraged their children to have friends of both sexes generally find that these children form more comfortable, casual relationships with both boys and girls, and this is an ideal start for a dating relationship.

If, however, your child would like to date a specific person, you need to use your best judgment to decide when your child is mature enough to handle dating. One good way to step into this slowly is to include your teenager's new friend on a family outing or two. This will give you an opportunity to see them together and get to know the other teenager before they spend a great deal of time alone.

And of course it isn't the dating you're worried about. It's the possibilities that arise in an intense male-female relationship. Sexual activity at an early stage changes the nature of a relationship in ways that adolescents aren't capable of handling. Talk to your child about your concern about early sex. The focus of your discussion should be on your teenager's health and well-being. It is vital for both boys and girls to be aware of the dangers of unprotected sex: pregnancy, AIDS, infections. Remember that it is your job to be certain that your teenager understands these issues. We recommend that you start these discussions long before your children reach adolescence. By the time they are teenagers, they are less open to listening to you, so it's important to get your message across early.

Dating is an important time for gaining more experience in relationships, and while there is certain to be emotional upheaval as your teenager goes forward in this area, it's also a very exciting and wonderful time.

HELPING YOUR TEENAGER THROUGH A ROMANTIC BREAKUP

To a teenager, first love can seem destined to be eternal love. Given the romance of this connection, it can be devastating for a youngster when a relationship ends. A breakup can also be the teenager's first taste of rejection and heartache, and as such it can consume the youth's entire life and seem to be the only thing that matters. Although you cannot erase your teenager's pain, the way you handle the situation will greatly influence how your child responds:

1. ACKNOWLEDGE, and do not underestimate, the pain your child is going through after the breakup. You might be tempted to say, 'The two of you were only together for two months. You've been upset for a week! Get over it already!' Meanwhile, your teenager may feel unwanted and unlovable: 'If Danny doesn't love me anymore, no one ever will.' Remember that going through any difficult occurrence the first time is distressing, and breakups are certainly no exception.

2. ALTHOUGH YOUR TEENAGER may ask to be alone to think, cry, or brood, let him know that you are there for him. He needs people around to lessen the pain of rejection, so make yourself available. Also encourage him to spend time with close friends and to seek out people he can talk to. Loneliness is one of the main reasons teenagers have such difficulty with a breakup, and afterwards some teenagers fear that they will be social outcasts and that no one will want to be with them.

3. LISTEN, BUT DON'T INTERFERE. Sometimes kids just need to talk. Resist the urge to give advice: 'Forget about her. She wasn't good enough for you.' 'Get out and start dating someone else. There are other fish in the sea.' These suggestions are usually not helpful and your teenager may resent them. Only time and unconditional support from family and friends can help your teenager feel better.

4. SOMETIMES PARENTS ASSUME that boys aren't as susceptible to hurt as girls. Perhaps this assumption is held because young men are more hesitant to show their emotions by crying and talking about feeling rejected. Boys often become stoic or put on an 'I don't care' attitude, but they may be in worse shape than most girls are after a breakup. They often fall in love more quickly than young women and may lack the social support necessary to overcome the breakup.

5. KEEP AN EYE OUT for signs of depression following a breakup. Because it is a form of loss, kids commonly react with sadness, grief and depression. One relatively common reason for teenage suicide attempts is the dissolution of an important relationship. If your teenager remains involved in school activities and stays in touch with friends, you can breathe a little easier, but if he doesn't seem to be coming around, talk to a professional immediately. (See also Depression, p. 184.)

Cutting Class and Skipping School

(See also Building Self-Esteem, p. 42; Speaking So Your Child Will Listen, p. 68; Setting Limits, p. 74; How to Handle a Brush with the Law, p. 149.)

Most adolescents skip school at least once. However, for some adolescents, cutting class or skipping school can become chronic, and the teenager may become involved with alcohol or drugs or may engage in sex.

Sometimes kids cut because they are anxious about something or because they're depressed and don't have the energy to go to school. Cutting is most common after a child changes schools. It is difficult to be the new kid at secondary school age.

If you learn that your child has cut class more than once or twice, you need to step in immediately and talk to your teenager, the school counsellor and any other person who might have a beneficial influence on your child. If you discover that something at school is the reason she hasn't been going to class, you will have a specific problem that you can probably solve.

If you and your mate work outside the home, consider asking a nearby relative whom your teenager likes to keep a watch on things. This person could come round to be sure your teenager hasn't come home in the middle of the day, and he or she can also give your teenager another caring person with whom to talk.

If you're having serious difficulty with your teenager, consult your teen's counsellor or the school psychologist. They may have strategies or referrals that will help.

How to Handle a Brush with the Law

(See also Building Self-Esteem, p. 42; Finding Quality Time, p. 53; Setting Limits, p. 74.)

When parents ask us how they should react if their children get in trouble with the police, we generally recommend that they allow the legal system to be the enforcer. For minor offenses, most kids will get a warning from a police officer or judge and that will be the end of it. Many parents are so angry and embarrassed that their child has got into trouble that they want to impose a tougher sentence at home. In this case, parents are underestimating the very strong impact that a court appearance or a severe warning from a police officer has on a child. Most are terribly afraid of getting in trouble with a law enforcement official, and chances are your teenager will try to stay out of trouble in the future.

This isn't to say that you should pretend nothing happened. Be supportive of your child and help him face whatever consequences may loom in the future. Of course, you should stress that his crime was wrong, but focus on the fact that the behaviour was wrong, not that your child is bad.

Opening channels of communication as quickly as possible is vital. To begin with, offer your child an opportunity to tell her side of the story. Ask your child to explain what happened. Your child may be reluctant to talk about the problem, but be patient and understanding. If he got into trouble because he was bored and had nothing better to do, you can work on helping him become engaged in extracurricular activities. If your child denies his guilt, keep an open mind and listen to what he has to say. It is possible that he is innocent of the charges. An explanation like 'Yes, I hit the other car, but I was swerving to miss a cat' doesn't make the traffic accident go away, but it does permit you to have a useful conversation about refining driving skills.

If your mistakes have played a part in your child's trouble, be honest and admit it: 'I've been irresponsible in not picking you up from those parties. If I'd come to get you, you wouldn't have gone with that gang of kids looking for trouble.'

Because police trouble is upsetting for any family, the stress level at home tends to rise to an all-time high. Therefore, you'll do well to remember these 'don'ts' if your child has a brush with the law:

➤ **DON'T OVERREACT.** Even though you're likely to be very angry, don't become abusive.

➤ **DON'T USE DEROGATORY NAMES** like 'juvenile delinquent', 'deviant', 'antisocial' or 'troublemaker'. Kids tend to live up, or down, to the labels you give them. They reason that if they are perceived as a troublemaker or other comparable label, they might as well act however they want – they have nothing to lose.

➤ **DON'T REJECT YOUR TEENAGER.** This is the worst thing you can do. Teenagers in trouble need help, and although they may not indicate it, they need you very badly at times like this.

➤ **DON'T BREAK THE LAW YOURSELF.** Be a good role model. We've seen parents who have knowingly purchased stolen merchandise become outraged when their kids are caught stealing. There's something terribly wrong with this.

AFTER THE CRISIS is over, pay particular attention to your adolescent and praise him for staying out of trouble. In some cases, kids get into trouble because negative attention is better than no attention at all. Make sure your teenager is positively rewarded for being a good kid.

Remember, too, that a child who gets in trouble once isn't doomed to a life of crime. Many who have a brush with the law go on to be focused students and build very successful lives.

part three

MENTAL DISORDERS AND FAMILY DIFFICULTIES

HOW TO USE PARTS THREE AND FOUR

PART THREE examines the various psychological or psychiatric problems that children or adolescents may have. While most of these conditions are rare, parents need to be aware of them, because early intervention can often make all the difference in how well a child copes with a disorder.

In Chapter 15 we present general information about what may contribute to certain disorders, including factors ranging from temperament to the environment. You'll also read about the resilient child and what seems to keep some children healthy despite having risk factors for certain psychiatric disorders.

Specific disorders, listed alphabetically, are explained in Chapter 16. In each entry we describe the disorder and explain what may cause it, what parents should watch for and what they can do in coping with it. You'll also find additional entries concerning problems that sometimes trouble children and adolescents such as AIDS, fire-setting, running away, suicidal behaviour and substance abuse.

In Part Four, Chapter 17, you'll read about mental health professionals. A good professional can provide the support, information and counselling a family may require. We also discuss the differences between psychiatrists, psychologists, social workers and counsellors, and we outline what these people do and how they might treat your child. Chapter 18 is a discussion of the role of the government in the lives of children and our concept that 'it takes a country to raise a child'.

You will read about psychiatric or psychological disorders from which children sometimes suffer. These disorders are described in great detail in the *Diagnostic and Statistical Manual of Mental Disorder*, 4th edition, known as the DSM-IV, published by the American Psychiatric Association. US mental health professionals regard this as their bible. Our descriptions of the disorder are based on the practical information contained in the DSM-IV and on our clinical experience in treating the various disorders.

DON'T JUMP TO CONCLUSIONS

When reading through this section and hearing about all the possible psychological disorders that children can have, it is natural for parents to say, 'Hey! my child has this problem . . . and this one too . . . and this one!' However, as you'll see, there is a big difference between average kids and kids with psychological disorders.

The key to understanding whether or not your child may have a disorder is whether or not your child suffers impairment as a result of it. Ask yourself if your child is handicapped in day-to-day life because of a particular problem. If a child is depressed for a couple of days and then feels fine, she does not have a psychological disorder. However, a nine-year-old boy who is depressed for weeks, who does not play with his friends anymore and who does not do his schoolwork is impaired and clearly has a problem.

If you think your child has a particular problem, ask yourself three questions:

1. **Is this symptom – let's say inattention – causing problems in school, with friends, with family, or in some other important part of my child's life?**
2. **Is my child upset because he or she has this symptom?**
3. **Am I upset or worried that my child has this symptom?**

If you answered no to all three questions, you probably don't need to worry about it. If you answered yes, then consider consulting with a family physician or mental health professional. The information contained in this book is intended to inform you about potential problems children may have, but you need a professional to provide the ultimate diagnosis.

WHAT TO EXPECT DURING ASSESSMENT

Most mental health professionals who treat children or adolescents like to have the parents involved in the treatment. Parents know the child better than anyone else and can provide a great deal of information to the therapist or physician.

After meeting you and your child, a professional's first task is to evaluate your child to decide what kind of treatment will be most helpful. This period is called the assessment. Expect to be asked a lot of questions, especially during the first few visits. Only by arriving at a better understanding of the situation can a clinician decide what your child's problem is and what kind of treatment will be most beneficial.

Some of the questions asked of you may be a little embarrassing or may seem invasive (questions may concern yourself, your marriage and other parts of your life), but please be aware that the person asking them is just trying to assess how to help your child. The clinician does not want to make you feel uncomfortable. He or she is simply trying to understand what your child's life is like and you, of course, are an important part of your child's life. If you are uncomfortable, tell the clinician how you feel, so that the two of you can solve the problem.

WORKING WITH THE CLINICIAN

Many of the difficulties from which children suffer can be treated by having parents and other important adults in the child's life, such as teachers and grandparents, make changes in the child's environment. For that reason, once treatment is under way, you may be asked to perform certain tasks or make changes in the way you are raising your child. Remember that the clinician is not saying that what you've done previously is wrong; he is simply putting in place strategies that he thinks will be more helpful to your child. For example, behavioural therapy is used for many problems, such as depression, anxiety, conduct problems and eating disorders. These techniques usually require that the parents structure a child's environment a certain way: Parents of a child with conduct disorder may need to create more structure for a child; parents of a child with depression may need to spend more time with their child, focusing on positive social activities.

The more interested and active you are in your child's treatment, the more likely he or she is to make steady progress.

chapter fifteen

FACTORS THAT CAN CAUSE OR CONTRIBUTE TO PSYCHIATRIC DISORDERS

Researchers are making enormous headway in better understanding the factors that contribute to psychiatric disorders. While there is still a great deal to be learned, the progress affects not only how a disorder is diagnosed but also how it is treated.

Here is the latest information about how the environment, the human brain, genetics and temperament affect mental disorders. This chapter concludes with information about resilience, so that you may do what you can to develop your children's protective factors.

Environmental Factors

We know that environmental factors do affect a child's growth and behaviour. The home, the school, the neighbourhood, the community and the country all affect the way children's personalities develop and the way they see themselves.

Parents, of course, are the most important people in a child's environment. Having good relations with his parents can do wonders in helping a child develop into a healthy person. Kids who have problems getting along with their parents may feel alienated or isolated and may develop all sorts of problems.

Personal problems of those around them may have a poor effect on a child. A caregiver who is depressed, for example, may cause a child to become depressed or socially withdrawn. Parental anxiety seems to have similar impact. Children with anxious parents may be anxious themselves or avoid playing with peers.

Therefore, one of the best things you can do for your child is to make sure that you take care of yourself and are healthy. And if you feel that you are experiencing a mental health problem, seek help. This is one of the most loving things you can do for yourself, your child and your family.

A major stressor for many children is parental divorce. Children from divorced families sometimes lose contact with one of their parents, which can lead to sadness and grief. The consequences of divorce can include behavioural problems, particularly for boys. However, parents should remember that the research seems to show that a peaceful divorce is far less problematic for children than a marriage full of conflict, anger and revenge. Parents can help their children by getting along with each other, even if this means that a divorce must occur.

An environment in which physical or sexual abuse occurs is, of course, unsafe for any child. Abuse can lead to depression, anxiety and problems with other children. Unfortunately, many of the hospitalized children we see have been sexually abused, and they often have a hard time adjusting to this terrible stressor as well as other stressors in their lives. If you think your child is being abused in any way, seek help at once. Also refer to the additional information on page 217.)

Maintain a healthful environment for your child by following the recommendations in this book to reduce conflict in the home and make your child feel wanted. If you provide your child with a loving home, he or she will be less likely to have difficulties.

The Brain and Behaviour

The brain plays a major role in determining a child's behaviour and emotions. It is a complex part of the human anatomy, and having a better understanding of it can help anyone who is trying to grasp better why a child behaves the way he does.

The parts of the brain that are particularly important for a child's behaviour and emotion are the cerebral cortex, the basal ganglia and the limbic system.

The cerebral cortex is the outside layer of the brain, and it is what distinguishes our brains from those of animals. If you have seen pictures of the brain, you may remember the cerebral cortex as the part that is grey and wrinkled. This is where most higher order thinking happens, such as speech and memory.

The basal ganglia seems to receive messages and then send them out to other areas of the brain. It is kind of like a gatekeeper and may control the brain in some ways. If the basal ganglia is not working properly, it may cause certain problems, such as Tourette's disorder (see page 230) or attention deficit/hyperactivity disorder (page 175).

The limbic system consists of several brain structures and seems to control emotions and aggression. Animals that have the limbic system removed seem to lose control of their emotions and may become aggressive towards things that are not threatening, such as a puff of air.

HOW DOES THE BRAIN WORK?

During childhood the brain grows and develops very quickly. Part of this development is the growth of connections (synapses) between brain cells. The more connections the child has between different parts of the brain, the more intelligent and better able to solve problems she will be.

During development, brain chemicals, called neurotransmitters, play an important role in brain communication and behaviour. Over thirty different kinds of neurotransmitters have been identified by researchers. Three neurotransmitters in particular, however, seem to have the greatest effect on the child's behaviour. These are dopamine, norepinephrine and serotonin.

HOW DO NEUROTRANSMITTERS AFFECT THE BRAIN?

For messages to be sent from one area of the brain to another, chains of neurons (brain cells) have to communicate with each other. This happens much the way messages move along a telephone wire: the neuron receives a message from its neighbour and then passes it on to the next neuron in the chain.

Each neuron operates rather like a starter pistol. It has to be fired for its neighbour to hear the message and pass it on to the next neuron. For the neuron to be fired, there has to be the right amount of a neurotransmitter at the beginning of the neuron. If there is too much or too little, then it will not fire and pass along its message. The brain is then out of balance, and certain parts of the brain will not be able to communicate. This situation can lead to behaviour and learning difficulties.

The neurotransmitters seem to be key to normal functioning. These chemicals help modulate or regulate the brain and keep it running smoothly. If the child's brain contains the right amounts of these neurotransmitters, the child will have an easier time adapting to his environment. If these chemicals are out of balance, however, the child may have problems controlling his behaviour or emotions.

Too much dopamine, for example, seems to cause increased activity and aggression in a child, whereas too little seems to lead to poor motivation and follow-through. Too much norepinephrine may lead to anxiety and withdrawal from social situations, whereas too little seems to cause inattention. Too much serotonin may induce good impulse control, but too little may lead to aggression and poor impulse control.

These chemicals also probably work together and with other neurotransmitters to cause a child's behaviour and emotions. For instance, childhood mood and anxiety disorders seem to develop when the brain has disturbances of norepinephrine and/or serotonin.

Researchers have learned that some disorders, often those related to depression or anxiety, respond well to medications that affect one or more of these neurotransmitters – in other words, the medications increase or decrease the amount of dopamine, norepinephrine, or serotonin in the brain, and when this happens, the condition improves.

How Do We Know the Level of a Neurotransmitter in a Child's Brain?

Levels of neurotransmitters are measured through tests of urine, blood and cerebrospinal fluid, obtained through a spinal tap. Researchers are regularly coming up with new and improved diagnostic methods, such as the PET (positive emission tomography) scan, which is kind of like a brain map that shows which parts of the brain are active. These new procedures may help us better understand the brain and how it works.

Do the Levels of Neurotransmitters Always Stay the Same?

The levels of neurotransmitters seem to go up and down. This change may be caused by normal cycles in the child's body or by other things. For example, when children experience certain emotions, the brain releases specific chemicals.

A child with depression may get some really terrific news – about winning a spelling bee, for instance, or making a sports team. This excitement may cause the child's brain to release more or less of a certain chemical. The resulting change in chemical balance may mean that parts of the brain (such as the limbic system which regulates emotions) can work and communicate better for a time, and this, in turn, may make the child feel better and be less depressed.

Conversely, a child who is doing fine may receive some bad news, such as hearing about the death of a close friend. This trauma may lead the brain to release or stop releasing certain chemicals. This chemical change could cause depression or some other kind of problem.

HOW PARENTS CAN HELP

Recent research findings show that a child's brain structure is affected by his or her environment. If a child is spoken to, played with and interacted with frequently during her early life – say, from birth to age three, then she has a better chance of being more intelligent in the long run.

For that reason, the most important thing you can do for your child is to enjoy him. Talking, singing and playing with him from infancy on is a good way to give him a strong start. Stimulating a young child by playing with him or reading to him will help make connections between neurons in the brain.

The more connections there are between neurons, the more flexible the child's thinking will be, which helps the child solve problems and develop other important skills. This is great news for parents, as it indicates that they can influence the intelligence of their children and help them reach their full potential.

We still have a great deal to learn about the brain. However, current research has greatly aided clinicians in determining many new treatments for childhood problems.

Genetic Influences

Each person has twenty-three pairs of chromosomes, which are threadlike structures made up of genes. One of the genes in each pair is contributed by the mother and the other comes from the father. This is how parents pass along traits such as height, intelligence and eye colour. The genes contain DNA, which builds cells that are put out into the body and which cause the person to develop in certain ways.

Some medical diseases seem to be carried by genes and passed on from parent to child. Sickle-cell anaemia, for example, is a blood disease that comes from the parents. Huntington's disease is also genetic. Mental health disorders can be genetic. Bipolar disorder (mania), schizophrenia, tic disorders and ADHD may be at least partially caused by genes. Children with these disorders are likely to have relatives with the same or similar disorders.

Some genes are dominant, which means that a child with this gene will definitely have a certain trait or disease. Other genes are recessive, which means that a person may or may not have that trait or disease but could pass the genetic predisposition for it on to his children. This helps explain why two parents

with red hair can have a child with brown hair. At least one of the parents with red hair had a recessive gene for brown hair. This same dominant-recessive system works for genetically inherited diseases: some children may not develop the disease, but they can still pass it on to their children.

Sometimes whether or not a disease develops has to do with environmental circumstances and personal stress. For example, a child who has the genes to develop a mood disorder may or may not ever have a mood disorder. On the one hand, if the child lives in an environment that is relatively free from major stressors, such as parental conflict, illness, abuse and so forth, he may not develop the disorder. On the other hand, a child who has only a weak genetic predisposition towards the disorder may develop the problem if he is beset by many stressors.

How do we know if a disorder is passed on genetically? Researchers look to see whether children and their parents or other relatives develop the same disorders. However, if a parent is depressed and the child later becomes depressed, we cannot assume that depression is genetic; too many other factors are involved. For example, the home environment created by a depressed parent may be one of the reasons the child becomes depressed; the depression may not be genetic.

Researchers sometimes do twin studies to determine whether a disorder is genetic. They compare identical twins, who have the same genetic makeup, but who were separated at birth and adopted by different families. Because these children are raised in different environments, commonalities between them are probably due to genes. For example, if twins are raised in different families and both of them later develop ADHD, then there is some evidence that ADHD may be genetic.

The study of genes is a fast-growing field. If researchers gain a better understanding of the influence of genes on children's behaviour, then mental health professionals will be better equipped to treat, and possibly prevent, some childhood disorders.

Temperament

Imagine that you turn on a loud radio in a hospital nursery full of sleeping infants. Each baby will react in a distinct manner to the music. Some children will be startled and will cry. Others will awake and listen silently. Still others might sleep through the disruption.

This unique response depends on the child's temperament, or the manner in which a person reacts to environmental stimuli including noise, taste, smell, touch and sight. Your child's temperament will determine, among other things, whether she is shy or outgoing, energetic or quiet and regular or irregular in her sleeping habits. Children's individual reactions are biological in nature and will affect them throughout their lives.

THE NINE COMPONENTS OF A CHILD'S PERSONALITY

For many decades, scientists have talked about individual differences in people. It took a long time for these individual differences to be examined in children, however,

especially infants. Researchers Alexander Thomas and Stella Chess first investigated this subject and identified nine behavioural components of temperament. All children's personalities comprised a combination of these nine elements:

1. **ACTIVITY LEVEL:** how much your child moves.
2. **RHYTHMICITY:** regular versus irregular schedules of eating, sleeping and having bowel movements.
3. **ADAPTABILITY:** the amount of time it takes your child to adapt to new situations.
4. **APPROACH-WITHDRAWAL:** whether your child tends to approach or avoid new things or people.
5. **THRESHOLD LEVEL:** sensitivity to stimuli, particularly pain.
6. **INTENSITY OF REACTION:** magnitude of crying or other reactions.
7. **QUALITY OF MOOD:** happy versus unhappy.
8. **DISTRACTIBILITY:** degree to which the child is distracted from current activities.
9. **PERSISTENCE AND ATTENTION SPAN:** length of time the child continues with one activity.

THREE BASIC TEMPERAMENTS

Based on children's tendencies regarding these nine basic characteristics, three different general temperament types have been identified:

1. THE EASY CHILD is happy most of the time and generally has a cheerful outlook. Her moods are mild or moderate, and she is regular and predictable in her eating and sleeping habits. The easy child adapts quickly to new situations and people and gets along well with others. Most people enjoy being around such children, and child-rearing usually proceeds smoothly. About 40 per cent of children are believed to have an easy temperament.

2. THE DIFFICULT CHILD often exhibits an unhappy mood. He takes a long time to accept change and reacts poorly to new situations and new people. His reactions are likely to be intense, and he may cry easily. He may be active, irritable and hard to be around, and his eating and sleeping habits are generally irregular. Many parents assume they are responsible for a difficult child's demanding behaviour, and this can make child-rearing arduous.

3. THE SLOW-TO-WARM-UP CHILD is usually inactive and moody. She is like an engine that takes some time to warm up. She finds change difficult, and it takes her some time to adapt, but she is less disruptive and unpleasant than the difficult child. She may be cranky in new situations, but she doesn't tend to yell or scream, as a difficult child might. She is generally mild in nature, but she has mood changes and is unpredictable in her daily activities. She is also likely to be shy or withdrawn, and she'll do what she can to avoid new situations.

Based on these descriptions, you should have a general idea which temperament your child has. Most children have characteristics from more than one category, but one temperament type will be most appropriate in describing them.

It is important to keep in mind, however, that each child's temperament is unique. Though your three-year-old may be a slow-to-warm-up child, your new baby will not necessarily follow suit.

As a parent, you will find life easier if you take your child's temperament into account. For example, if you know your difficult child is likely to react poorly when the family moves to another house, you can start implementing strategies to help him feel more comfortable with change. You might start by bringing home brochures about interesting children's activities in the new community, and you can eventually take him with you to visit the new community before you actually move.

A child's temperament will also affect the way others respond to her. The easy child is usually well liked by teachers and is likely to excel in school, but this doesn't mean that your difficult or slow-to-warm-up child is doomed. You'll just have to help this type of child find other ways to approach new acquaintances.

The temperaments of family members will also affect the general household atmosphere. Those with difficult temperaments may make the household feel very tense at times, making it helpful if there is an easy family member who can make everyone laugh now and then. And of course children who are regular in their patterns and normally sleep through the night tend to lead the way towards a calmer household, partially because other family members have been able to get enough sleep.

Parents may have different temperaments from their children, and sometimes this causes difficulty. Because of her own shyness, a mother who is slow to warm up may find it particularly hard to smooth the way for a difficult child. However, by taking your own temperament into account, you will find a way to work with your child towards a satisfactory outcome.

You need to be flexible in your parenting. For example, if your child is easily distracted, make sure that you have her full attention before you make a request. Don't ask her to take out the rubbish when she is engrossed in a favourite television programme. If your child is slow to warm up, expose her to other children frequently so that she will become more adept at making friends.

Remember that you are not to blame for having children who are fussy or in a bad mood for long periods of time. Parents should also know that temperament is not affected by pampering or by the type of punishment the child receives. Temperament is something each person is born with, and it can't be radically changed.

Although you cannot change or control your child's basic temperament, you can modify your own response to it. Doing what you can to bring out the best in your child by helping him with transitions, modifying his sleeping and eating patterns so they suit the family, and working with rather than against his bad moods. With your help a child of almost any temperament can learn to lead a happy, comfortable life.

Factors That Protect and Build Resilience

Some kids seem to be relatively sturdy emotionally. They find ways to cope with the stress in their lives. They bounce back when they have a failure in school or in their personal relationships. They pick themselves up, dust themselves off and start again after something goes wrong. What is it about these kids that makes them so resilient? Here are some of the things that seem to protect children from having emotional difficulties. By understanding the qualities and circumstances that can increase resilience, you may be able to help your children avoid emotional problems.

➤ **PARENTAL SUPPORT.** You can help your child by being available and by being helpful and supportive. Mentally healthy adults usually report that they had a loving relationship with at least one parent or with another adult in their environment.

➤ **SOCIAL SUPPORT.** Encourage your child to make friends and make your home available if kids need a place to hang out. Try to be available to drive your kids to a friend's house, to the movies, or to the shops with their friends.

➤ **GOOD SELF-ESTEEM.** Kids who feel good about themselves, their skills and their lives tend to have fewer mental health problems. Parents play an important role in building their child's self-esteem.

➤ **INTELLIGENCE.** Children who are intelligent are often good at solving problems, so they are able to find ways to change, end, or avoid whatever is troubling them. Parents can enhance their children's intelligence by talking with them, being affectionate and playing with them, particularly during infancy and toddlerhood.

In sum, good parental and social support, self-esteem and intelligence appear to be the major elements that allow some children to avoid emotional problems and grow into well-adjusted and productive adults. Even children who are born with some kind of problem, such as a handicap, can be resilient if they are raised in the right kind of environment. (For help with any of these issues, refer to Part Two and particularly to Chapter 6, Bringing Out the Best in Your Children.)

chapter sixteen
PSYCHIATRIC DISORDERS

Acting Out/Behaviour Problems (Conduct Disorder)

(See also Setting Limits, p. 74; Anger in Daily Life, p. 82; Stealing, p. 115; Anxiety, p. 173; Attention Deficit/Hyperactivity Disorder, p. 175; Depression, p. 184.)

WHAT IT IS

Children and adolescents with conduct disorder show a chronic pattern for six months or more of either (1) violating age-appropriate rules, such as staying out past curfew, running away from home, or being truant from school; or (2) violating the rights of others by bullying, lying, initiating physical fights, using weapons, being physically cruel to people or animals, stealing, fire-setting, or purposely breaking into or destroying private property.

WHAT CAUSES IT

In some instances, children may have a relative, neighbour, or friend whose behaviour is deviant. Other times, kids learn that they can get what they want by illegal means. It seems easier to them to steal a stereo than to get a job and save money to buy one.

In other cases, a problem early in the child's life, such as lead poisoning or fetal alcohol syndrome, caused by prenatal alcohol consumption by the mother, may partially contribute to conduct disorder.

Conduct disorder is often accompanied by other disorders, including attention deficit/ hyperactivity disorder (ADHD), depression, or anxiety.

Kids with ADHD have trouble controlling their impulses and may do things that get them in trouble. Youngsters who are anxious or depressed may be in a great deal of pain and feel that the only way they can cope with it is by behaving badly.

In most instances youngsters seem to develop conduct disorder because they do not have enough structure or discipline in their lives. Many youngsters report that they steal or behave violently because they are bored and know that they will probably not get in trouble for it. Youngsters with conduct disorder, however, need to experience consequences for their behaviour. It is important for their parents not to protect them from disciplinary action by authorities at school or in the community.

WHAT TO WATCH FOR

About 10 per cent of children and adolescents have conduct disorder (it is typically more common among adolescents). These youngsters usually get into trouble in obvious ways – by staying out late, running away, being truant, setting fires, starting fights at school and stealing. It is likely that you are well aware if your child has a behaviour problem. As a matter of fact, you may be relieved to hear there is a name for it. While kids who act out are sometimes referred to as juvenile delinquents, mental health professionals avoid that judgmental term.

WHAT PARENTS CAN DO

A carefully structured environment with known limits is most helpful to a child with behaviour problems. In addition you can take these three measures:

1. Reduce conflict and anger in the household. If there is a great deal of conflict or anger in your home, you should consider family therapy with a qualified family counsellor or therapist. Frequently, such therapy will focus on helping your family communicate more clearly and pleasantly. Problem-solving training (see Chapter 5) may also help to reduce the amount of conflict in your family.

2. Work to make your relationship with your child more pleasant. Again, family therapy may help. A therapist may request that you and/or your spouse spend more time with the youngster doing enjoyable activities, such as walking in the park, seeing a movie, pursuing a hobby together, or just talking. If you have several children, this may entail spending separate time with each of them, which is time-consuming. However, families we've counselled agree that it is worth the effort and leads to a more pleasant home life.

3. Increase discipline, monitor the child's behaviour closely and be consistent. Changing the family approach to discipline and rules can make a big difference. Although they usually don't admit it, kids like to have rules. If they understand the limits, they begin to work out what they can and cannot do, and this makes them feel more secure. By supervising your child, you'll be able to ensure that she is following the rules and staying out of trouble.

A therapist can help you establish a few important rules – the child may not skip school or stay out past 9:00 P.M. on a school night, for example. If the youngster breaks these rules, predetermined consequences are put into effect – the loss of telephone or television privileges, perhaps. In addition, you should offer rewards for good behaviour.

If Your Child Is Already in Trouble with the Legal System

If your youngster already has a criminal record and has been assigned a juvenile officer or case manager, work with this individual to determine what kind of help your child needs.

You also need to work closely with personnel from the school to make sure that your child is facing appropriate consequences for behaviour problems at school.

ALTHOUGH CONDUCT disorder isn't easy to treat, parents who follow through with consequences tend to have some success and can improve the parent-child relationship.

Adjustment Disorder

(See also Building Self-Esteem, p. 42; Acting Out, p. 167, Anxiety, p. 173; Depression, p. 184.)

WHAT IT IS

Adjustment disorder is a fancy way of saying that a child is having trouble adjusting to a major stressor in her life. (To be defined as an adjustment disorder, the trouble needs to begin within three months of the onset of the stressor.)

Adjustment disorder can cause social withdrawal, declining school grades, reluctance to participate in extracurricular activities, distorted and negative thinking, excessive worry, suspension from school and even legal problems.

WHAT CAUSES IT

Adjustment disorder may result from one or a series of stressors. Sometimes the stress is something that affects only the child or adolescent (being dropped from a team, the breakup of a romantic relationship). In other instances it can affect the entire family (divorce, sibling discord, family financial problems) or even the entire community (threat of violent crime, loss of a favourite teacher).

WHAT TO WATCH FOR

Most kids worry sometimes or seem upset, but the child who is suffering from adjustment disorder may be anxious or depressed, or he may get into trouble. However, in sum, these problems add up to a general discomfort, with none of the symptoms being strong enough individually to lead to a diagnosis of anxiety disorder, major depression, or conduct disorder.

WHAT PARENTS CAN DO

Be supportive and understanding. Though most adults rarely consider it, children frequently experience stress. It's not easy to face challenges like starting a new year in school, making friends, losing people you care about, having a teacher you don't like, or being the last one picked for a team.

If your child is sad because he is doing poorly in school, try to find out what is going on and get help. Sometimes a session or two with a tutor can make a difference.

AIDS

WHAT IT IS

AIDS (acquired immune deficiency syndrome) is a viral disease that weakens the body's ability to fight off infection.

WHAT CAUSES IT

AIDS is acquired through sexual contact, contaminated drugs, or contact with blood products or fluid from someone infected with the virus. The virus attacks the immune system and breaks it down by destroying the T cells that kill viruses.

WHAT TO WATCH FOR

A person may be infected with AIDS for years before any symptoms emerge. Early symptoms may include fever, muscle and joint pain, rash, hives and diarrhoea. Of course, these can be caused by many conditions, including the flu. In later stages of the disease, the person may develop pneumonia or a type of skin cancer called Kaposi's sarcoma, which is characterized by dark brown or purple nodules.

WHAT PARENTS CAN DO

As a parent you need to talk to your kids about AIDS. Most children have heard of AIDS through the media and have absorbed at least one message: AIDS kills. However, if children get the majority of their information about AIDS from the media or from other kids, they are likely to harbour some misconceptions.

For example, some kids think that AIDS can affect only adult homosexuals. They don't realize that heterosexuals and children can develop the disease as well. Parents need to stress that AIDS is not an 'us-them' disease that only happens to people who do certain things; it can happen to anyone. Encouragingly, one study showed that about 85 per cent of parents had had at least one discussion of AIDS with their elementary school children.

With preschoolers and primary school children, you need only discuss the disease the way you might explain about a grandmother who has shingles or a neighbourhood teenager who has mononucleosis. If the topic comes up because someone you know or someone in the media has the disease, you can say something as simple as this: 'People who have AIDS get weak, so their body gets sick.'

Primary school children may be afraid that they will get AIDS by drinking from a fountain, sitting on a toilet, or playing with other kids (with or without AIDS). Assure your child that the AIDS virus dies when it is exposed to air. You may explain that AIDS is transmitted by having sex and doing drugs. A detailed explanation of how the virus is transmitted is probably not yet necessary.

For children over age ten, however, you'll need to provide more details about the transmission of the disease. You might explain that the exchange of contaminated body fluids – blood, semen, vaginal fluid – causes AIDS. Explain that you cannot get AIDS from someone who does not carry the disease, but it is hard to tell who has AIDS; you cannot tell just by looking, because AIDS may not become apparent for many years.

Parents of older children should also describe protected, or safer, sex. Some parents may balk at giving such information to young teenagers. Unfortunately, some kids become sexually active at a very young age. We definitely think it is more important to prevent the spread of AIDS than to moralize about sexual activity. Of course, you can discuss abstinence at the same time. Talk with your kids about the permanence of AIDS. Sometimes kids feel that they will never contract AIDS or that they will conquer the disease if they get it.

Overall, perhaps the most constructive thing parents can do is to educate themselves about AIDS. Parents are often surprised at the complexity of the questions kids ask, and it will make your discussion easier if you have a thorough understanding of the topic. You must feel comfortable talking to your kids about these issues if you are to provide accurate and useful information.

If you suspect that your child has AIDS, you should seek medical attention immediately. An AIDS test should be done as soon as possible. The sooner it is caught, the more effective treatment can be. If your child is at high risk for developing AIDS, you may want to consider having him tested even if he or she does not have any symptoms.

If your child is diagnosed with AIDS, find a trusted physician and follow his advice. You should also consider finding support groups to help you and your child deal with your frustration and fear. Individual therapy may also be helpful.

New methods of treating the disorder are being researched and used all the time, and knowledge about AIDS is changing rapidly. Contact your local health department, family physician, or public health clinic for precise up-to-date information about AIDS. Hopefully, there will soon be a cure.

Anorexia

(See also Bulimia, p. 182.)

WHAT IT IS

Anorexia is a loss of appetite. Anorexia nervosa is a condition whereby, in an effort to be thin, a child does not eat enough to maintain a normal body weight. The problem is more common in girls, but it can also affect boys.

WHAT CAUSES IT

Anorexia can have a number of medical causes, including problems of the hypothalamus, a part of the brain. However, scientists have not conclusively documented the reasons why youngsters develop anorexia.

In some cases, anorexia arises because youngsters feel that they have no control in their lives, and they struggle to find ways to gain control. During a parental divorce, for example, a youngster may become anorexic, hoping subconsciously that her problem will reunite the family. However, this does not mean that the child is purposely creating a problem to be manipulative or that the parents are to blame for the anorexia.

WHAT TO WATCH FOR

The child or adolescent with anorexia nervosa doesn't eat very much and is usually severely afraid of gaining weight or becoming fat. The child is also likely to have a distorted view of her body shape or size. A child with anorexia nervosa may think she is fat even though she is grossly underweight. When drawing pictures of herself, she is likely to depict her body as fat.

Another sign of anorexia in adolescent girls is that they will stop having their menstrual period. This condition is known as amenorrhoea and usually suggests that the youngster has not been eating enough for quite a while.

You may be reassured to learn that the following notions about anorexia are just myths:

MYTH #1: *Youngsters with anorexia nervosa never eat.* These kids may eat some food. They will eat less than their bodies require for good health, however. Also, they may avoid high-fat foods and eat only certain low-fat foods, such as vegetables.

MYTH #2: *Youngsters with anorexia nervosa lose their appetite.* Appetite can be very high; a complete loss of appetite is rare. Indeed, some kids may suffer stomach cramps from hunger, which they either ignore or endure.

MYTH #3: *Youngsters with anorexia nervosa have been sexually abused.* There is no direct relationship between sexual abuse and anorexia.

MYTH #4: *Youngsters with anorexia nervosa always lose weight.* Anorexia nervosa is also displayed through failure to make expected weight gains. Children and adolescents grow, gain weight and fill out. A child with anorexia nervosa may continue to grow taller, but not gain much or any weight.

MYTH #5: *Youngsters with anorexia nervosa are always girls.* Males with the problem are overlooked because many people incorrectly assume that only females develop anorexia.

MYTH #6: *Youngsters with anorexia nervosa think that they are fat.* They may view certain parts of their bodies – thighs, buttocks, or stomach, perhaps – as fat or flabby.

MYTH #7: *Youngsters with anorexia nervosa come from dysfunctional or unhealthy families.* Although this situation is sometimes the case, youngsters with anorexia nervosa come from all kinds of backgrounds.

MYTH #8: *Youngsters with anorexia nervosa are always Caucasian.* Some ethnic minorities do have this problem.

Children have different body types and will develop different eating patterns in order to maintain good health. Some children and adolescents have small appetites and do not need to eat very much to be healthy. Others can eat a great deal and not gain much weight. It is important to know your child's normal eating patterns so that you can be aware of any changes.

While exact weight is not really the issue, your child's paediatrician can provide guidelines as to an ideal weight range.

WHAT PARENTS CAN DO

If you suspect that your child has anorexia, you need to consult a physician. In a mild case or a case in the early stages, she can be treated on an outpatient basis. Advanced anorexia is very serious, however, and can lead to death. Immediate hospitalization may be necessary.

Your first task is to make sure that your child is medically stable. In severe cases, she may have to be fed through a tube in order to ensure that she gets enough nourishment and can start to gain weight.

Curing the immediate problem is only part of the solution, however. Unless other changes are made in the youngster's life, she will probably become anorexic again and lose weight as soon as she is discharged from the hospital. For that reason, cognitive therapy is often used with these youngsters. Because they tend to have a distorted view of their bodies, they may also have distorted thoughts – for example, 'I am fat; if I eat a banana, I'll gain three pounds.' In therapy they are taught to evaluate the validity of these thoughts. If they determine that a thought is not valid and may be harmful, they learn to replace it with a more practical one: 'I need to eat to live.' By changing her thinking pattern, the youngster can learn to be satisfied with her weight and body shape, and this can help prevent further bouts of anorexia.

A nutritionist will probably help develop a nutrition plan for the youngster to make sure that she is eating adequately and healthfully. The youngster will also benefit from periodic weigh-ins.

You'll be an important part of the treatment process. Although the problem may not have been caused by the family, it definitely becomes a family problem because it affects everyone. A therapist may make special requests of you, such as spending additional time with your youngster or monitoring her food intake, and it's important that you do whatever is recommended.

Anxiety (Generalized Anxiety Disorder)

(See also Obsessive-Compulsive Disorder, p. 201; Panic Disorder and Agoraphobia, p. 204; Phobia, p. 208; Post-Traumatic Stress Disorder, p. 211; Separation Anxiety, p. 215.)

WHAT IT IS

Anxiety is a natural emotion that aids in survival. However, youngsters with anxiety disorder have a system that overreacts to stressors. Children with generalized anxiety disorder worry so much that they start to have problems in their lives because of worrying all the time. Because of their concerns, these youngsters also have physiological symptoms, including restlessness, getting tired easily, difficulty concentrating, stomachaches or headaches, or muscle tension. Falling asleep may be difficult because they worry after going to bed. As a result, they are sometimes tired and irritable from not sleeping. A child who has experienced excessive anxiety or worry for at least six months may be diagnosed with anxiety disorder.

WHAT CAUSES IT

Being overly anxious tends to have a biological component, and it sometimes runs in families. However, family or society stressors can certainly aggravate the condition. For instance, if the family is moving, the parents are divorcing, or things aren't going well at school, the anxious child will become even more anxious.

Youngsters with generalized anxiety disorder may also have what is called anxiety sensitivity, which means that their anxiety creates more anxiety. Children and adolescents with high anxiety sensitivity tend to become anxious when they have the bodily symptoms of stress. For example, if their body feels tense, they may worry about why their muscles are tight: 'Why is my body acting this way? I must be sick or something. I hope I don't throw up.' Feeling this way makes them even more anxious, which then makes their body even more tense and their muscles tighter. The circular thought pattern simply heightens their anxiety until the cycle is broken.

WHAT TO WATCH FOR

All children worry and get anxious sometimes, and it is not usually a problem. Kids tend to worry about things that are new or challenging – doing well in school, for example, or playing sports well, or having friends. An adolescent is more likely to worry about fitting in with a group, dating, peer pressure, or the future (going to college or getting a job). Most kids get through these challenges unscathed and learn to manage their stress. In some ways, worrying about something can even be useful, because it motivates people to work harder.

However, for about 5 per cent of children, excessive worry and anxiety become problematic; they find everything overwhelming and frightening. These kids are worriers. Anxious kids often want to be perfect – they want to get perfect results, to look perfect and to have everyone like them. They are frequently oversensitive and react strongly to any criticism. Getting a bad result on a test can seem like the end of the world to them. Also, kids who worry tend to think that the absolute worst thing that *could* happen *will* happen. They ask a lot of 'what if' questions. If an anxious child has to give a speech in front of her class, her thinking might go something like this:

'I have to give a perfect speech on China. What if it isn't perfect? If my speech isn't perfect, the class will laugh at me because they don't like me. The teacher will probably laugh too and give me a bad mark. What if I get a bad mark? My parents will be so mad at me. Then, they'll never let me go to the movies this weekend. Everyone is going to be at the movies. They'll think I'm a total dork if I can't go. I'll die if they don't let me go.'

WHAT PARENTS CAN DO

For a large majority of kids who worry, the problem tends to go away. If your child's worry or anxiety is occasional, she probably just needs stability and reassurance that she's doing well and that things will work out fine because she tries hard. Be patient. If you become frustrated with having to reassure her, you will simply heighten her anxiety.

However, if the anxiety is truly affecting your child's life – if he won't go to school or he's having difficulty with friends – we recommend that you seek help from a therapist. For many kids, cognitive-behavioural therapy is quite helpful. This type of therapy deals with social-skill and problem-solving training as well as cognitive restructuring techniques and behavioural assignments.

Antianxiety medication is seldom and only briefly used for children and adolescents. Mild antianxiety medications may be prescribed for some children or adolescents, particularly if the problem is likely to be short-lived – for example, if a child is going through a parental divorce.

Attention Deficit/Hyperactivity Disorder (ADHD)

(See also Setting Limits, p. 74; Handling Aggressiveness, p. 113; Acting Out/Behaviour Problems, p. 167; Learning Disorders, p. 195.)

WHAT IT IS

Children who are diagnosed with attention deficit/hyperactivity disorder (ADHD) have difficulty sitting still and paying attention. If the condition is mild, the child may simply be fidgety all the time. If it is extreme, however, the child will be unable to stay in his seat at school and may even wake in the night and run around. Because of poor concentration, these children are easily distracted, and something like a ticking clock may disturb them when they are reading. Some children cannot even concentrate long enough to watch a fifteen-minute cartoon.

These children are also sometimes clumsy and may injure themselves frequently. They may forget to pick up after themselves, break things, create a lot of noise and bother people around them. They are often frustrated because they are constantly getting into trouble.

Neither the child nor the people around him realize that he has a disorder, and though he may desperately want to behave, it may be difficult for him to do so without help and treatment.

The disorder must be diagnosed by a qualified child psychiatrist or psychologist through observation, history-gathering from parents and teachers and testing. No layperson can diagnose this disorder, so if a teacher or another parent suggests that your child has ADD or ADHD, ask the school or your paediatrician for a referral to someone who can offer a definitive diagnosis. Once diagnosed, the disorder can be treated through medication and behaviour modification.

Normally the hyperactivity aspect of ADHD diminishes with age, but the difficulty paying attention may continue into adulthood.

WHAT CAUSES IT

While the exact cause of ADHD is still subject to debate, scientists feel that children with the disorder are born with the problem. Studies do show conclusively that ADHD is not caused by parental indulgence, family problems, or diet.

WHAT TO WATCH FOR

Here are some of the symptoms of ADHD:

➤ **HYPERACTIVITY:** Because he has a motor that never stops and is always on the go, this child may have trouble sitting in his seat for more than a few seconds. He may run or climb constantly, even when his peers are sitting quietly.

➤ **INATTENTIVENESS:** The child has difficulty focusing for long periods of time because she is easily distractible.

➤ **IMPULSIVITY:** This child may blurt out answers to questions or interrupt others, saying things or acting out without thinking. He may also do dangerous things like running out into the street without looking.

➤ **ACTING YOUNGER THAN THEY ARE.** A twelve-year-old who has difficulty concentrating, cannot sit still and acts younger than his age might have ADHD.

➤ **POOR SCHOOL PERFORMANCE.** Because these kids often disrupt the class, they are often scolded by their teachers. If the problem is not diagnosed and treated, a cycle of disruption, reprimand and failure begins.

➤ **DIFFICULTY WITH RELATIONSHIPS.** It is hard for these children to make friends and keep them. Often other kids describe them as obnoxious, loud, or mean. Adults may also be irritated or annoyed by these children. These kids want attention and affection, but they behave in such a way that others don't want to be near them.

Though any child may be impulsive and have difficulty focusing or sitting still occasionally, most youngsters' actions are not problematic, and the kids will grow out of them. The child who has ADHD will regularly act in a way that is inconsistent with normal development, and the problem behaviour will also occur in more than one setting. A ten-year-old who squirms during a church service but is fine in the classroom does not have ADHD.

Parents may begin to suspect a child has ADHD when he starts preschool or nursery school, since school requires children to pay attention and sit still for long periods of time, but mild cases may not be spotted until a child enters primary or the first stage of secondary school. Here the academic demands become more rigorous and an even more structured work style is necessary, and as a result, children with mild problems that have gone unspotted can no longer keep up as easily.

WHAT PARENTS CAN DO

Because ADHD causes problems for the child in different settings and in different ways, it is important that each case be considered on its own merits. Appropriate treatment may include medication or behaviour therapy or a combination of the two. Both therapies are discussed in detail below. When recommended, the medication can help the child with focus and self-control. The behaviour therapy will help him gain new skills.

Medication

Medications are frequently prescribed to decrease the child's activity level and increase his attention span. When the symptoms of ADHD are diminished, the child is often able to improve his peer relations, academic performance, classroom behaviour and family relationships.

Most of the medications used for children with attention deficit/hyperactivity disorder are stimulants. It may seem surprising to provide a stimulant to an overactive child, but this is effective because stimulants increase alertness and help a child concentrate better and be less active. Stimulants are thought to work through increasing the release of norepinephrine and dopamine, which are natural chemicals in the body, into the child's system. Three commonly prescribed stimulants are methylphenidates, such as Ritalin; dextroamphetamines, such as Dexedrine and magnesium pemoline, such as Volital.

These medications are fast-acting and generally take effect within a few hours. They also do not stay in the child's body for long, so they usually have to be taken a couple of times a day. The fact that drugs move quickly through the body means that the dosage can be adjusted so that the medication will be in effect for only the hours when the child is in school. When the child is at home, parents can use behavioural techniques to help control the child's behaviour.

About 70 per cent of children with ADHD will benefit from taking stimulants. Children who do not respond well can be given other medications such as an antidepressant, which may work.

These medications may produce some side effects, including decreased appetite, sleeping problems, headaches, irritability and stomachaches, but these conditions are not long term and are not likely to cause major problems. However, check with your doctor immediately if your child does not seem to be adjusting well to the medicine.

Because of the possible side effects, parents should carefully consider their decision to have their children go on stimulants. Though teachers sometimes request putting a child on medication because he or she is disruptive in the classroom, you have to consider what will be best for your child.

The media have reported cases of people using large quantities of Ritalin or other stimulants to get high. These are rare situations, however, and the majority of cases have involved adults. Most children recognize that the stimulants help them, and they do not report craving them or feeling addicted.

Behaviour Therapy

Behaviour therapy is often used, with or without medication, for children with ADHD. The goal is to enforce faithfully and consistently consequences of good and bad behaviour. Working with a mental health professional, parents can map out clear guidelines describing appropriate and inappropriate behaviour and the consequences for each. Once these guidelines are put in place, parents and teachers must work together so that reinforcement is consistent.

The basic components of behaviour therapy are explained below. While some of the techniques may seem simple enough to try on your own, balance and consistency may be difficult to achieve unless the behaviour modification plan is designed and monitored by a mental health professional.

DEVELOPING BEHAVIOURAL CONTRACTS.

Contracts are often used as a part of behaviour therapy. A contract is a document designed by the therapist, with the assistance of the child and his parents or care-takers and signed by all who are involved. The contract describes acceptable behaviours and specifies the reward that will be given to the child for success or the punishment for refusal to carry them out.

Contracts work best when you start with a relatively minor behaviour pattern so that your child will experience immediate success, boosting her self-esteem and sense of competence. A child with ADHD, for example, may not be able to sit still during the entire dinner hour. However, if you specify in the contract that she has to sit still for the first ten minutes of dinner, she may be able to do so with relative ease. You can increase the difficulty of the tasks as the child progresses.

Rewards are an important part of behavioural contracts. Instead of offering toys or money, select special treats that are appropriate for the behaviour. If your child sits still for the first ten minutes of dinner, you might agree to watch a favourite television programme with her. If dinner isn't disrupted, you can get the dishes done so that you are free to watch with her.

We recommend that you also include important behaviours in the contract – the actions that are most disruptive to family life or to your child's life. A contract might read: 'If Mary stays quietly in bed until 7:00 A.M. on Saturday, she may stay up an extra half hour on Saturday night.' Type up an actual document, sign it and have your spouse and the child sign it, too. Then put the contract somewhere where everyone can see it, perhaps on the refrigerator or a kitchen bulletin board.

When the family is ready to try to change another behaviour, you should create a new contract.

IGNORE CERTAIN INAPPROPRIATE BEHAVIOUR.

For the duration of a contract, ignore other things that bother you – though of course you should never ignore dangerous conduct such as running out into the street without looking. For example, if you are not currently treating your child's impulsive behaviour, you should ignore him when he shouts out answers to questions before you are finished. However, if you 'catch' him waiting quietly for someone else to finish speaking – something you know is very difficult for him – you should certainly praise him.

Ignoring certain types of behaviour is often difficult for parents, but it can be a helpful part of an overall treatment package.

OFFER FULL-TIME SUPPORT. Children with ADHD frequently face criticism from teachers and classmates, so it is important to

be supportive of your child at all times. Make sure that he knows you love him regardless of his behaviour. Explain to him that, even though his behaviour can sometimes be irritating, you like being around him and care about him. Also praise him for every success, being very specific. For example, if your child sits quietly and colours during a thirty-minute car ride, don't just say, 'You were good in the car.' Say, 'I love the way you sat with your seat belt fastened and made this picture for me. You also let your baby sister sleep, and that was important to me. Thank you.' But be realistic and don't give false praise. Children know when adults are just paying lip service.

WHAT ELSE YOU CAN DO

Support and consistency on the part of the parents is an important aspect of helping a child with ADHD. For that reason, you will want to work closely with your child's school once you have a definitive diagnosis. Start with the classroom teacher and include the staff counsellor or psychologist as well. The school needs to be informed of the diagnosis and your approach to treating it.

Many school systems have good resources for working with children with special needs, and you should begin to explore what is available. The school may recommend that your child be pulled out of class for special help during the day. Many communities also have active parent groups that deal specifically with ADHD, and from other parents you can learn more about how to help your child.

It will be important to stay in touch with the school administration from year to year to be certain that your child is placed in a classroom where the teacher will take the time to work with him.

If you keep the school informed and work with them in planning what will be best for your child, you will likely find that you have created a strong and important support system that can make all the difference for your child in both his academic work and his self-esteem – both of which are important for his future success.

Autism and Other Developmental Disorders Rett's Disorder, Childhood Disintegrative Disorder and Asperger's Syndrome

WHAT THEY ARE

A pervasive developmental disorder is a problem a child has from birth that impairs the way she functions. These disorders are said to be pervasive because they can affect the child in a number of different ways, often impairing her speech, her social relations and her motor function. These disorders are generally diagnosed before a child starts school.

There are four major pervasive developmental disorders.

1. AUTISM. Children with this disorder have problems with socialization. They may make eye contact infrequently, resist playing with or making friends with other children and be unable to show pleasure and love. Many also have difficulty communicating. Some children with autism do not speak at all.

Others develop odd speech patterns – overusing nonsense phrases, for example, or constantly repeating what others say (echolalia). These children also repeat actions that serve no purpose. For example, one child we treated used to tie a piece of wool to his middle finger. He would then bounce his hand up and down and would sit for hours at a time watching the wool. The average child would quickly tire of such a task, but children with autism do not.

2. RETT'S DISORDER. Children with Rett's disorder seem to develop normally for the first five months or so of life. However, after this period of normal development, a number of things happen: The child's head ceases to grow at the same rate as the rest of his body. He loses hand movement skills he previously had and develops repetitive hand movements. The child also exhibits problems with social interactions and communication, and when he learns to walk, his physical movements are abnormal.

3. CHILDHOOD DISINTEGRATIVE DISORDER. Children with this problem develop normally for the first two years of life. Then they lose some of the functions they previously had. This may include language skills, social skills, motor skills and bowel or bladder control.

4. ASPERGER'S SYNDROME. Children with Asperger's syndrome display many of the same behaviour patterns as do children with autism, including repetitive movements and problems in social relations. However, they do not have the same speech problems as do children with autism.

WHAT CAUSES THEM

Researchers do not yet know what causes pervasive developmental disorders. However, it appears that there are anatomical changes in the brain. The reasons for the changes are not known. The child may have been exposed to a virus before birth, or a problem with his immune system may cause the disorder.

If your child has a pervasive developmental disorder, don't blame yourself. Scientists do not yet understand the causes well enough to identify anything parents could have done differently to prevent a disorder from occurring.

WHAT TO WATCH FOR

Delayed development is one sign of a pervasive developmental disorder. Children with these problems may not reach the usual developmental milestones, such as crawling by about age nine months or speaking in short sentences by the age of two. However, don't overreact. Children develop at different paces, and most who develop somewhat slowly are perfectly fine. If you have any concerns, check with your paediatrician.

Among the pervasive developmental disorders, autism seems to be the most common, although it is still relatively rare. It is also the best understood and most studied.

WHAT PARENTS CAN DO

Take your child for frequent medical check-ups. Generally, a doctor will pick up on the early signs of autism and other developmental disorders, and she may refer you to a developmental paediatrician, a child psychiatrist, or another mental health professional.

Treatment for these disorders is usually called habilitation and involves helping a child learn some of the basic life skills, such as eating by himself, talking, or taking care of his own hygiene. Although these disorders do not typically disappear the way a successfully treated phobia might, the child can learn many new skills that will help him function better.

Many parents also find it helpful to join a support group. Because the child with a pervasive developmental disorder generally requires a great deal of care, finding others who are in the same situation helps many parents feel less isolated. Check with nearby hospitals, community mental health centres, or universities to see what groups are available in your area.

Bed-wetting (Enuresis)

(See also Setting Limits, p. 74; Soiling, p. 222.)

WHAT IT IS

When children over age five regularly wet the bed or wet their pants, the condition is known as enuresis. Nocturnal enuresis occurs at night, and diurnal enuresis happens during the day. Boys have enuresis more often than girls.

WHAT CAUSES IT

Some children who wet the bed have a medical problem, such as a urinary tract infection. Others have sleep-arousal difficulties and simply cannot wake up in time to use the toilet. However, in most cases, there is not one simple reason for the bed-wetting. Kids who have small bladder capacity will not be able to postpone urination for as long as children with a normal bladder. It is important, therefore, for parents to recognize that children usually have little control over their problem and don't do it intentionally.

WHAT TO WATCH FOR

Until about age four, many children cannot remain dry through the entire night, but the problem usually lessens as kids grow older. If your child is over age five and has trouble staying dry, day or night, you may want to set up an appointment with your child's paediatrician.

WHAT PARENTS CAN DO

Enuresis can be one of the most embarrassing problems for a child to have. Many children with enuresis are afraid to sleep over at friends' houses because they might wet the bed. Because of the stigma attached to bed-wetting, you need to be understanding with your child.

Make an appointment with your paediatrician or family physician for a thorough medical examination for your child. If there is no physical cause of the bed-wetting, it is likely you can treat the problem yourself at home. By far the most common technique is the urine alarm, or bell and pad, which can be purchased at drugstores and some major department stores. This device consists of a urine-sensitive pad that is placed on top of the child's mattress but underneath the sheets. The pad is connected to a bell, buzzer, or bright light that is activated when the child starts to urinate, thus awakening him as he begins to wet the bed. Over time, the child's body sets up its own alarm system so that he can get to the lavatory in time. The success rate for those who use the pad consistently is about 77 per cent. If your child resists using the alarm or is scared of it, ask your doctor about other options.

If you decide to use the alarm, explain the procedure to your child. Talk about what the alarm is (a device to help him stop wetting the bed) and how the system will work: If the alarm goes off during the night, your child should go to the lavatory to finish urinating, clean up and change his pyjamas. Then he should return and change the bed himself, using the clean sheets you've left out. Reassure your child that you are there to help him overcome this problem.

Though the alarm may also wake other members of the family, everyone needs to be patient. Avoid disparaging comments – 'Did you wet the bed *again*?' – or names, like pee-head or baby.

Praise your child enthusiastically for dry nights: 'You did such a great job of staying dry last night. I'm so proud of you.' Even when he accidentally wets the bed, you should acknowledge his effort to stay dry: 'I know you are trying really hard to stay dry. I know it's hard for you.'

Don't expect instant results. Although some kids learn to wake up after just a few nights, it might take a month or more for others. Be patient and do not scold or punish your child for the bed-wetting. However, if

your child is not following the treatment steps by going to the lavatory and changing the sheets after urination, you might give him appropriate consequences such as a time-out.

If your child suffers a relapse, he can use the alarm system again, and this repetition is usually effective.

Other methods are sometimes used for treatment, but they are more restrictive and complex than the bell-and-pad technique and do not lend themselves to easy use by parents. Additionally, some medications, such as Tofranil, Ditropan and Desmopressin, have been shown to be effective for the treatment of enuresis. Because of potential side effects, however, these medications should probably not be considered until you have tried behavioural treatments such as the bell and pad.

Daytime Accidents

If your child is five or over and still wets her pants during the day, book an appointment with your paediatrician. The doctor can rule out a physical cause – urinary infection, diabetes, or sexual abuse are the better-known possibilities – and is likely to refer you to a mental health professional. In the meantime, be supportive and don't punish your child. Except in rare cases, the urination is accidental and your child is probably already embarrassed. Don't add to your child's problem by becoming angry or punitive.

Bulimia

(See also Anorexia, p. 171; Depression, p. 184; Obsessive-Compulsive Disorder, p. 201.)

WHAT IT IS

Bulimia nervosa is an eating disorder characterized by binging and purging. A youngster will binge by eating a much larger amount of food than most other people would eat. Following a binge, the person will avoid gaining weight by vomiting or taking laxatives. This is called purging.

WHAT CAUSES IT

Bulimia sometimes has a medical cause. It also seems to be linked with depression in some youngsters, particularly those who have a hard time controlling their feelings. They think they will find some relief from their depression through binging and purging, but that only makes them feel even more depressed.

Most cases of bulimia seem to be caused by a youngster's desire to be thin. In Western society, there is a tremendous pressure on youngsters, especially girls, to be slender, but some youngsters' metabolisms may make it difficult for them to be thin. This frustration can lead to binging and purging in the hope of losing weight.

WHAT TO WATCH FOR

Youngsters with bulimia will usually not tell people about the problem. If you suspect your child may be bulimic, start monitoring the food in the house. You should also keep a close eye on your child, as inducing vomiting by sticking a finger down the throat is the preferred method of purging. Some youngsters with bulimia nervosa may immediately go to the lavatory after a meal, particularly if they have eaten a great deal.

You may also notice scars across the knuckles – some children involuntarily bite down on their hand when they use their finger to induce vomiting. Your dentist may also be able to spot some clues: frequent vomiting can lead to dental decay because the acid from the stomach wears down the teeth.

Here are some commonly held myths about bulimia:

MYTH #1: *Youngsters with bulimia nervosa always throw up to get rid of food.* Some may also use laxatives or diuretics, and others exercise incessantly to avoid gaining weight.

MYTH #2: *Youngsters with bulimia nervosa binge primarily on junk food.* Actually, they often prefer foods that are sweet or high in carbohydrates, like hamburgers, doughnuts, pie, or chips. They may also eat an overabundance of salads, vegetables, fruits and even condiments such as ketchup or mustard. Because the child is probably trying to hide her problem she may eat foods that will not be missed from the refrigerator or cupboard.

MYTH #3: *Youngsters with bulimia nervosa are always female.* A small percentage of youngsters with bulimia nervosa are boys. Males with bulimia are sometimes not diagnosed because no one thinks to look for the disorder in boys. However, they too sometimes face pressure to be thin. For example, some members of school wrestling teams are instructed by their coaches to lose weight so they can wrestle in a lower weight class.

MYTH #4: *Youngsters with bulimia are always thin because they purge.* Actually, these kids vary greatly in body weight. Some are thin, but others may be overweight and use purging to avoid gaining additional weight.

WHAT PARENTS CAN DO

Seek help. Bulimia can result in a number of physical problems, including kidney difficulties, fluid loss, dental problems and even death. In severe cases, hospitalization is the only treatment option. In other cases, group or individual therapy may work well.

The most common treatment for bulimia is exposure and response prevention. During the exposure phase, the youngster is encouraged to eat a well-balanced meal. Following the meal, the child will probably have a desire to purge, so the response prevention treatment is introduced: to prevent the purging, the child can simply be told not to go to the lavatory for thirty minutes or so, but she is monitored during this period by her parents or by the medical staff. In severe cases, the parents or medical staff may need to hold the child's hand or even use physical restraint to prevent her from purging. The child gradually learns to eat balanced meals and to avoid the binge-purge cycle.

Cognitive therapy is also used to help combat a youngster's negative thoughts about eating. The child is taught to identify a distorted thought and then challenge and replace it.

Parents can help prevent bulimia by de-emphasizing the importance of physical appearance. However, this is difficult be-cause of the influence that the media can have on a child's perception of beauty. Thin is considered beautiful in our society, and this attitude is not likely to change radically in the near future. You need, therefore, to talk with your child frequently about avoiding the need to be thin for appearance's sake. Instead, emphasize good physical health and feeling good.

Depression (Major)

(See also Explaining the Concept of Death, p 118; The Brain and Behaviour, p. 158; Depression (Dysthymic Disorder), p. 186; Manic Depression, p. 197; Post-Traumatic Stress Disorder, p. 211.)

WHAT IT IS

A major depression is one that lasts for a long time, usually two or more weeks. Prolonged irritability and sadness are the cardinal signs of depression. In addition, children or adolescents must have at least four of the following symptoms for the diagnosis to be conclusive:

1. **DECREASED INTEREST or pleasure in activities that the child previously enjoyed, such as going to school, being with friends, reading, watching television.**
2. **WEIGHT LOSS without dieting or failure to gain weight; or greater than expected weight gain.**
3. **TROUBLE SLEEPING or sleeping too much.**
4. **RESTLESSNESS or feeling slowed down.**
5. **FEELING TIRED or suffering loss of energy.**

6. **FEELING WORTHLESS** or having inappropriate guilt.
7. **SUFFERING** a decreased ability to think or concentrate.
8. **REPEATED THOUGHTS** of death or suicidal behaviour.

Youngsters with depression often have distorted perceptions. They may have a low opinion of themselves and may think they are bad or unattractive. They may also feel hopeless about the world or the future, believing that things will never get any better.

WHAT CAUSES IT

Depression can have a number of different causes. Sometimes it is caused by problems with brain chemicals called neurotransmitters (serotonin and norepinephrine). Other times, depression occurs after a loss. It is common for a child to feel sad and depressed after the death or departure of a loved one. The condition is considered major depression only if it lasts for more than two weeks or is unusually severe.

Children and adolescents may get depressed for a variety of other reasons, including social or family problems. A youngster's social life is extremely important to him and any disruption of it, such as a relationship breakup, can be shattering.

WHAT TO WATCH FOR

Most people feel sad at least part of the time, and children are as likely as anyone to have these feelings. However, there is a big difference between feeling a little sad and being truly depressed. Childhood depression is such a major problem today that it is important for parents to understand the condition. Consider these different children and adolescents.

Michael is a ten-year-old whose parents recently divorced. His father moved out of the area, and Michael has not seen him for two months. Michael was very close to his father and feels sad that he cannot see him every day, as he used to. Michael mopes around the house a lot and cries more easily than he used to, but his behaviour has not changed much otherwise. He still enjoys being with friends and is doing well in school.

Jacey is a fourteen-year-old who has always got along well with her parents. For the last several weeks, though, Jacey has been irritable and difficult to be around. About three months ago her best friend committed suicide. Jacey does not seem sad, but talks about feeling guilty that she is still alive even though her friend is dead. She has trouble sleeping and is not interested in eating. As a result, she has lost five pounds. Jacey's marks have dropped and she has not hung out with her friends lately.

Larry, age sixteen, comes from a stable family. He does well in school and has plenty of friends. Lately, he's been wearing black clothing all the time and he talks about death quite a bit. When Larry's parents asked him why he was acting this way, he said, 'This is the cool way to act. Everyone talks about death. That's how all of my friends are.' Larry does not seem sad and says that he has never thought about attempting suicide.

WHICH OF THESE youngsters most likely has major depression? Technically, only Jacey is depressed, even though she does not seem sad. In children, depression is often shown through irritability. Michael is sad, but his sadness is appropriate. He is mourning the loss of his father, but this sadness has not overwhelmed him or caused impairment in school or friendships. Finally, Larry is an interesting example. His symptoms seem to be attributable to peer pressure rather than depression. Some teenagers do consider it cool to act morbid and brooding.

Even though Larry and Michael may not be depressed, each of these situations can be troubling to parents and cause concern.

WHAT PARENTS CAN DO

It's sometimes hard to understand why a child gets depressed over what parents may view as little things – a fight with a friend, peer pressure, difficulty with maths. However, you should always take your child seriously if you think he is depressed. Not all children who are depressed think about suicide, but some do. If you are in doubt about whether your child might be depressed, consult a mental health professional.

For depression that does not respond to therapy, medication can be helpful.

One type of depression seems to be biological in nature. It is called seasonal affective

disorder (SAD) and occurs during winter. Researchers theorize that SAD is caused by a lack of sunlight, and it is treated with light therapy – having the youngster sit in front of bright lights for a few hours each week.

For other types of depression, different therapies are used. When distorted thoughts are a problem, cognitive therapy is helpful: the youngster is taught to identify, challenge and change disturbing thoughts that may be causing him trouble.

When kids with depression isolate themselves from family and friends, behaviour therapy is sometimes recommended. The goal here is to help the child find more pleasurable things to do. Treatment may involve spending more time with the family, going out with friends and doing enjoyable things.

Just as there are many different causes of depression, there are also many treatments. If your child is depressed, find a competent mental health professional who can plan your child's treatment and work with this clinician to help your child.

Depression (Dysthymic Disorder)

(See also Handling Aggressiveness, p. 113; The Brain and Behaviour, p. 158; Acting Out, p. 167; Depression, p. 184.)

WHAT IT IS

In many ways dysthymic disorder is similar to major depression. The primary symptoms are feeling depressed or feeling irritable, but dysthymic disorder is the 'low-grade fever' of depressions – it is less severe than major depression, but it lasts longer. It can affect children of all ages, even those as young as preschool.

WHAT CAUSES IT

The causes of dysthymic disorder are similar to those of major depression. Many children with the disorder may have problems with brain chemicals (neurotransmitters) such as dopamine, serotonin and norepinephrine. For others, stress and trouble adjusting to problems may better explain its presence.

WHAT TO WATCH FOR

Youngsters with dysthymic disorder tend to feel bad – depressed or irritable – for a year or more. These kids seem to be down in the dumps, or blue, more often than not for very long stretches of time. They may also be pessimistic, always anticipating the worst. Though they are not depressed enough to receive a diagnosis of major depression, they may have a variety of symptoms related to depression, including the following:

1. Decreased or increased appetite and weight loss or gain
2. Sleeping more or less than usual
3. Fatigue or low energy
4. Low self-esteem
5. Poor attention or difficulty making decisions
6. Hopelessness

Younger children with dysthymic disorder may also have somatic complaints, such as headache, stomachache, or leg pain. This is probably because children have difficulty showing that they are in distress and display it by complaining about bodily problems. These kids may be aggressive, again because they are unable to show their pain in other, more mature ways, such as talking about the problem.

Because dysthymic disorder symptoms last so long, the child or adolescent usually develops problems with schoolwork, friends and family members. Other people may assume that the child has always been this way and may find him unpleasant to be around. The youngster may have periods when he becomes more severely depressed and suffers major depression. This is called double depression, since both disorders are present at the same time. After the major depression clears, however, the youngster will still be depressed, as the dysthymic disorder may still be present.

WHAT PARENTS CAN DO

Dysthymic disorder can be a serious condition, and parents should consult a mental health professional. Because the disorder lingers for so long, it can be very demoralizing for the youngster and have long-lasting effects. In addition, if the child is feeling hopeless, he may behave recklessly or try to hurt himself.

Treatment usually involves the entire family. They may be encouraged to undertake more pleasant activities together – having family dinners, going on picnics, taking trips together, reading, or just talking together more frequently. The parents are also usually encouraged to praise the child for every success, whether it's getting good results or participating in sports.

Since these children tend to become socially withdrawn or isolated, they are generally encouraged to interact more with peers. Antidepressants may be used as well, although these normally are not prescribed until other techniques have not worked.

Overall, the intent of intervention is to create a more supportive and accepting home environment for the youngster. Fortunately, treatment for dysthymic disorder can be very effective, particularly when the family is involved.

Emotional Attachment, Lack of (Reactive Attachment Disorder of Infancy and Early Childhood)

(See also Anxiety, p. 173; Autism, p. 179.)

WHAT IT IS

In this condition the attachment of the infant or young child to her parents or caregiver is problematic. Normally, children form early and firm attachments to those who care for them. This early attachment is a particularly important developmental milestone as it lays the foundation for later successful parent-child relations as well as attachment to friends and future spouse and children.

WHAT CAUSES IT

In contrast to autism, which has some of the same symptoms and seems to be a biological condition, reactive attachment is usually caused by inadequate parenting. The fact that you are reading this book shows that you are a caring parent, and it is therefore unlikely that your child has this disorder.

The parents of children with reactive attachment are generally not affectionate or responsive. For example, when the child cries, the parents may ignore the child or perhaps even hit the child to stop him from crying.

Some teenage parents may interact with their children in this manner because they don't have the same level of life experience and knowledge that more mature parents have. Children who are moved from one foster care home to another may also develop this disorder.

Reactive attachment may also result when a child is born prematurely or with a medical problem and has to be hospitalized for a long time. If the child does not have much physical or emotional contact with others because she is in an incubator, then attachment may be underdeveloped. When the child comes home, however, the problem usually disappears, and the baby becomes attached to his parents. Hospitals today encourage staff and parents to hold these infants as often as possible. They even recruit volunteers to come in and hold and rock the babies in order to provide emotional warmth when the parents can't be there.

WHAT TO WATCH FOR

Infants and children younger than age five may display two types of reactive attachment:

1. *Inhibited.* This is a lack of attachment. The child does not initiate much social contact with the parent or care-taker and may seem to be uncomfortable being around people.

2. *Disinhibited.* These children exhibit poor attachment to the parent but seem to attach randomly to others. Instead of displaying stranger anxiety, which is normal, the baby may become immediately attached to a stranger who picks him up.

WHAT PARENTS CAN DO

The primary treatment for this disorder involves strengthening the parent-child bond. Parents may be instructed to take parenting classes to learn how to take care of the child and how to show warmth and affection. Parents may also be trained in how to have fun with the child. Fortunately, when the parent is highly motivated, treatment for this disorder is usually quite successful. Parents should also consult with a developmental paediatrician or child psychiatrist or psychologist.

Fire-Setting (Pyromania)

(See also Building Self-Esteem, p. 42; Setting Limits, p. 74.)

WHAT IT IS

Pyromania is a serious disorder in which a youngster establishes a pattern of purposely setting fires. These fires sometimes cause profound damage and even bodily harm or death to others, making this a very worrisome problem that should be dealt with by mental health professionals.

WHAT CAUSES IT

Youngsters who suffer pyromania may use fire-setting as a way to decrease their anxiety. They may have problems in their lives such as a lack of friends or academic failure, so they turn to fire-setting as a way to try to find relief.

Boys are more likely to have pyromania than girls are. However, true pyromania in children is relatively uncommon.

WHAT TO WATCH FOR

Many children are fascinated by fire. Some kids build fires in the back garden or try to barbecue food without their parents' permission. Or they might play with matches or try to build torches. If a major fire occurs, it's generally accidental. These children are usually experimenting with fire the way they might experiment with water or any other interesting substance.

Youngsters with diagnosable pyromania set fires not out of curiosity but because they have an abnormal attraction to fire. They may start by setting a minor fire – burning a bush, perhaps. They may then set fires that become increasingly destructive. They intend their actions to cause damage, and they take pleasure in the chaos that surrounds the discovery of the fire. They may even want people to get hurt.

Some youngsters with pyromania also show a peculiar interest in fire-related items such as alarms, fire departments, fire engines and firemen. Setting off fire alarms at school or in public buildings is often part of the pattern.

WHAT PARENTS CAN DO

Though curiosity about matches and small fires is common in children four to ten years old, the wise parent who finds a child experimenting with flame will discuss the dangers of fire and set clear consequences, such as cleaning up and grounding, if the child is caught playing with matches or fire again. Additional supervision will also be necessary. Most children will quickly outgrow the problem and will adhere to parental rules on this issue.

If a child is diagnosed with pyromania, treatment by a mental health professional is necessary. Treatment is likely to consist of behavioural methods to focus on shaping and changing the child's behaviour. For example, a programme might be developed whereby the child receives a small reward or praise for each day he goes without setting a fire. The negative consequences of setting a fire should also be clearly defined. The entire family is likely to be involved in the treatment, as the parents will be the ones who implement the behavioural programme. Close supervision of the child during this period is also absolutely necessary.

Many local fire departments will arrange for firemen to meet with children who set fires. Some even pair up a child with a firemen who acts as a big brother to help the child channel his interest in fires and better understand the problems that fire can cause.

Gambling (Pathological)

(See also Building Self-Esteem, p. 42; Setting Limits, p. 74; Depression, p. 184.)

WHAT IT IS

Pathological gambling – a condition where someone has consistent difficulty controlling his urge to gamble – is rare in children. Adolescents can sometimes become involved in gambling, however, and some may become obsessed with the thrill, the action and the excitement of it. When this happens, the gambler will bet on almost anything – a casual card game, a school football game and whether or not a substitute will teach English class that day. Pathological gamblers may report that they have tried unsuccessfully to stop betting.

Pathological gambling in adults is a very serious problem. Some gamble away their entire pay cheque, and their financial problems may become so serious that they lose their homes or their spouses leave them. In Las Vegas, the local hospital has an inpatient unit for persons who gamble and many people are placed in psychiatric hospitals for this problem.

WHAT CAUSES IT

To date, researchers have not firmly established what causes pathological gambling. The problem seems to be similar to other addictions. A few people feel it is biological, possibly relating to problems with particular brain chemicals (neurotransmitters) or other brain irregularities. Other people gamble because they are depressed or have low self-esteem and want to escape from their lives.

WHAT TO WATCH FOR

Most kids gamble occasionally, and betting now and then just for fun isn't pathological. Some children bet small amounts of money when playing card or board games. Other kids may bet that they can outperform others in a race or on a test. Some even bet on the speed at which they can finish certain chores.

Loss (or temporary gain) of valuable items – money or prized possessions your child wouldn't normally give up – can be a sign that your child is gambling inappropriately. Some parents report that their child begins to steal in order to have money or objects with which to bet. Youngsters almost always try to cover up their problem and are likely to deny it if confronted.

WHAT PARENTS CAN DO

Setting firm limits is the first step in arresting this problem. Sit down with your child and the rest of the family and work together to establish some rules about leisure time. You may completely ban gambling, or you may limit it to situations where money or objects aren't used.

If your child's time has been consumed by gambling, look for alternative activities. You might also spend more time with your child doing activities that both of you enjoy.

Rewards may also be effective. Start by praising gambling-free days. Later on, you may want to increase the reward base: For three days without gambling, you might let your adolescent have an extra hour of telephone time. For a longer period of success, take him to a professional football game or ask him what he would enjoy doing.

Sometimes the problem may be too great for you to handle. Your teenager may have got into serious financial difficulties and may be mixing with an objectionable crowd. In this case, enlist the help of a mental health professional. He or she will offer guidelines on what you can do as a parent and will also meet with the child to work on any problems that may be causing the gambling, such as depression or low self-esteem.

Most large cities have branches of Gamblers Anonymous or other types of self-help groups. They will have knowledge and advice for working with teenagers. You can find their number by looking in the phone book or by calling Directory Inquiries.

Hair-Pulling (Trichotillomania)

(See also Anxiety, p. 173; Depression, p. 184; Pica, p. 210.)

WHAT IT IS

Trichotillomania is a disorder in which children pull out strands of their hair until the hair loss is noticeable. Usually this disorder involves pulling hair from the scalp, eyebrows, or eyelashes, but some children may pull hair from their arms or legs or, more rarely, the pubic region. The hair-pulling seems to relieve stress or anxiety, and sufferers of this disorder rarely report that it causes them pain.

On occasion, a youngster may eat the hair (this is known as trichophagia), which can cause hair balls to form in the stomach. In other cases a child may try to pull hair from other people or even animals.

Although trichotillomania is not always a serious condition, it can embarrass the child and cause her to withdraw socially. It can also cause real damage to the scalp and sometimes results in permanent baldness.

WHAT CAUSES IT

Stress is the most frequent cause of hair-pulling. The child may be going through a family move, starting a new school, or enduring a parental divorce. Some youngsters say they pull their hair because of an itching sensation, which may or may not be caused by a dermatological problem.

WHAT TO WATCH FOR

Some children pull their hair occasionally, and girls in particular may play with, twist, or fiddle with their hair until it breaks. This behaviour is normal and not a cause for concern.

If your child develops a bald spot somewhere on her body, however, then hair-pulling has become problematic.

WHAT PARENTS CAN DO

If there are no problems with baldness or eating of the hair, you can probably ignore the behaviour for a time to see if it's just a phase the child is going through. Sometimes parents set up a system of small rewards – a trip to the park, a small amount of money – to help a child break the hair-pulling habit.

If the trichotillomania is accompanied by anxiety or depression, medications may be prescribed to help with the problem.

If it does become severe, consult a mental health professional. Because trichotillomania is frequently caused by stress, family therapy may be in order to help find ways for your child to reduce the stress in her life.

Hostile Behaviour (Oppositional Defiant Disorder)

(See also Setting Limits, p. 74; Anger in Daily Life, p. 82; Acting Out, p. 167.)

WHAT IT IS

Oppositional defiant disorder is seen when children or adolescents behave belligerently for six or more months. They may be hostile or rebellious to adults, including parents and teachers. Their offences may include four or more of the following:

1. losing their temper
2. arguing with adults
3. refusing to follow rules
4. purposely annoying people
5. blaming other people for their mistakes
6. being very touchy or easily irritated
7. getting angry frequently
8. being spiteful

Of course, most youngsters (and most adults!) will occasionally act in any one of these ways. For that reason, hostility is not referred to as oppositional defiant disorder unless the youngster has four or more of these symptoms for at least six months.

WHAT CAUSES IT

Some researchers assert that oppositional defiant disorder is a mild form of conduct disorder and that it has similar causes. As with conduct disorder, oppositional defiant disorder may be caused by an underlying problem, such as ADHD, depression, or anxiety. Sometimes ODD arises because parents are too harsh with the child or because they have neglected to establish limits or to express approval of the child.

Even if parents have not caused the disorder, it is important for them to be part of the solution.

WHAT TO WATCH FOR

Children as young as preschool may show signs of hostility by openly refusing to comply with certain requests from a parent, teacher, or other authority figure. However, adolescence is certainly the peak time for expressions of defiance. To a certain extent this is normal adolescent behaviour as a teenager tries to move away from parental control.

For most, limit-testing will not grow into a problem, and teenagers will quickly learn what they can and cannot get away with at home and at school. Some youngsters push things too far, however, and may ultimately be diagnosed with oppositional defiant disorder. They may get in trouble with parents or at school. While school problems may cause them to get detention or to be suspended for a day or two, adolescents with oppositional defiant disorder usually don't get into the kinds of legal problems that youngsters with conduct disorder may experience.

WHAT PARENTS CAN DO

Some children or adolescents with oppositional defiant disorder may require therapy. However, the behaviour of other kids may not yet be completely out of hand and the following guidelines may be enough to turn the situation around:

1. PARENTS MUST FIRST DECIDE what behaviour they can live with and what has to be changed or stopped. Your child may be doing some things that annoy you such as not making her bed, but her transgressions are minor things like that. For other things, such as talking back to teachers or staying out past curfew, you may need to set up some rules and consequences. For example, if the youngster comes in on time for two weekends in a row, you might offer a reward, such as extending the curfew by fifteen minutes the following weekend. If he's late, you might keep him from going out the following weekend night. Changing this type of behaviour requires careful monitoring on your part.

2. THE PARENT-CHILD RELATIONSHIP needs to be improved. You may need to spend more leisure time with your child. Sit down with him and come up with a list of things that the two of you would enjoy doing together: going to the park or to a museum, for example, or making pottery or going fishing. You should avoid focusing on the child's minor problems and not constantly correct the child.

3. INCREASE THE AMOUNT OF PARENTAL SUPERVISION your child receives. Oppositional defiant disorder sometimes escalates into conduct disorder, which can lead to serious legal consequences. If you carefully monitor your child's behaviour, keep track of the kids she hangs out with and check up on what she does at school, you may be able to prevent the problem from developing into conduct disorder.

Kleptomania

(See also Stealing, p. 115; Obsessive-Compulsive Disorder, p. 201.)

WHAT IT IS

Youngsters with kleptomania have periods when they compulsively steal things, generally things they don't need or that they could afford to buy. For example, a young boy who suffers from kleptomania might steal an inexpensive hairbrush meant for a girl. Kleptomania differs from shoplifting, which tends to be intentional and motivated by a desire to obtain the stolen object for its usefulness or monetary value. Only about 5 per cent of people who steal actually have kleptomania, and it is relatively rare in children and adolescents.

Many kids steal something – a packet of chewing gum, perhaps, or a chocolate bar – at least once, but an adolescent who steals once does not have kleptomania.

Children with kleptomania usually steal alone and are unlikely to enlist an accomplice. They also don't steal for revenge or out of anger. They simply cannot control their impulse to steal and they feel increasing tension before stealing. After the theft, the child feels relieved or pleased or excited because she was able to release the tension she felt. She may hoard the stolen items, but she will probably never sell them for profit.

Generally, the youngster realizes that it is wrong to steal and may even want to stop doing it, but it is difficult for her to stop. In fact, she may later return what she took and feel guilty about what has happened.

WHAT CAUSES IT

Very little is known about the causes of kleptomania. In some cases, the compulsive stealing may be a way for a youngster to discharge her anxiety about other things in her life.

In contrast to many other child disorders, kleptomania appears to be more common in females.

WHAT TO WATCH FOR

Most children and adolescents who steal do not have kleptomania. However, you may want to consult a professional if you observe a pattern of theft, particularly of items that are useless or inexpensive. You may also notice signs of guilty behaviour, or your child may act embarrassed if you discover something in his bedroom that he has stolen. Youngsters try to hide what they have done, not only to avoid punishment but because they are embarrassed and cannot explain why they do it.

WHAT PARENTS CAN DO

Establishing consequences for stealing is generally effective. However, this doesn't work for kleptomania because youngsters with this disorder cannot solve the problem by just wanting to stop. If they do not steal, they have a lot of tension that they still need to get rid of somehow. If true kleptomania is suspected, parents should seek the aid of a mental health professional.

Learning Disorders

(See also Autism and Other Developmental Disorders, p. 179; Speech Problems, p. 223.)

WHAT THEY ARE

Children with learning disorders (also known as learning disabilities, the term that seems to be preferred by teachers) have difficulty processing certain types of information. There are a wide variety of learning disorders, and a child might be classified as having a disorder because he or she has difficulty with any number of things – reading, sequencing, maths, writing, or organization, for example.

While you need to stay informed about what your child needs, the law guarantees that all children with learning disabilities must receive an appropriate education, so you'll have the school on your side helping you.

Keep in mind that learning disabilities are not the same as mental retardation or low intelligence. Most children with learning disabilities are of average intelligence; some are quite intelligent. Having a learning disorder does not mean that your child is stupid or will never have a normal life or a good job.

WHAT CAUSES THEM

Most learning disorders seem to be biological. The child has a problem in one part of his brain that makes it hard for him to read, do maths, write, or process incoming information. Bear in mind that nothing you did as a parent caused this to happen, nor is it the fault of your child's teacher. Learning disabilities do not happen because of inadequate education or poor teaching.

Remember, too, that your child is not to blame. Just because he has difficulties in school does not mean he is lazy or does not try. He may be trying harder than other children, but without results. Imagine how frustrating!

WHAT TO WATCH FOR

If your child is having difficulty learning long division or doesn't seem able to get through a novel yet, it is likely that he's just not ready; the ability will develop with time.

The child with learning disabilities exhibits difficulty with certain processes and is consistently unable to keep up with his classmates in certain areas. This does not preclude him from excelling in other areas, though. A child who suffers from dyslexia may be a whiz at maths.

A diagnosis of a learning disorder should be made only after official testing has been conducted. Technically a child has a learning disorder only if his skill level on a standardized test in reading, maths, or writing is below what it should be based on his age, education and intelligence.

If your child complains regularly about something ('I can't read this; the letters are all jumbled together') or if he frequently makes the same types of mistakes in writing or maths, you may want to talk to his teacher. Or the teacher may have noticed something and will suggest that your child be tested.

WHAT PARENTS CAN DO

Evaluation generally includes tests of intelligence, achievement and perhaps adaptive functioning. Usually your child's school will do the testing for you, especially if your child's teacher recommends it. You can also contact a psychologist who specializes in testing (psychologists are normally the only mental health professionals who conduct psychological testing).

If your child has a learning disorder, you should work closely with the school and teachers. Full cooperation is necessary from everybody involved. Thought will be given to how your child can do her best in the regular classroom. She may be given extra time to complete tests or work assignments, for example.

In addition, if your child has difficulty learning in a normal classroom setting, you can help him by following some of these recommendations:

1. Praise your child at every opportunity. Look for small actions that deserve praise. For example, if your child has a reading disability and correctly reads a sentence, be very congratulatory and make a big deal out of it.

Praise non–learning related activities too. For instance, if your child neatly makes his bed without being told, tell him how great it looks and how special he is. Do not be afraid of appearing silly when praising your child; do it with gusto.

2. Set appropriate study and work limits for your child. Because they are frustrated about being different, children with learning disorders sometimes try to rebel against the extra study time that may be required. If your child gets upset or has a tantrum, you may be tempted to relent, not wanting to cause your child further distress or embarrassment. However, you are not doing your child a favour by allowing him to avoid study time. Generally, study difficulties are remediable, but it will require extra time on his part. Point out that it's better to master some of the shortcuts and study techniques being taught him now rather than to wait until secondary school. You can reassure him that things will get a lot easier. And even if it doesn't really get easier, you will have established a routine, and he'll be less resistant as he gets older.

3. Help your child find activities at which she excels. A child who has difficulty learning in one area needs other areas where she can feel proud of her accomplishments. Your child may excel in hockey, netball, or football, or she may write, paint, or draw well. Doing well at a task will help your child gain a sense of competence and self-worth. In addition, she may become more independent, which will help when dealing with the learning disorder.

4. Tell stories to your child and encourage make-believe play. Many children with learning disabilities have great imaginations, which may develop because of a lag in other areas of learning. Encourage your youngster to stretch his imagination and praise him for being creative. Everyone wants to feel that he is good at something; kids with learning disabilities often have the focus placed on what they don't do well, such as reading.

5. Do not let a label of 'learning disabled' rule your child's life. Remember that she is a person first and a child with a learning disability second. That is why we use the term 'a child with a learning disability' instead of 'a learning disabled child'.

6. Don't feel guilty if you sometimes resent your child's problem. Having a child with a learning disorder can cause a lot of extra work for a parent. What's more, you may have unfulfilled expectations concerning your child's accomplishments. However, don't take out these feelings on your child through anger or other unpleasant emotions. Instead, talk with someone you trust about these feelings. For example, you might discuss these problems with your spouse, a parent, a friend, or the psychologist your child is seeing. Your feelings are common, and if you're able to air them, you'll find it easier to come up with a new approach.

Also, you must separate your child from the problem. Your child is not the problem; the learning disorder, which your child cannot control, is the problem.

7. Be aware of the signs of depression (page 184) and suicide (page 228). Unfortunately, kids with learning disabilities often feel a tremendous amount of pressure from adults. In addition, they may be picked on at school for being 'stupid' or 'slow'. Many of these children develop low self-esteem, feel isolated or alienated and may develop depression or thoughts of suicide.

ALTHOUGH a learning disorder can cause many problems for children, help is available. Make sure you demand attention and help from the school and work closely with them to make certain your child gets what he needs.

Manic Depression (Bipolar Disorder)

(See also The Brain and Behaviour, p. 158; Depression, p. 184.)

WHAT IT IS

A manic person is one who has extreme mood swings. For example, most kids feel very happy before an exciting trip or prior to the Christmas holidays, but a child suffering from mania can feel this way at any time, and the mood lasts longer than would be expected. Kids with this problem may also report feeling high even though they aren't taking any drugs. Because of these feelings, the youngster may talk in a grandiose manner and think she can do almost anything. While being in a good mood may seem like a fine condition, in reality it's like being perpetually high, and the speed effect has a harmful impact on the child's life. Sufferers are usually easily distracted and as a result may not do well in school.

In addition to an elevated mood, a number of other behaviour patterns are also associated with mania. One of the most common is a lack of sleep. A youngster may get only three or four hours of sleep at night and report that she feels rested. She may also be extremely talkative and her speech may be very rapid. Many also report that their thoughts come very quickly, and as a result, they seem to jump from thought to thought without finishing things. Adolescents with mania may talk inappropriately about sex or become promiscuous.

Most people who become manic also become depressed from time to time. They may cycle between mania and depression and rarely have a normal or stable mood. This is called bipolar disorder.

Mania is rare in children, but it's more common among adolescents.

WHAT CAUSES IT

Mania seems to be genetic. The disorder is also biological and seems to be related to a lack or an excess of brain chemicals known as neurotransmitters. This is probably why medication works so well for mania; the medication replaces or takes away neurotransmitters and helps the brain go back to normal, which results in stabilizing a person's mood.

WHAT TO WATCH FOR

The symptoms of mania are similar to those of other mood disorders – the elevated mood may be accompanied by irritability, distractibility and depression. A child who is depressed may also be irritable. For a diag-nosis to be made, a cluster of symptoms has to be present for a period of time, and they must represent a change from the way the adolescent was acting before. The child's actions may also lead to dangerous behav-iour. For example, she may become sexually promiscuous, spend a great deal of money, or begin using drugs.

Youngsters with mania or bipolar disor-der usually give certain signs that they are starting to cycle into a manic episode. Ado-lescents who are becoming manic may begin to speak more rapidly or may take on a lot of projects.

Work with your youngster's clinician to help identify what actions seem to signify the onset of another episode. Then you can take appropriate steps to help the child.

WHAT PARENTS CAN DO

A consultation with a mental health profes-sional is the first order of business, as this disorder can often be controlled with med-ication. A number of antimanic medications are effective, are relatively safe and cause few side effects. The best-known one is lithium, which has been on the market for a long time and is relatively inexpensive. Antiseizure medication, such as sodium val-proate, also has been prescribed in recent years for youngsters with mania and has produced satisfactory results.

While using these medications, the person has to have blood drawn regularly (initially quite frequently but later on, every three to six months) to see whether the med-ication in her system is at the therapeutic level – in other words, whether she has enough of the medication in the body to treat the disorder. Sometimes, an SSRI such as Prozac, Seroxat, or Lustral, is used to treat the depression component of bipolar disorder. However, if the medication is continued after the person is no longer depressed, it can spur a manic episode.

Parents can help their children by closely monitoring their behaviour and mood. Even though mania or bipolar disorder can be largely controlled with medications, there is no guarantee that the youngster will never become manic again. In addition, some children or adolescents with this disorder may stop taking the medication because they miss being manic and having those highs.

Mental Retardation

WHAT IT IS

Mental retardation is characterized by below normal intelligence and a lack of adaptive skills, such as the ability to care for one's hygiene needs. It can be mild, moderate, severe, or profound. Youngsters with severe or profound mental retardation tend to have many difficulties, including physical handicaps.

WHAT CAUSES IT

Many times, this condition is present from birth. It may be genetic, or sometimes something happens right after the baby is born. The umbilical cord may get wrapped around the child's neck, for example, leading to decreased oxygen and damage to those parts of the brain that determine intelligence.

Brain damage may also be caused later on by abuse, such as when a child is vigorously shaken. Poisoning may also lead to mental retardation. Substance abuse, particularly sniffing lighter fuel, paint thinner, or glue, can also cause mental retardation.

The problems in intellect and adaptive functioning must occur before the age of eighteen years in order to be considered mental retardation. A nineteen-year-old who suffers brain damage in a car accident would not be classified as mentally retarded.

WHAT TO WATCH FOR

Differences in growth and development are the usual signs of mental retardation. Profound cases are easy to spot, but a mild case may go unnoticed at first. If you're concerned that your child isn't learning things at the same rate as her peers, talk to your paediatrician. Testing will be in order. You may find that your child is simply delayed in development or has a learning disorder. If a diagnosis of mental retardation is made, the earlier you are aware of it, the easier it will be to help your child.

WHAT PARENTS CAN DO

Good prenatal care is the first important step in avoiding mental retardation. Prospective mothers should give up smoking and drinking even before they get pregnant. During pregnancy they should go to the obstetrician for frequent checkups and follow her advice.

If your child is diagnosed with mental retardation, a number of resources in your community will be able to help you. Most cities or counties have centres with trained personnel. These services typically include habilitation, which helps the child learn basic life skills, such as hygiene, feeding herself and basic work skills. These resources can also help you if your child is aggressive or not cooperating in some way; professionals can suggest strategies and offer support.

Most persons with mental retardation, particularly if it is mild or moderate, can function in society. Workshops and other places of employment offer jobs that are well suited to people with a variety of levels of ability.

Being the parent of a youngster with mental retardation can be a full-time – and very rewarding – job, but it's important not to neglect your own needs. Consider joining a support group. The camaraderie can help you feel less isolated and you'll benefit from shared experiences, resources and information.

Remember to take time off and do things for yourself and continue to do things with your spouse. Take a walk, go shopping, dine at a nice restaurant. Make sure that you take care of yourself so that you can take care of your child.

Mutism (Selective)

(See also Helping the Shy Child, p. 44; Anxiety, p. 173; Hostile Behaviour, p. 192; Speech Problems, p. 223.)

WHAT IT IS

Children with selective mutism are consistently unwilling to speak in certain situations, even though they are able to speak. The child may refuse to speak at school, for instance, and instead use hand gestures or facial expressions to communicate. True selective mutism will persist for more than a month, and it is relatively rare.

If a child does suffer selective mutism and the condition persists, he may have difficulty making or keeping friends or may be teased by peers, who assume he is mentally retarded or just bizarre. In school he may be punished or given low marks because teachers and administrators assume he's being contrary or trying to get out of certain tasks such as giving an oral book report, answering questions out loud, or participating in group activities.

WHAT CAUSES IT

In some cases selective mutism results when a child has an extreme form of social anxiety and feels a great deal of tension or nervousness when he is with other people. In other cases the children refuse to talk because they have a speech problem, like a lisp or a stutter, that makes them feel self-conscious. In these cases, the child's language impairment is generally the focus of treatment, and when that is corrected, the mutism ends.

WHAT TO WATCH FOR

At various times, most kids will go mute about something. Some kids may play a game where they can't talk for a certain amount of time. Other kids may not talk when they are angry, giving everyone the silent treatment. During the first month of school, some kids are extremely shy and do not speak very much. However, in each of these cases the child will probably stay silent for only a little while. Most kids have a hard time staying quiet for long!

If your child has a diagnosable case of selective mutism, he will consistently refuse to talk in certain settings, such as school or summer camp, even when it's important. In school, for example, he may not respond to a teacher's questions and may not even ask to go to the lavatory.

WHAT PARENTS CAN DO

Behavioural techniques are often used in treating selective mutism. If a child is anxious, she may be taught relaxation techniques. A reward programme, where a youngster receives small rewards such as a piece of chocolate for making small responses, can also work. To get the reward next time, the child has to talk a little more than she did previously. These programmes work best when set up by a mental health professional.

Usually the family must be closely involved in treatment, partly because they can offer encouragement in ways that few others can. For example, members of the family may have learned that when the child points at the refrigerator, she wants a glass of juice. The family may be told to refuse to get her the juice until she asks for it orally, thus reinforcing the importance of spoken communication. This type of therapy may sound a bit unkind, but it can greatly help the youngster begin to feel more comfortable with oral communication.

Obsessive-Compulsive Disorder (OCD)

(See also The Brain and Behaviour, p. 158; Anxiety, p. 173; Post-Traumatic Stress Disorder, p. 211.)

WHAT IT IS

Obsessive-compulsive disorder, commonly referred to as OCD, consists of two types of behaviour: obsessions and compulsions.

Obsessions are recurrent and persistent worries that are not realistic or typical. For example, a child may worry about getting germs from touching doorknobs.

Compulsions are repetitive actions that the person feels will help drive away the obsessive thoughts. For example, a child who fears germs may wash her hands repeatedly, perhaps hundreds of times a day. Another child who irrationally fears being punished may pray hundreds of times a day.

Although a child may have either obsessions or compulsions, they typically go together. The compulsion is an attempt to get rid of the obsession.

Compulsive actions may take hours each day to perform. We worked with a young adolescent who spent approximately two hours each night getting ready for bed. This caused problems because she had to start getting ready so early that it was difficult for her to finish her homework or enjoy any free time.

WHAT CAUSES IT

Obsessive-compulsive disorder is a biological condition having to do with a lack of certain neurotransmitters in the brain. It is sometimes inherited – people who have relatives with OCD develop it more often than people who do not have relatives with this disorder.

However, the condition is exacerbated by stress or trauma. People with OCD often report that their symptoms worsen when they do not get enough sleep, have personal problems, or are ill. Obsessive-compulsive behaviour may be a way for stressed children to exert some control in their lives.

WHAT TO WATCH FOR

Obsessive-compulsive disorder may interfere with school, friendships and family life. Often children report that they don't understand why they have the obsessive thoughts and perform the compulsive actions.

Children with OCD often worry aloud and obsessively, about things that you consider nonsense, or they may repeat certain actions over and over. If you notice this tendency, then you should consult a mental health professional.

WHAT PARENTS CAN DO

Usually, children with this disorder need some form of therapy. Cognitive-behavioural therapy seems to be most useful.

The clinician working with the child will help her identify unrealistic thoughts such as 'I'll die if I touch that doorknob'. The child is then taught to determine whether these thoughts are accurate or distorted. Finally, the child learns to replace the exaggerated thought with a more realistic one: 'The door-knob may have germs on it, but people rarely get sick and die from touching a dirty doorknob.'

The next step in the treatment is to help the child stop the compulsive behaviour. The clinician helps the child build a hierarchy of tasks the child feels he must do, noting how strong the impulse to do each one is. The first items are things the child feels he should do but does not have to do. The child is then prevented from performing the compulsive behaviour. For example, a child who feels the compulsion to wash his hands is prevented from doing so after a non-messy meal. When the child can refrain from washing his hands without much discomfort, he undertakes the next item on the hierarchy, perhaps not washing his hands after a messy meal.

Medication also has a definite role in the treatment of OCD, and a child psychiatrist may decide to prescribe medication such as a selective serotonin reuptake inhibitor (SSRI).

One fine book that parents may wish to read for more information is *The Boy Who Couldn't Stop Washing* by Judith Rappaport. There is also an Obsessive-Compulsive Foundation.

Overeating and Obesity

(See also Stressing Physical Activity, p. 58; Bulimia, p. 182.)

WHAT IT IS

Although overeating and obesity are not technically considered eating disorders, they can be serious problems for children. Obesity is usually defined as being more than 20 per cent above the normal weight for one's height and build. Being overweight is not the same as being obese, and there is no strict definition of it. However, most children have a good concept of what 'overweight' means. Depending on height, carrying an extra $3\frac{1}{2}$ to $4\frac{1}{2}$ kilograms (8 to 10 pounds) over the ideal weight probably means that a child is overweight.

Obesity – and to some extent, being overweight – can result in rejection, low self-esteem, high blood pressure and potential diabetes.

WHAT CAUSES IT

Obesity results when the body uses less energy than it takes in through food. Obese youngsters typically eat more food than they need, perhaps because they are not very active or because their bodies use little energy due to a low metabolism. Obesity can also have a medical cause, such as a thyroid problem.

WHAT TO WATCH FOR

In general, parents are well aware of what to watch for. One child in the family may pick at her food, eating little, and she may also have unlimited energy. As a result, she may be toothpick-thin. Her less fortunate brother may love sedentary activities like the computer and video games, and he may also enjoy a good meal. He gains weight as a result of excessive food consumption and insufficient physical activity.

Fear of having a fat child plagues both thin and overweight parents; the social ramifications of being overweight are so burdensome. Overweight kids are often last to be picked for a team, may have more difficulty making friends and may have few dates, for example. But it's important not to overreact about your child's food intake and start nagging him about eating less. Sometimes parents of a child with a stocky build worry that he is overweight; your paediatrician or family physician can offer you guidelines as to what's normal for your child. Some people will never be rail-thin.

Many people hold certain incorrect beliefs, or myths, about overeating and obesity:

MYTH #1: *Youngsters who are overweight are lazy and lack self-control.* This is an inaccurate picture of youngsters who are obese. Most people who are overweight are productive members of society who are energetic and resourceful.

MYTH #2: *Weight problems are lifelong in nature.* Although it can be exceedingly hard to lose weight and keep it off, it is possible. Indeed, if you can help your child lose weight now, he will be much less likely to continue to be obese.

WHAT PARENTS CAN DO

If your child is overweight, consult a paediatrician or your family physician, who can recommend a nutrition and exercise programme that the entire family can follow – an enormously supportive and helpful way to approach weight control.

Because youngsters are still growing and

need adequate food and nutrition, they should not usually diet and should not be on a restrictive diet. In fact, most overweight children should not lose weight. Instead, their body weight should stay steady or increase slightly as they grow taller and sturdier. This may not be true, however, for youngsters who are severely overweight or for whom being obese has created other health problems.

The Stoplight Eating Plan

We often use a method called the stoplight diet. We sit down with the family and establish categories for various foods, particularly foods that the child likes.

'Red' foods are ones that are high in fat or calories and are not generally very healthy – chips, hamburgers, fried chicken, gravy and pie. These red light foods should not be eaten very often – maybe only once or twice a week.

'Yellow' foods may be somewhat high in fat or calories, but they are not as bad as red foods, and they may contain important nutrients like protein. Yellow light foods like baked chicken, mashed potatoes and pancakes may be eaten occasionally, perhaps three to five times a week.

'Green' foods are those that are healthy and low in calories and fat – fresh vegetables, fresh fruit and raisins. These foods can be eaten almost any time and make great snacks.

This system seems to be helpful because it makes sense and is simple for kids to remember.

The other important component of a healthy lifestyle is exercise. You should help your kids develop an active lifestyle by taking them on walks, biking with them and playing football with them. Make sure that they get outside in the fresh air.

By establishing early healthy eating and exercise habits, you'll have given your child a gift that will last a lifetime.

Panic Disorder and Agoraphobia

(See also Anxiety, p. 173; Depression, p. 184.)

WHAT IT IS

Panic disorder is an anxiety disorder that does not arise from any specific cause. It seems to come out of nowhere, but the feelings are extremely intense. During the attack, a youngster may feel a sense of impending doom, and this feeling of desperation can last from ten to thirty minutes.

Because of the intensity of the anxiety, a child may become very worried about it happening again, so he starts avoiding situations that he feels might trigger an attack. If he has had several panic attacks at the swimming pool, for example, he may avoid going swimming.

Some people with panic disorder also have agoraphobia, a fear of being in places where one might have a panic attack or where it would be difficult to escape if a panic attack occurred. For example, a youngster with agoraphobia might fear riding in a car over a long bridge because she couldn't escape from the car if she started to have a panic attack. People with agoraphobia are often thought to be afraid to leave their homes. This may occur in severe cases, but most youths with agoraphobia will be afraid only of certain places.

Some people with panic disorder go on to develop depression; some adults with the problem even attempt suicide to escape the attacks. Thus it is important for youngsters with this disorder to be reassured that they are not crazy, that others suffer from it, too (about 5 per cent of the population suffers from, or has suffered from, some form of panic disorder) and that there is help for them.

WHAT CAUSES IT

Most people who develop panic attacks have high anxiety sensitivity, meaning they fear the symptoms of anxiety. If they become a little anxious, it makes them more anxious, sometimes triggering a panic attack.

Panic disorder may also have a genetic component. Many sufferers have a relative with some type of anxiety disorder.

WHAT TO WATCH FOR

Panic disorder is generally not diagnosed until after a youngster has had several attacks. During these attacks, the sufferer may have multiple symptoms, including the following:

1. heart palpitations or pounding
2. sweating
3. shaking or trembling
4. shortness of breath or feelings of smothering
5. feelings of choking
6. chest pain
7. upset stomach or nausea
8. dizziness, light-headedness, or fainting
9. feeling that things are not real or feeling detached from oneself
10. fear of losing control or going crazy
11. fear of dying
12. numbness or tingling
13. chills or hot flushes

As you'll note, many of the symptoms are physiological, though some involve internal fears such as a fear of going crazy.

WHAT PARENTS CAN DO

Fortunately, effective treatments have been developed to help combat panic disorder. Although these techniques have been used primarily with adults, preliminary research seems to show that they can also help children and adolescents.

One of the major treatments was developed by David Barlow and his colleagues at the State University of New York at Albany. It is called the MAP programme – Mastery of Your Anxiety and Panic. Because many children and adolescents with panic disorder feel embarrassed by this problem, education about the disorder is a major part of the MAP programme.

In addition, a number of exercises are included in the MAP programme. For example, because many youngsters with panic attacks tend to hyperventilate, or breathe too fast, the child is taught how to breathe properly – slowly and from the diaphragm. The youngster is also taught to identify bodily symptoms and evaluate whether they are serious or benign. Using the MAP programme, about 80 per cent of adults experience marked improvement in their panic disorder and many stop having panic attacks completely. Although this programme works best when a trained and experienced mental health professional serves as a coach, the programme was developed as a self-help manual and can be administered by parents. The MAP programme can be ordered from the US Psychological Corporation: +1-800-211-8378.

Paralysis, Temporary (Conversion Disorder)

WHAT IT IS

A person with temporary paralysis, or conversion disorder, loses the ability to use some part of his body. This is a psychological condition, however, not a physical one. This paralysis, typically of a hand or an arm, may last a few minutes or a few weeks. It's important to understand that this paralysis is completely real to the sufferer.

Conversion disorder is most common among women and is relatively rare in children.

WHAT CAUSES IT

Conversion disorder is usually caused by some kind of stressor. For example, a child may have high anxiety about something, such as sexual abuse, and try very hard to repress her feelings about it. Extreme anger is also sometimes exhibited as temporary paralysis.

WHAT TO WATCH FOR

A child with conversion disorder may have trouble walking or difficulty swallowing. Some sufferers have unexplained seizures.

WHAT PARENTS CAN DO

A thorough medical checkup by a physician is the first step in looking for a solution. If a medical problem is not discovered, then you'll want to consult a mental health professional. Sometimes the problem will go away on its own, but usually it indicates a more serious problem.

Personality Disorders

(See also Chapter 15.)

WHAT THEY ARE

A personality disorder is a pattern of thinking and behaving that is notably different from the way others think and behave. People with these disorders often have problems interacting with others. Personality disorders differ from other psychiatric disorders in that they are more enduring and difficult to change.

The more common kinds of personality disorders include the following:

PARANOID: A pattern of distrust and suspicion where the person assumes that others are out to get her.

SCHIZOID: A pattern of extreme aloofness from others paired with few expressions of emotion.

SCHIZOTYPAL: A pattern of feeling very uncomfortable in interpersonal relationships and exhibiting bizarre social behaviour or beliefs, such as believing that others can read your mind.

ANTISOCIAL: A pattern of behaviour whereby the rights of other people are ignored – violence, stealing and so forth. Many antisocial people commit serious crimes and feel no remorse about what they do. They have no guilt and no empathy.

BORDERLINE: A pattern of behaviour where the person has unstable interpersonal relationships, views of himself and moods. This person may idealize his wife and, ten minutes later, think she is the worst person who ever lived. Persons with this disorder may engage in self-destructive behaviour, such as using sharp objects to cut themselves or banging their heads.

HISTRIONIC: A pattern of behaviour where a person seeks attention by being dramatic, flamboyant, or seductive.

NARCISSISTIC: A pattern of very strong beliefs that one is better, more attractive, or 'special' and that one's needs are more important than the needs of others.

AVOIDANT: A pattern of behaviour where a person avoids others, has low self-esteem and is extremely sensitive to criticism.

DEPENDENT: A pattern of being very needy and wanting to be taken care of. The person may be unable to make minor decisions, such as what clothes to wear to work, without advice from a spouse.

OBSESSIVE-COMPULSIVE: A pattern of needing extreme order and control over things and people. This personality disorder is different from the psychiatric disorder described on page 201.

WHAT CAUSES THEM

Personality disorders can have a number of different causes, including chronic trauma such as sexual abuse, genetics and environment. Learned behaviour also seems important in the origin of personality disorders. A child may learn that when he wants something from his parents, withdrawing and giving them the silent treatment may work. The child may be rewarded by the parents' attention or by receiving money or treats. Later, when the child is grown, this pattern of withdrawing may destroy an adult romantic relationship. However, the person may be unwilling to give up this behaviour because he has not learned other ways of acting.

WHAT TO WATCH FOR

Because the personality is formed during childhood and adolescence, these patterns usually start to emerge when people are young. However, because this is also a time when people 'find themselves', brief changes aren't a cause for concern. One day a teenager may be quiet and introspective and the next day she may be overly dramatic and extroverted. This behaviour is not something to worry about. Because of this normal experimentation, children are rarely diagnosed with a personality disorder. In fact the DSM-IV (the primary manual of mental disorders used by mental health professionals) specifies that a person should be eighteen years old before being given a personality disorder diagnosis.

Occasionally, adolescents are diagnosed with a personality disorder but generally only if the behaviour is severe. For example, one symptom of borderline personality disorder is repeated suicidal gestures that aren't serious, such as cutting the arms and legs. An adolescent who displays this behaviour would be likely to receive a personality disorder diagnosis.

WHAT PARENTS CAN DO

Consult a mental health professional if you suspect a personality disorder. Although effective treatments have been developed, most people with a personality disorder require a great deal of therapy before they get better. Thus early intervention is helpful.

Phobia

(See also Overcoming Fears, p. 117; Anxiety, p. 173; Obsessive-Compulsive Disorder, p. 201; Panic Disorder, p. 204; Phobia, Social, p. 209; Post-Traumatic Stress Disorder, p. 211; Separation Anxiety, p. 215.)

WHAT IT IS

A phobia is an intense fear reaction to a specific object or situation. Phobias differ from general anxiety, which is a more free-floating concern about the future. Although children and adolescents fear a number of different things, four general categories of fear have been identified by mental health professionals: (1) animals; (2) the natural environment (storms, tornadoes, heights, water); (3) getting injections, seeing blood and getting hurt; and (4) situations (being on an aeroplane, in a lift, or in a small place).

WHAT CAUSES IT

Fear actually plays an adaptive role in life as it helps warn children that they may be in danger. Without fear, children might go off with strangers, pet strange dogs, or cross a busy street without looking. However, for some children a certain fear can get out of control, sometimes because of a bad experience, such as becoming phobic about dogs after being bitten by one. In other cases, a child may become fearful after seeing or hearing about someone else having a bad experience. We treated one child for a bee phobia: his mother was extremely allergic to bee stings and demonstrated a severe fear of bees. Even though the child was not allergic, he was phobic about bees (a learned reaction).

WHAT TO WATCH FOR

Many people have heard of phobias and probably know the names of some specific types of phobias. For example, fear of being trapped in small places is called claustrophobia. Children with a phobia react with *extreme* fear and distress when they are near the feared object. Some children may run away, scream, or even faint. Generally, the fear does not subside.

It is normal for toddlers, preschoolers and early primary school children to be afraid of the dark, storms, dogs and other large animals, spiders and snakes, strangers, monsters, bogeymen and other frightening things. Being afraid of the dark at age sixteen, however, is less common and therefore not age-appropriate.

Phobias are also different from fear in that a phobia impairs one's life because of the time and effort spent worrying about or avoiding the feared object. A child who is afraid of insects, for example, might avoid playing in the grass, walking through fields, or even going to school, and one who is phobic about dogs may refuse to visit a home where there is a dog. However, young children and some adolescents may not recognize that their phobias are irrational or excessive.

WHAT PARENTS CAN DO

Some of the techniques noted in 'Overcoming Fears', page 117, may be helpful. However, if your child seems to have developed a true phobia, you are best advised to consult a mental health professional. Children can be helped through a variety of means, and there is no sense in his life being hampered by a phobia.

Phobia, Social

(See also Helping the Shy Child, p. 44; Overcoming Fears, p. 117; Phobia, p. 208.)

WHAT IT IS

Social phobia is anxiety or fear that arises from social situations. While everyone feels a little nervous about some social situations, a social phobia is fear that has got out of control. The affected child tries to avoid social situations because they make him so anxious. Youngsters with this problem generally fear not measuring up to the expectations of others. They worry about being laughed at or teased.

WHAT CAUSES IT

Some children are born with a temperament that makes them want to withdraw from social situations. Others develop a social phobia following a pattern of unpleasant social experiences. For example, kids who are rejected socially or teased frequently may develop a social phobia.

Because it can cause problems in peer relations – a vital part of maturation during childhood – the social phobia should be treated. Generally, this means exposing the child to social situations, starting with simple, nonthreatening situations like being with one or two people and working up to being in larger groups. Most kids with social phobia realize they have a problem and want to get better.

WHAT TO WATCH FOR

Each child with a social phobia will develop a unique pattern, but children and adolescents with social phobia usually have difficulty making friends. They are often described as shy, and they feel uncomfortable talking to people they don't know well. Some get along well with adults but do poorly with peers. Or some may have particular difficulty getting along with peers of the opposite sex. These youngsters often try to avoid situations that they find stressful, such as parties, dates, slumber parties and dances. They may also avoid doing things that are necessary, such as eating in public or giving presentations in class because they fear being judged.

WHAT PARENTS CAN DO

If you think your child has a social phobia, consult a professional. The condition is treatable, but it may take time.

Pica

(See also Setting Limits for Toddlers, p. 128.)

WHAT IT IS

Pica is a disorder in which a person eats inedible substances or objects such as hair, dirt, rocks, plaster, paint chips, leaves, paper, or even faeces.

Ingesting harmful objects can cause intestinal problems, vomiting, or choking. Kids who live in older homes with lead paint can get lead poisoning from eating paint chips. Lead poisoning is quite serious and can cause long-term problems, including learning difficulties.

WHAT CAUSES IT

Sometimes pica is caused by a vitamin or mineral deficiency, particularly a deficiency in zinc. Other times, lack of supervision causes children to eat things that they shouldn't. When this problem occurs in older children or adolescents, it is often associated with mental retardation.

WHAT TO WATCH FOR

Many kids like to experiment, and sometimes this involves tasting different things. Infants in particular go through a period when they stick anything they can find straight into their mouths. However, most kids outgrow this phase and don't usually actually swallow much – they just put it into their mouths and spit it out again.

Children who suffer pica fail to move beyond this stage. They not only put odd items in their mouths, but they may chew and swallow anything from leaves to little pieces of paper.

WHAT PARENTS CAN DO

To begin, make your home safe. Set all plants up high so that kids can't eat the leaves or the potting soil. Place dangerous objects in childproof drawers or cabinets. However, no matter how careful you are about putting things away, there is no substitute for careful supervision.

If a child is beyond toddlerhood and is still eating odd things, take her to the paediatrician for a checkup, since pica may be caused by a medical disorder or a vitamin deficit. In some cases, the paediatrician may recommend vitamins or some other dietary supplement. If you have lead paint in your house, request that your doctor check your child's lead level.

In some cases, the doctor may feel that your case should be handled by a mental health professional who will probably set up a behavioural programme for you. In addition, you should take the following steps:

➤ Find out in advance who to contact in an emergency. There may be a day when you need the number quickly.

➤ When your child is about to eat something, like the ribbon from a toy, take it away from her and give her a verbal reprimand, 'No!' With an older child, you can use a time-out.

➤ Distract the child with other activities. Talk or sing and make him forget about eating the object.

Parents ask us about tactics such as washing a child's mouth out with soap or having her gargle with an unpleasant liquid. We find this is ineffective and does little to prevent a child from eating other things in the future.

Post-Traumatic Stress Disorder

(See also Anxiety, p. 173; Depression, p. 184.)

WHAT IT IS

Post-traumatic stress disorder, also known as PTSD, occurs as a result of personal exposure to a major trauma, usually one that is outside the normal range of human experience.

WHAT CAUSES IT

Post-traumatic stress disorder is one of the few disorders whose cause can usually be identified. A child may develop this disorder after being attacked by a dog, sexually or physically assaulted, seeing a parent die in a car accident, or seeing someone get shot. It can happen if the child experiences the trauma herself, or sees someone else experience a trauma.

Some people can go through a traumatic experience and not develop a problem. Others may be bothered by it, but sometimes not immediately.

WHAT TO WATCH FOR

A period of anxiety following any serious event is natural. Following the death of a loved one, for instance, most kids will feel bad and think about it a lot, but the death does not generally cause PTSD unless the child witnesses it. Children who are present during a traumatic event, however, may not be able to forget about it so easily.

A child who suffers post-traumatic stress disorder will re-experience the trauma in the form of nightmares or intrusive, recurrent thoughts about the event. In his play he may act out the trauma repeatedly, or he may have flashbacks to the event and feel as though he is reliving it.

Avoiding certain things may be part of PTSD. However, what is avoided may not be totally predictable. For example, a child who was in a serious car accident may refuse to ride in a car, or she may refuse to ride through the section of town where the accident happened. If the accident happened when the child was being driven to a sports practice, she may insist on dropping out of the team. She may also refuse to talk about what happened, or she may forget certain important parts of the event.

Anxiety is also a part of PTSD. The child may worry excessively that she will be traumatized again, or she may have trouble falling asleep, perhaps because she fears having nightmares. Hypervigilance – being on guard or on the lookout all the time – is also common. Additionally, the child may be easily startled. Some kids may appear to be depressed and may not take part in activities they used to enjoy before.

WHAT PARENTS CAN DO

Anytime a child experiences a severe trauma, seek the advice of a mental health professional. Often the child will not want to talk about the experience, which will lead parents to believe that she is all right. Talking about it is usually healthy, however, and is one way to process what happened and make meaning of it.

Given the difficulty of talking about the experience, finding a clinician with whom the child can feel comfortable is essential.

Treatment for children or adolescents with PTSD usually involves having the youngster tell and retell the story of what happened. This process is sometimes called abreaction. As this is an anxiety disorder, exposure techniques are the best treatment, and abreaction is a type of exposure technique. However, the key is not to rush the child. If the child tells the story before she is ready, she may be overwhelmed by anxiety or other overpowering feelings, which may damage or stall therapy.

The child may also be encouraged gradually to do things that she has avoided since the trauma. For example, if she has avoided playing with friends, then this may become a focus of treatment. Rewards may be used to encourage her to do these things.

Therapy may include some education about safety (avoiding certain areas of town alone, walking home from school with a friend) in order to increase a child's comfort level about day-to-day life. What is taught will of course depend on the nature of the trauma and the child's age. The goal is to help the child feel that he can protect himself from whatever is on his mind.

Treatment for youngsters can be tricky, partly because the family may be unsettled by the traumatic event or the fact that their child has developed PTSD. Your natural tendency as a parent is to protect your children. If he has already been traumatized, you are probably even more intent on protecting him. However, successful treatment involves having him get back out into the world again and stop avoiding things that are not harmful, such as riding in a car. This may be difficult for your child and therefore may be hard for you. If you are uncomfortable about what your child is doing, you should talk to the clinician. That way, the two of you can figure out ways to help make everyone feel more comfortable while also making sure that your child receives quality treatment.

Running Away

WHAT IT IS

The clinical definition of a runaway is a child 'between the ages of twelve and eighteen who leaves home with the intention of running away and stays away for more than forty-eight hours without parental permission'. As you might note, children under age twelve are not mentioned, presumably because kids this young rarely run away for more than a short period; they are more likely to hide in the garage, prepared to come back when they feel less angry or when they are convinced that everyone is in a panic about them.

WHAT CAUSES IT

You may think kids run away because they do not want to listen to authority, follow rules, or go to school. Actually, kids are more likely to run away because they feel rejected by their parents, and they hope this will bring them attention. Many others who run away report that their parents reject them emotionally by calling them names and so forth. Physical or sexual abuse is often a part of the picture; about two-thirds of runaway kids report being the target of significant parental violence.

WHAT TO WATCH FOR

Youngsters usually give some signals that they are considering running away. Some adolescents may be direct and tell their parents that they have such plans. For others, the signs may be more subtle. Look closely at the relationship you and your spouse have with your child. That will help determine whether your child is at risk for running away from home. If you find yourself arguing with your child more than praising her, then you could be heading for trouble.

Because children often run away from home after being abused, parents also need to be alert to signs of abuse (see page 217) by the other parent, a friend, or a relative. If abuse is occurring, do everything in your power to seek refuge for your child. This may involve getting help from law enforcement agencies or leaving your home with your child and finding a new place to live. These steps are drastic but necessary if you want to help your child and prevent her from running away.

Few stressors can compare with having a child run away and knowing that she is on her own and in potential danger. Parents obviously want to do all they can to prevent this from occurring.

WHAT PARENTS CAN DO

Most kids who run away come back within a day. In fact, most of them hide out at a friend's house, a local shopping centre, or somewhere else nearby. If your child does leave home, call the police immediately. They will usually be helpful and understanding. Often they cannot do much until the child has been missing for twenty-four hours, but letting them know right away will put them on alert.

If your child contacts you or returns home, be supportive. You may be extremely angry, but if you direct this anger at your child, she will be likely to leave again. Your goal should be to mend the relationship, which is going to take a great deal of work. Family therapy is usually helpful in these situations, and your child may need extra therapy time for help in overcoming personal problems.

If your child does not return home, contact a national organization that helps parents seek runaway children such as the National Missing Person Helpline (0500 700 700). Although this situation is frightening for parents, there are hundreds of shelters nationwide that help kids who run away from home.

Schizophrenia

WHAT IT IS

Schizophrenia is a serious disorder characterized by loss of contact with the environment, by a deterioration of the ability to perform everyday functions and by disorganized thinking, feeling and conduct. Fortunately, schizophrenia is relatively rare in children, and if it does appear, it does not usually start until about age fifteen.

There are five major symptoms of the disorder:

1. DELUSION. Youngsters with delusion may have bizarre beliefs. We worked with one patient who believed that Abraham Lincoln was insane. He wanted to ride his bike to the state capital, forty miles away, to protest. Another common delusion is the belief that one is being watched, followed, or spied upon.

2. HALLUCINATIONS. This involves seeing or hearing things that others cannot see or hear. A child may hear voices inside or outside of his own head. He may see totally bizarre things such as cars floating, people who don't exist, or religious figures. Keep in mind, however, that certain hallucinations are considered normal: seeing visions when falling asleep, for instance, or waking and seeing a ghost of a recently deceased loved one.

3. DISORGANIZED THINKING. This problem typically presents itself when the person is talking. She may tell stories that make no sense, or she may answer a question in a bizarre manner. For example, an adolescent with schizophrenia may respond to the question 'Where do you live?' by saying something like 'Wheels on farm tractors are square'.

4. GROSSLY DISORGANIZED BEHAVIOUR. A youngster with schizophrenia may stop attending to personal hygiene, or she may pace or seem agitated. She may also display inappropriate behaviour, such as public masturbation or shouting for no reason.

5. CATATONIC BEHAVIOUR. If a child becomes catatonic, he withdraws from the environment. He may sit in the same position for hours on end or seem completely unaware of his surroundings.

WHAT CAUSES IT

There is no single cause for schizophrenia, but it is generally believed to be an organic and genetic disorder. Not all children who have schizophrenia in the family develop the disorder, so researchers think that other factors, such as outside stressors, play a role in its development.

WHAT TO WATCH FOR

Schizophrenia is not easy to hide. Look first for the symptoms described above. In addition the child will seem to lose skills and abilities that she had before and will behave in extreme ways.

WHAT PARENTS CAN DO

Seek immediate assistance from a mental health professional. This problem can be severe, and hospitalization is sometimes required.

On a positive note, antipsychotic medications are available to help with schizophrenia. Like some other medications, they can cause side effects. However, new medications with fewer side effects are constantly being tested and approved.

A person with serious and chronic schizophrenia is unlikely to be able to take care of herself and usually cannot live on her own. Therefore, many who suffer with schizophrenia live in group or residential homes. These facilities are similar to a normal home, but trained staff members are available to assist residents with taking medications and accomplishing the necessary day-to-day tasks such as eating, bathing, doing laundry and shopping.

Separation Anxiety

(See also Helping the Shy Child, p. 44; Temperament, p. 162; Anxiety, p. 173.)

WHAT IT IS

Separation anxiety disorder occurs when a child doesn't want to be separated from a parent (often the mother) or someone else to whom he is attached. This is an entirely normal stage for young children and becomes problematic only if the child fails to outgrow it. A child older than five or six who refuses to go to school or a friend's house alone has reached the point when separation anxiety may have become a disorder. Possible solutions ought to be explored so that this child won't miss out on normal social development.

WHAT CAUSES IT

Some children are temperamentally disposed to worry more than others about separation, and many children who suffer separation anxiety are shy, which is often inborn. Other times separation anxiety arises because a child is stressed or is facing a very real type of separation. For example, during a parental divorce, the child may worry that his parents do not love him any more and may react by clinging to one or both of them.

WHAT TO WATCH FOR

Age is the determining factor as to whether or not you should worry about your child's difficulty in separating. If your eighteen-month-old cries when you go out for the evening, rest assured that she will almost certainly cheer up five minutes after the door closes behind you and that her separation anxiety is perfectly normal.

If, however, you find yourself the only parent remaining at playgroup or if your primary school child is suddenly having trouble with your leaving for work or going out for the evening, there may be cause for concern.

Excessive clinging is another sign of separation anxiety disorder. If your child's teacher reports that your daughter is at her side all day and not interacting with the other children, consider whether you're observing clinginess at home as well.

You may also notice complaints of sudden illness. Sometimes, just before the parent is to leave, a child will complain of a stomachache or headache. The complaint may be real but caused by worry, not a physiological cause. Or it may be a ploy to try to get the parent to stay at home. Some of the children we treat for this problem say they worry about their parents being hurt; others worry for their own safety – about being in a fire or being kidnapped.

Separation anxiety may display itself at bedtime. Your child may be reluctant to have you leave the room and may demand that you stay with him until he falls asleep. Occasionally, children or adolescents may have nightmares about being separated from their parents. In these nightmares they may see their parents being hurt.

Separation anxiety can cause a lot of problems for children. Making friends may be difficult as they may not want to leave their parents to venture out into the neighbourhood. They may also rush home from school to be with their parents and thus avoid going to a friend's house to play or doing extracurricular activities. Some may even resist attending school. Sleepovers at friends' houses are probably also out of the question until the problem is solved.

WHAT PARENTS CAN DO

As with any other anxiety disorder, a gradual approach to treatment is wise. The goal is to help your child become more independent and feel less anxious when away from the parent. Parents who are firm but compassionate can often bring about improvement on their own.

With some children, encouragement will do the trick ('You'll do fine at Grandma's house for an hour without me. She wants to make biscuits with you, and you'll have a terrific time while I do some shopping'). Try to keep your separations short in the beginning. That way you can build on your child's successes.

Some kids, though, will need more intensive help, and that is when parents may want to consult with a mental health professional. Behavioural therapy is often used and involves a step-by-step shaping procedure with a system of rewards for the child's increased independence. First, the clinician will probably have the child come up with a lot of different scenarios involving being separated from you. Each item is then rated on a scale of 0 to 10, depending on how hard it is to do. Such a list, or hierarchy, may look like this.

ITEM	RATING
Being right next to Mummy	0
Being $\frac{1}{2}$ metre (2 feet) from Mummy	1
Being $1\frac{1}{2}$ metres (5 feet) from Mummy	2
Being in my bedroom with Mummy in the kitchen	3
Being in my bedroom when Mummy is outside in garden	4
Having Mummy go to supermarket without me	5
Going to school without Mummy	6
Going to a friend's house for thirty minutes	7
Going to a friend's house for two hours	8
Sleeping over at a friend's house	9
Going to Grandma's house in another city without Mummy	10

The child is then encouraged to do one of the easier items until she feels comfortable and praise and small rewards are earned at each step. The best rewards are those that further encourage the child to be independent, such as getting to go somewhere special with Grandma.

This approach works quite well with most kids, so long as the steps aren't pushed too quickly. The trick is to challenge the child without pushing him too fast to become independent.

Treatment may also be hard for you, the parent. Like most good parents, you probably enjoy being with your child, and you may not like being separated. You probably want to protect your child, and you understand that the world can be dangerous. If you have these kinds of feelings, tell the clinician about them. That way, you and the clinician can figure out ways to help you feel more comfortable as well.

Sexual Abuse

WHAT IT IS

There is no legal definition of childhood sexual abuse in the UK, while the US definition states that it occurs anytime a person has sexual contact with a youngster under the age of eighteen and the perpetrator is five or more years older than the youngster. In other words, a nineteen-year-old who has sexual intercourse with a fourteen-year-old has committed sexual abuse.

Sexual contact obviously includes sexual intercourse and oral sex, as well as exposing oneself to a child, showing a child pornography, fondling, kissing and other kinds of sexual acts. Both girls and boys can be sexually abused, and the perpetrators can be either male or female.

Obtaining accurate estimates of the incidence of sexual abuse is difficult, but an example from the state of Missouri in the US may help to illustrate the extent of the problem. In 1993 alone, 52,231 incident reports of child abuse or neglect were filed, with 2,756 of these cases involving child sexual abuse of some kind. It is truly frightening to consider the actual number of sexually abused children in the US.

Keep in mind that child-to-child sexual exploration is relatively common and that there is a difference between abuse and normal sexual exploration. If done without coercion, it is relatively common and normal for children to be curious about each other's bodies and to want to look at and touch each other. When same-age children touch each other or play doctor, it is very different from when an older person performs similar acts. Generally, parents probably should not punish this exploratory behaviour between children or make the child feel ashamed. Instead, begin to explain to the child about appropriate and inappropriate behaviour and contact.

WHAT CAUSES IT

Two kinds of people sexually abuse children. Paedophiles have a mental disorder and prefer to have sex with children rather than with adults. Other abusers prefer an adult sexual partner but may abuse children when they are under extreme stress.

However, it is important to keep in mind that the causes of child sexual abuse have to do with the adult abuser. The child is clearly not responsible for the abuse.

WHAT TO WATCH FOR

Ideally, your child will tell you if he or she is being sexually abused or has been abused in the past. However, even if you and your child communicate well, something may prohibit him or her from talking to you. Some children feel ashamed; others worry that the abuser – often a friend or relative – will get in trouble; some are embarrassed or blame themselves; and young children often lack the vocabulary to explain what has happened. Children also assume that they are bad if they felt physical pleasure during the abuse.

Adolescents sometimes do not report sexual abuse, perhaps because they blame themselves. Often the abuser will tell the adolescent that she was seductive and 'asked for it'. Male adolescents are particularly reluctant to discuss sexual abuse, especially if the abuser was a male. They fear being labelled a homosexual, queer, faggot, or worse if they report the incident.

Even though children may not verbally tell you about sexual abuse, they will usually give other signs that sexual abuse may have occurred. Parents should be aware of these signals so that they can seek help for the child:

1. **PHYSICAL SIGNS.** Girls who are sexually abused may have vaginal bruising or blood in their underwear. Boys might have anal bruising or blood in their underwear.

2. **ACTING OUT SEXUALLY.** This behaviour, often exhibited by younger children, can include sexual play with dolls, masturbation and precocious sexual knowledge or language. Their drawings of people may include the genitalia or show sexual activity. Older children may begin to sexually abuse younger siblings.

3. **SEEMING WITHDRAWN.** A child may become emotionally distant or cry a lot. He or she may suddenly refuse physical affection from parents and others or greet it with fear. Adolescents may begin to spend more time in their bedrooms.

4. **MENTIONING HAVING 'PLAYED GAMES' WITH CERTAIN ADULTS.** For example, kids might describe nude wrestling, tickling, playing doctor, playing farm animals and so forth. Sometimes they may be talking about totally innocuous games, but you should ask questions.

5. **SIGNS OF AGGRESSION.** Abused children may frequently or increasingly hit siblings or even adults. They can also harm themselves. For example, young children may beat their heads against the floor because their emotional pain is so overwhelming. Adolescents may use needles or razor blades to inflict cuts on their arms or legs.

6. **PROBLEMS AT SCHOOL OR WITH EXTRA-CURRICULAR ACTIVITIES.** A dramatic drop in performance may occur. Keep in frequent contact with your child's teachers, even if your child does not have any problems. That way, the teacher will be more likely to call you

if your child begins to have school problems, regardless of the cause.

7. RUNNING AWAY. This is particularly likely to happen if the abuser is someone the child knows well. The child may also use drugs to escape from reality.

8. SUICIDE ATTEMPTS. Parents should be aware of any signs of potential suicide (see page 228). Our research has shown that some kids from abusive families attempt to commit suicide. If this fails, they may murder a family member or another person in an attempt to end the abuse.

While some of these symptoms, taken individually, may not be a cause for distress, if a child suddenly begins to show a pattern of these problems, you should suspect sexual abuse. Ask your child about it. The child may deny it, but his or her reaction might help you decide if it is true.

WHAT PARENTS CAN DO

Teaching children about sexual abuse is a good first step towards preventing this problem, and education has been increasingly emphasized. This may be due to recent horror stories regarding children who have allegedly been sexually abused by preschool staff, priests, coaches, relatives and others. Additionally, as parents become more aware of the problem and educate their children, youngsters become more likely to report sexual abuse.

Formerly, many people thought that only dirty old men and strangers sexually abused children. Today most people are aware that sexual abuse can be committed by a person of any age, educational level, family background, sex and income level. Most child sexual abuse is perpetrated by someone who is known to the child.

By far the best way to prevent your children from being sexually abused is to educate them about it. Although sexual abuse is widespread, less than one-third of parents discuss the topic of sexual abuse with their children, and others often do not initiate the discussion until the child is nine years old.

Unfortunately, many children are sexually abused at a much earlier age. Males are most likely to be sexually abused during the preschool years, from about two to four years old and during adolescence, from about twelve to fourteen. For females, the likelihood of being sexually abused increases throughout development, peaking during adolescence.

Parents often teach children to avoid strangers, yet the majority of reported sexual assaults involve someone who is known to the child. Children therefore need to know that almost anyone could try to hurt them. Teach your children that they have the absolute right to refuse to do anything that makes them feel uncomfortable or threatened. They do not have to let anyone touch them.

Children need to be familiar with the most common threats, promises and lies that abusers will use to prevent a child from reporting them. Usually, an abuser will try to befriend a child before the abuse occurs. They often give gifts or show affection to the child.

They might use bribes to persuade the child to endure the abuse. To prevent a child from reporting the abuse, some abusers also use threats: 'I'll kill you if you tell,' or 'I'll hurt your parents if you tell,' or 'No one will believe you,' or even 'You'll be blamed for this'.

Emphasize to your child that children are *never* responsible for abuse and are not punished if they tell. Keep open communication with your children and let them know that they can tell you anything. With younger children, you may want to read stories or use puppets to help teach them about sexual abuse.

The following recommendations will also help prevent abuse.

1. Leave your child only with people you trust absolutely. Don't have blind faith in people. Most parents would not hesitate to leave a child with a relative. However, male relatives are responsible for a large proportion of sexual abuse. Although you should not be paranoid, no one should be above suspicion.

2. Start talking to your kids early. Even toddlers and preschoolers are sometimes sexually abused, so you cannot wait until your child is older to begin this education. Some parents are reluctant to talk about sexual abuse with their young kids; they want to begin sex education when the children are older. Educating your child about sexual abuse is not the same as educating your child about sex.

3. Teach your child about good versus bad touching. Bad touching makes a child feel bad or uncomfortable. You might explain to your child that bad touching happens when someone older touches you in any place that would be covered by a bathing suit – on the buttocks, genitals and chest, in other words. Tell your child that if she is uncertain, she should tell you about an incident so that you can help.

4. Make sure that your child would report abuse if it occurs. You might play 'what if' games. Ask your child questions such as 'What would you do if someone touched you on your bottom?' or 'What would you do if someone threatened you?' Asking these types of questions will help you determine what actions the child would take if abuse occurred.

5. Make sure your child can say no to adults. Stress that it is perfectly okay for your child to say no to an adult if she feels threatened. Again, play the 'what if' game to make sure your child understands.

If your child is being sexually abused, your first step must be to remove the child from the abusive situation. Unfortunately this process may be incredibly disruptive for everyone involved. You may have to leave your spouse and stay with relatives or even in a shelter. No matter how hard this is to do, it is absolutely necessary. Remember that you are the only person who is looking out for your child and you need to protect him.

If your child is sexually abused, it is crucial that you do not blame him in any way for what happened. Clearly, your child was not responsible. The adult abuser is always responsible when sexual contact occurs.

Sometimes kids feel guilty because they did not fight off the abuser, because they were curious, or because the sexual abuse felt good. In fact, the child may have been mildly flirtatious to the abuser. However, the child is still not responsible and should not be blamed.

Finally, you need to seek professional help for your child. There are several sources to which you can turn. You probably should begin by getting a physical examination for your child. Your paediatrician or family physician can recommend good mental health resources that exist in your community.

Sexual abuse can lead to depression in a child (see page 184), or a child may develop post-traumatic stress disorder (see page 211), particularly if a sexual assault or rape has occurred. These incidents can lead to extreme emotional distress for a child. Mental health professionals can help your child and your family cope with the distress.

Sleep Disorders

(See also Anxiety, p. 173; Depression, p. 184; Post-Traumatic Stress Disorder, p. 211.)

WHAT THEY ARE

While infants may sleep erratically, most children acquire a normal sleep pattern as they grow older. Occasionally a child may suffer a sleep disorder such as insomnia, hypersomnia, or narcolepsy.

A child with insomnia has trouble going to sleep or staying asleep. Before a diagnosis can be made, the problem must last for at least one month. Hypersomnia causes a child to sleep too much or to nap often during the day; the problem must continue for at least one month. Narcolepsy – falling asleep suddenly and unexpectedly – can be diagnosed only after it has continued for at least three months. This disorder is especially dangerous because sufferers can fall asleep at almost any time, resulting in accidents. It is not particularly common in children, however.

Any one of these disorders can cause problems. Whether the child is getting too little or too much sleep, she is likely to feel tired and lethargic. It may be difficult for her to get to school on time or pay attention in class. The youngster may also feel too tired to live a normal life outside the classroom.

WHAT CAUSES THEM

Each disorder stems from a different cause, so a medical professional would need to make the final diagnosis. In general, however, generalized anxiety, post-traumatic stress disorder and depression can all cause sleep disorders. Narcolepsy tends to come from a biological cause and may have a genetic component – people with the disorder often have relatives who also suffer from it.

WHAT TO WATCH FOR

A child who occasionally has difficulty sleeping does not have a sleep disorder. The symptoms of a true sleep disorder last for a long time and are not related to how tired the child is.

WHAT PARENTS CAN DO

Your first task is simply to try to help your child get normal sleep. Provide a quiet, relaxing environment – turn off the television and out-law telephone calls after a certain hour – and help your child find ways to calm down before bed. Reading quietly or listening to music right before bed helps many people relax.

You can try aids such as a nice bath and a glass of warm milk to help calm your child, but don't give her over-the-counter sleep medications. These were developed for short-term use with adults.

If you feel your child needs professional help, your paediatrician may refer you to a sleep lab (usually a part of the department of neurology at a medical centre). If admitted into such a programme, your youngster may have to sleep – or try to sleep – in the lab so that her sleep patterns can be analyzed.

Soiling (Encopresis)

(See also Bed-wetting, p. 181.)

WHAT IT IS

Encopresis is a disorder where children start or continue having bowel movement acci-dents long after most children are toilet-trained (at least one a month for three months). For a diagnosis to be made, the child has to be chronologically and mentally older than age four.

Most children who soil do not do so intentionally, and they are usually terribly ashamed. If the problem occurs during the daytime, the child may be ostracized by her friends.

WHAT CAUSES IT

Encopresis is sometimes caused by a medical problem that responds to surgery; other times the condition results from constipa-tion: a blockage causes the faeces to leak out rather than come out through a normal bowel movement. Constipation can also cause an anal fissure, making it painful to have a bowel movement. This then makes the child anxious about having a bowel movement, and because the faeces are with-held, they overflow at unplanned times.

Encopresis can also result from stress in a child's life such as starting school or the birth of a sibling. In some cases, severity in toilet training may cause it. If the parent yells at or punishes a child who is learning to use the toilet, this child may develop the problem because she becomes afraid of going to the lavatory and tries to avoid it.

If the child is intentionally soiling, the problem may be a way of indirectly express-ing other problems, such as extreme anger. In some cases, it may be caused by sexual abuse, but this is not the most likely basis for the encopresis.

Encopresis can also be related to mental retardation, but most children and adoles-cents with mental retardation can be suc-cessfully toilet-trained.

WHAT TO WATCH FOR

Needless to say, you'll be very aware if your child is suffering from encopresis. (Older children may try to launder their underwear or bedding in order to cover up the problem, but it is a difficult condition to hide for long.) Between the time you realize you have the problem and when you consult a profession-al, you should note the circumstances when the problem occurs in order to speed a diagnosis. For example, if your child seems afraid of having a bowel movement, this might help a paediatrician narrow the possible causes.

WHAT PARENTS CAN DO

Take your child to a paediatrician in case the problem calls for medical or surgical treatment. If the child avoids using the toilet because of anxiety, relaxation techniques may be helpful. Keep in mind that it is important to be discreet since your child may be embarrassed by the problem and not want others to know about it. If the child becomes embarrassed during the medical examination, the problem is likely to worsen.

When the soiling is intentional, family therapy is usually recommended. In particular, communication training may be used to help the child express himself more directly and feel comfortable doing so. In some cases, a reward system may be recommended.

Speech Problems (Communication Disorders)

(See also Autism and Other Developmental Disorders, p. 179; Learning Disorders, p. 195; Mutism, p. 200.)

WHAT THEY ARE

Speech problems, or communication disorders, occur when a child has difficulty expressing herself orally. These are the most common disorders:

1. EXPRESSIVE LANGUAGE DISORDER. These children don't speak as well as they should based on their level of intelligence. They may have a very limited vocabulary, or they may often repeat a few words or phrases. These children may also speak slowly and have trouble finding the words they want to use. Others make many errors, such as leaving out important parts of sentences or phrasing all of their statements as questions. All children may exhibit some of these problems as they learn to talk; a problem is considered a disorder only if it doesn't go away by a certain age.

2. MIXED RECEPTIVE-EXPRESSIVE LANGUAGE DISORDER. This disorder is similar to expressive language disorder, but kids with this problem also have difficulty understanding what other people say.

3. PHONOLOGICAL DISORDER. Youngsters with this disorder have difficulty pronouncing certain speech sounds. This is totally normal in very young children who are learning to talk, but an eleven-year-old who cannot pronounce the *th* sound, for example, may have phonological disorder.

4. STUTTERING. Kids who stutter may repeat certain sounds or syllables: 'ch-ch-ch-ch-check.' They may also pause in the middle of words. Typically, they have difficulty with the same words or sounds, so they may avoid using certain words because they know they are likely to stumble over them.

WHAT CAUSES THEM

Most speech disorders are caused by neurological problems. The connections between certain parts of the brain do not work as well as they should. (See 'The Brain and Behaviour', p. 158.)

Anxiety and stress may also contribute to speech disorders. Giving a speech in class will almost certainly bring out any child's speech difficulties. Stressful situations are particularly painful for stutterers who may do relatively well with their problem when they are talking to family members or friends but who stutter when talking to strangers, members of the opposite sex and others who make them nervous.

Some medical problems, such as head trauma, can also lead to communication disorders.

Speech problems are not diagnosed as communication disorders if they are caused by a lack of education or a strong regional accent or dialect.

WHAT TO WATCH FOR

Many young kids say certain words improperly, but this speech difficulty is age-appropriate. Think of the number of times you've heard a child say 'wabbit' for 'rabbit' or 'free' for 'three'. These mispronunciations are normal at an early age and generally disappear as the child grows older.

Children with communication disorders have more severe problems, and each disorder brings with it difficulties of its own. Check with your paediatrician for a referral to a speech pathologist if you are overly concerned about any of the following:

➤ Vocabulary that is inappropriately limited.

➤ Very slow speech or difficulty retrieving words.

➤ Any speech difficulty combined with difficulty understanding what other people say.

➤ Failure to outgrow difficulty with pronunciation.

➤ Stuttering.

Your paediatrician can tell you whether this problem is one that your child will outgrow or whether it bears further exploration with a speech pathologist.

WHAT PARENTS CAN DO

If a problem is diagnosed, find out what resources are available to you. Most schools do some testing to help identify kids who might need some help. Additionally, speech therapy may be provided by many schools. If you do not have access to such services, you may have to consult with a speech therapist who works at a hospital or in private practice.

Speech therapy generally consists of having children do exercises to improve their enunciation of words or sounds or to decrease stuttering or whatever communication problem they have. Ask what you can do to reinforce the work at home.

Substance Abuse

(See also Setting Limits, p. 74; The Importance of Peer Relationships, p. 142.)

WHAT IT IS

Alcohol and drug abuse is a serious health and social problem for the youth in the US. According to the U.S. Department of

Education, almost 5 million teenagers have an alcohol problem and 4 per cent of high school seniors in the US report drinking alcohol daily. Young people lose their lives every day in alcohol- or drug-related car accidents, drownings, suicides and homicides. In fact, alcohol-related accidents are the leading cause of death for people fifteen- to twenty-four-years-old. Some teenagers who use drugs develop critical health-related problems such as damage to the brain, heart, or kidneys after years of abuse.

There are five basic stages of alcohol use, and these same basic stages could apply to drug use:

1. *Abstainers* don't drink or drink less often than once a year.

2. *Light drinkers* consume alcohol on occasion, one to three times a month. Their primary motive is not to get drunk or feel high but to fit in at a social gathering.

3. *Moderate drinkers* actively seek alcohol and want to get drunk or high to experience these sensations. These kids drink about once a week but they do not binge-drink.

4. *Moderate to heavy drinkers* are likely to be preoccupied with drinking, and their peer relationships and results may suffer.

5. *Heavy drinkers* are likely to be dependent upon alcohol. These teenagers usually drink several times a week.

WHAT CAUSES IT

Children and adolescents typically start to use substances because of boredom, to escape from hassles, because of peer pressure, or just for fun. Most start out using a substance recreationally, in social situations. Some kids may find that they are more relaxed when they are drunk or high. Because substance use initially may make them feel really good, the behaviour is reinforced.

As youngsters drink more alcohol, tolerance builds up and they have to drink more in order to have the effect they used to get from smaller amounts. They may also become physically or psychologically dependent on the drug and feel that they may not be able to stop.

Alcoholism or substance abuse does tend to run in families. This may be due to genetics – a certain part of the brain may malfunction and lead people to seek substances. It may also occur because kids may see their parents or other relatives having fun using substances and try them for themselves.

WHAT TO WATCH FOR

Most kids experiment with alcohol or other substances during their teenage years. This experimentation is usually the result of curiosity and does not cause any problems. Indeed, some parents do not particularly disapprove of their teenagers' occasional alcohol or recreational drug use and are thankful that their kids are not using more dangerous substances such as cocaine and acid.

To identify your teenager's alcohol or drug use before it becomes problematic, watch for some of the following symptoms:

1. Cutting classes or entire school days.
2. Poor school performance, particularly declining marks.

3. Breaking curfew.
4. Unexplained cuts, bruises, abrasions, or other injuries.
5. Withdrawal from family activities or decreased closeness with family members.
6. Secretive behaviour such as refusal to answer questions about where he was.
7. Poor personal hygiene.
8. Trouble with the police.
9. Low frustration tolerance (easily annoyed or angered).
10. Signs of intoxication or being high such as garbled speech, lack of coordination, clumsy gait, boisterousness, depression, or severe mood swings.

WHAT PARENTS CAN DO

If your child's behaviour indicates substance use, talk to her about it. Be supportive and explain that no matter what, you will not be angry. Your goal is to help your child, not be punitive.

If the youngster has not used substances extensively and is not physically addicted, outpatient treatment can probably be used, but the child should be given a physical examination to make sure that she is okay and can withdraw from the substance safely. Private counselling can be useful; it may focus on helping the teenager identify triggers for substance use, such as feeling lonely or being with certain friends who drink. The teenager then learns to do other things when those triggers come up instead of using substances. Coping strategies can also be taught to help the youngster think of alternative ways to cope with problems, such as talking to a friend when she feels depressed instead of

using drugs. Support and groups, such as Alcoholics Anonymous, can also be helpful and are available in most communities; look in the phone book for the nearest AA.

If the youngster has been using drugs extensively, inpatient treatment may be necessary. If a teenager is dependent on the drug, improper withdrawal can cause medical problems, even death. Therefore, medically supervised detoxification is needed. Inpatient treatment also has the benefit of physically separating the youngster from drugs while he learns about triggers and coping strategies.

Remember, however that prevention is the best cure. If your child has not yet started to use substances, there are a number of things that you can do to help prevent it from becoming a problem.

1. BE AWARE OF THE RISK FACTORS for substance abuse: having a family history of addictive behaviour, feeling out of control, lacking parental supervision, having school problems, experiencing anxiety or depression, encountering peer pressure and being rebellious. Children who fit into these categories are more likely to experiment with substances and may become more easily addicted. Some children, regardless of their predisposition, are very determined to stay away from alcohol and drugs and will be successful. However, be cautious if these risk factors describe your child well.

2. ENCOURAGE OPEN COMMUNICATION with your child – a point we've stressed many times in this book. Listen to your child without being judgmental. If she admits that she has experienced peer pressure to use drugs, don't blow up or forbid her to see certain friends. Instead, listen carefully to what your child has to say. You might tell her, 'I know it's hard to resist peer pressure, but doing so will make you feel better about yourself. It's the right thing to do.' Be understanding and work with your child, not against her.

3. BE A GOOD ROLE MODEL. Parents may say one thing to their children and then hold themselves to a different set of standards. Few things are more frightening for a young child than to see her parent drunk or high or getting sick from drinking. However, if you choose, drinking in moderation is up to you. In fact, some believe that parents who drink responsibly in front of their children and who may even allow their children to taste alcohol on special occasions, seem to have fewer problems down the road with their children's drinking. Drinking becomes demystified in these families. Of course, this decision is personal and should be guided by your attitude towards alcohol. There is, however, no excuse for using illegal drugs, particularly in front of your children.

4. ESTABLISH FAMILY VALUES. According to the U.S. Department of Education, children who decide not to use alcohol or drugs usually have a firm set of values concerning the use of substances. Begin talking about these issues even when your child is a preschooler. Make it clear to your child that you do not approve of substance use. Don't wait until you suspect that your child has a problem.

5. PRAISE YOUR CHILD WHEN SHE AVOIDS USING SUBSTANCES. It's hard for kids to resist peer pressure, and unfortunately drugs are easily available, even in the schools. Your child deserves praise for remaining drug-free.

6. ENCOURAGE YOUR CHILD'S HOBBIES AND ACTIVITIES. Many adolescents experiment with drugs when they are bored and have nothing exciting to do. Religious and community youth groups can help keep adolescents engaged. Provide supervision and make sure you have a general idea what she is doing.

7. TEACH YOUR CHILD HOW TO RESIST PEER PRESSURE. Acknowledge that saying no to friends and schoolmates can be hard, but is necessary. If a child is offered drugs, the U.S. Department of Education offers the following recommendations:

➤ **ASK QUESTIONS.** Make sure that you [the child] understand the situation. For example, you might ask the person, 'What is it?' If you are invited to a party where you think drugs might be present, you should ask some additional questions such as 'Who else will be there?' and 'Will there be drugs there?'

➤ **SAY NO.** Be firm and do not argue about it. Do not let the other person change your mind.

➤ **GIVE REASONS OR EXCUSES, IF PRESSED.** For example you might explain, 'My parents would kill me if they found out.' This reason is clear, and most other kids will understand.

➤ **SUGGEST OTHER ACTIVITIES.** You might say, 'Let's go to a movie instead.' (At this point, you may feel your child shouldn't hang around with someone who does drugs. However, we have to be realistic here. The social networks of children and adolescents are complicated and tenuous. Ideally, your child will not want to be friends with someone who uses substances, but your immediate concern should be to help your child say no to drugs.)

➤ **LEAVE IF NOTHING ELSE WORKS.** Leaving might mean that you will lose a friend, but you are protecting your life.

Suicidal Behaviour

(See also Building Self-Esteem, p. 42; Depression, p. 184.)

WHAT IT IS

Suicidal behaviour consists of suicidal thoughts – planning to commit suicide, feeling that it would be less painful to be dead, or thinking about what it would be like to be dead – and suicide attempts, when a youngster actually tries to end his life. Suicide attempts may include obvious attempts, such as slitting one's wrists or shooting oneself, but it can also include more subtle acts, such as driving a car into a tree or drinking excessive amounts of alcohol when on medication.

Despite the best efforts of health care professionals, the number of youngsters who have suicidal thoughts or commit suicide continues to increase. Our research has shown that fully 6.6 per cent of *children* report having thoughts about committing suicide.

While young children rarely attempt to commit suicide, parents should be aware of the danger signs.

WHAT CAUSES IT

Feelings of depression or hopelessness precede the suicidal thoughts. These feelings can result from various causes including stress, loss, or a brain chemical imbalance. As a result, youngsters can feel hopeless; they get so caught up in their problems that they cannot see that a solution exists or that things will change and get better.

If a family member or friend has committed suicide, a child is at increased risk.

WHAT TO WATCH FOR

There is no single profile of the suicidal child or adolescent. For some, depression and despair have been a part of their lives for a long time, whereas for others, a brief period of distress can produce suicidal thoughts. Although females attempt suicide more frequently than males, males choose more lethal methods, such as handguns, and succeed more frequently.

Often, but not always, teenagers will display clues, sometimes quite subtle clues, that they are contemplating suicide. Sometimes they will openly discuss the subject; at other times they will be secretive and hide their suicidal behaviour. We have found that children and adolescents may show some of these signs if they are feeling suicidal:

1. Talking about suicide: 'I'm going to kill myself' or 'I should just end it all'.
2. Talking about death: 'I wonder what it would be like to be dead'.
3. Feeling hopeless.
4. Feeling depressed.
5. Feeling anxious.
6. Being moody.
7. Indicating that others would be better off without him.
8. Making suicidal gestures, such as hurting himself.
9. Being reckless – cutting himself with a knife, perhaps, or driving too fast.
10. Giving away treasured property to friends or family.
11. Using drugs or alcohol.
12. Skipping school.
13. Isolating himself from family and friends.
14. Expressing an unusual amount of anger.
15. Losing interest in daily activities such as school, sports and being with friends.

A youngster who has experienced a great loss or separation, such as a romantic breakup, is a particularly strong candidate for suicidal behaviour, so any of the above patterns should set off an immediate alarm.

WHAT PARENTS CAN DO

If you think your child is at risk, seek immediate help. Call your family doctor for a referral, or if the crisis is immediate, call 999. A teenager who may commit suicide is clearly in crisis and needs help right away.

Youngsters who have had thoughts of suicide often benefit from therapy. This can be provided on an outpatient basis, but only if the likelihood of suicide is judged by mental health professionals to be relatively low. In these cases, the mental health professional may often require that the youngster sign a no-harm contract. This is a contract between the mental health professional and the child in which the child agrees that if he is feeling suicidal he will either talk to his parents, call the mental health professional, or call 999, a crisis line, or go to the emergency department.

Other youngsters may require hospitalization, which will allow them to work on their problems in an environment that is safe and where it is exceedingly hard for them to hurt themselves. Additionally, being around other youngsters with serious problems often helps them realize that they are not alone and that other youngsters have similar problems.

Some parents hesitate to discuss their concerns with their child because they do not want to overreact, or they fear the possibility of alienating their child by indicating they are very worried about him. However, you must get over this because this is a case where help can really arrive too late. Occasionally, we have seen people ignore signs of suicidal behaviour in teenagers and pay the price later.

Ideally, suicide prevention starts long before the child actually considers committing suicide:

➤ Keep open communication with your child. Many suicidal adolescents feel isolated from their family members and report family problems.

➤ Work on building your child's self-esteem. Your child must feel loved, accepted and respected. Listen to your child and take her problems seriously. Your teenager's problems may seem inconsequential to you, but be sympathetic to your child and what she is going through.

➤ Keep in mind that youngsters do not always realize that things change and that today's problems will not seem as important in a week. The adolescent's problems may not seem severe, but we have seen many unfortunate cases where a youngster attempts suicide because of a romantic breakup or some other problem.

➤ Help your child problem-solve. Kids who feel that they are competent at solving problems will be more likely to see a solution to their current problems. Also help your child think of things she can do when she feels distressed – she can talk to you, talk to friends and so forth.

Tics

(See also Attention Deficit/Hyperactivity Disorder, p. 175.)

WHAT THEY ARE

Tics are involuntary rapid movements that appear abnormal but may not have a medical cause. Some tics, such as eye twitches or blinking or jerking of the head, involve motor control. Others are vocal, such as coughing, repeating certain phrases, or repeating what others say (echolalia). There are three primary types of tic disorders:

1. *Tourette's disorder.* This is probably the best-known tic problem. A child with Tourette's has multiple motor tics and one or more vocal tics every day for a year or more. The vocal tics sometimes involve the use of obscenities, which can bring notoriety to those who have the disorder.

2. *Chronic motor or vocal tic disorder.* The child has either a motor or a vocal tic but not both. The tics are present every day for a year or more.

3. *Transient tic disorder.* The child has either motor or vocal tics every day for between one month and one year. These tics may come and go.

WHAT CAUSES THEM

Tics may stem primarily from a genetic cause. However, stress or trauma also seems to play a role in whether or not a child develops a tic. In other words, a child may have a genetic predisposition to have tics, but the amount of stress (moving, parental divorce, or the death of a loved one) in a child's life may eventually determine whether or not tics appear and how severe they are. Having tics can cause problems for children in peer relationships, at school and in the development of self-esteem.

WHAT TO WATCH FOR

Tics can start at any time. If your child begins to display odd behaviour that seems tic-like, ask him about it. If he can control it, it is probably not a tic, although children with transient tic disorder can seem to control them. Tics also seem to be commonly associated with attention deficit/hyperactivity disorder and may be more common in these kids.

WHAT PARENTS CAN DO

Check with your paediatrician. After examining your child, the doctor may recommend medication or may refer you to a child neurologist or mental health professional. In some cases, the tic may completely disappear after treatment.

Other times, relaxation exercises and family therapy can be helpful. If a child feels calmer and more connected to his family, she may feel relaxed enough so that the tic will subside.

Violent Behaviour (Intermittent Explosive Disorder)

(See also Advocating Empathy, p. 50; Anger in Daily Life, p. 82; Handling Aggressiveness, p. 113; The Brain and Behaviour, p. 158; and Chapter 5.)

WHAT IT IS

Intermittent explosive disorder is present when a youngster repeatedly becomes seriously violent towards property or others. These children and adolescents may not seem angry or aggressive in between episodes, but then their anger explodes and they may hurt others or damage property.

Generally, kids become angry only when someone does something to them, such as calling them a name or taking one of their belongings. However, youngsters with inter-mittent explosive disorder may lose control and beat someone up for no reason at all or because of a small slight. They sometimes have a hard time telling when things are accidental and tend to believe that others are being hostile to them. For example, if a child like this is standing in the lunch queue and gets bumped by another child, the child with intermittent explosive disorder may assume incorrectly that the other child was trying to push him, and a fight may ensue.

Children with intermittent explosive disorder are not constantly angry; their rage may occur infrequently.

WHAT CAUSES IT

In some cases, a problem with the brain's neurotransmitters – low levels of serotonin, perhaps, or high levels of dopamine – may cause the outbursts. These youngsters may also have a short circuit of sorts in the front part of their brains known as the prefrontal cortex. Seeing violence in the home, on television, in the community, or elsewhere may also lead a child to be aggressive, and some children who have been physically abused may develop problems with aggression.

WHAT TO WATCH FOR

Almost all kids sometimes become really angry. They may have tantrums, throw things, or get into an occasional fight. However, intermittent explosive disorder is more severe and relatively rare. These kids may cause serious injury, or they may get into legal trouble because of property damage.

It is often difficult for youngsters to

explain what they were feeling before and during an attack. They often report that they 'just lost control'. Some youngsters say it was like blacking out – that they cannot remember losing their temper or committing the violent act that followed.

WHAT PARENTS CAN DO

Treatment for intermittent explosive disorder can be very tricky because it is hard to treat something that does not happen often. However, sometimes the outbursts are so violent that law enforcement authorities may be involved and treatment may be court-mandated. This means that the child or adolescent must seek therapy or she will receive other consequences, such as being sent to a juvenile facility or being placed on parole.

In treatment, the child may work on a couple of things. For example, problem-solving therapy is often used to help the youngster learn to solve her problems before they get out of control and lead to conflict with another person. The steps of effective problem-solving (see page 160 for our problem-solving protocol) are among the tools that are useful.

Kids with anger or aggression problems also frequently lack empathy, which is feeling warmth towards other people and wanting to avoid hurting others. Empathy training involves having the child think about how her victim may have felt when the child was hurting her.

part four

GETTING PROFESSIONAL HELP

chapter seventeen
MENTAL HEALTH PROFESSIONALS

JUST AS YOU MIGHT go to one type of doctor for a foot problem and another to remove a mole, there are a number of different types of mental health professionals. The purpose of this section is to provide you with what you need to know about the various types of professionals; it may help you assess what is right for your needs.

Although there are a number of differences between the mental health professionals, they all have a few things in common. Most of them offer therapy or counselling. If they treat clients or patients, they can call themselves therapists, counsellors, or clinicians. These are the general terms for these jobs.

Mental health professionals want to help you and your child. They have all received a great deal of training in the treatment of children's problems. They enjoy working with children and their families and want to do their jobs well. They also expect to work not just with the child but also with the parents and maybe even other persons in the family, including siblings and perhaps the child's teachers.

Of course, some mental health professionals are better qualified than others to treat certain problems.

PSYCHIATRISTS

A psychiatrist is a professional who has completed medical school and has chosen to specialize in psychiatry, which is the study of mental disorders, including depression, anxiety, schizophrenia and so forth. After medical school, the physician receives more training, including a four-year residency. A child and adolescent psychiatrist must complete an additional two years of training in child psychiatry.

After this training, psychiatrists must take several examinations before they can be licensed to practise medicine. The fact that someone has finished his training – medical school, internship and residency – does not mean that he can practise psychiatry. He must first show that he is qualified to practise medicine by passing exams that qualify him to become a licensed physician. In the US the most qualified psychiatrists are those who are board certified, or have a diploma. These are the ones who have passed the most rigorous examinations. Child psychiatrists must become board certified to adult psychiatry first and then take another series of examinations to become board certified as child psychiatrists.

Many psychiatrists work at hospitals, mental health centres, or other facilities. Others see patients in private practice in their own office or with other professionals. Some psychiatrists do research, some just see patients and others do some of each.

Child psychiatrists treat children with mental disorders like the ones described in this book. Because they are physicians, they can treat physical and medical problems as well as prescribe medications for mental disorders. When treating mental disorders, the child psychiatrist might try behavioural approaches or suggest other recommendations, but if she finds it appropriate, she might prescribe medication. Psychiatrists can also hospitalize a person if the patient has a severe mental disorder or is a danger to himself or others.

When you meet with a child psychiatrist, she will probably ask you many questions about what the child does and what you do so that she can try to work out how to treat the problem. Each of your first few meetings with the psychiatrist will probably last about an hour. After that, she may see you for a shorter time. If your child is taking medication, the psychiatrist will probably ask you questions to see whether or not the medication is working and whether the child is having any side effects.

PSYCHOLOGISTS

A psychologist is a professional who has an advanced degree in psychology. These degrees are called doctorates: Ph.D., Psy.D., Ed.D. It takes about five to six years to get a doctorate. There are several areas within psychology. The types of psychologists who see clients are clinical, counselling, developmental and school psychologists. Some of these psychologists specialize in research, others do therapy and some do a bit of both. They may work in hospitals, mental health centres, private practice, schools, day-care centres and other settings. Like psychiatrists, they generally work with mental disorders.

If they plan on seeing clients after they receive their doctorate, most psychologists have to do a one- or two-year internship where they receive specialized training in therapy. After the internship, they must take a series of tests to get their licence to practise. In the US, a person cannot advertise himself as a psychologist unless he has a doctorate and is licensed.

There is a great deal of overlap between clinical, counselling, developmental and school psychologists. However, clinical and counselling psychologists tend to see clients individually or for family or group therapy. Developmental and school psychologists do mostly testing and evaluation, particularly in schools or day-care centres. School psychologists may do therapy with children, although we should note that they are different from school counsellors, who specialize in helping kids adjust to school and plan their careers. Psychologists are the best prepared to administer psychological testing.

During your first couple of sessions with a child psychologist, you will probably be asked a lot of questions about your child and family. This is the 'getting to know you' stage. Later, you will probably be asked to do certain things, such as trying new ways of setting limits or doing new and pleasant activities with your child. Many psychologists will assign this kind of homework to you or your child. You will probably see the psychologist once a week for fifty minutes or an hour. This treatment might last a few weeks, months, or even years, depending on what the problem is.

SOCIAL WORKERS

In the US, social workers usually have a master's degree in social work. They are trained primarily to work with families or do counselling with individuals. Some of them work at hospitals, mental health centres, in private practice, or in schools.

One of the main ways they help people is by finding resources in hospitals, mental health centres, or the community, for clients. If a child has mental retardation, for example, a social worker can help the family get into the system to receive specialized services. She can give referrals, find placements for the child and so forth.

Some social workers work for local councils. For example, they may work for the Social Services and help investigate reports of child abuse. They may meet with troubled families on a regular basis to check up and see how things are going, try to solve problems, get needed services and so forth. Some social workers also do individual counselling or family therapy.

When you meet with a social worker, you will probably be asked questions about your family and your child. The social worker will also want to know about different systems the child is in, such as school programmes like special education and what services he receives. Social workers frequently use resources in the community to help treat the child, so they are interested in hearing about the resources the child currently has. Like the psychiatrist and psychologist, the social worker may also do traditional therapy and meet with the client weekly for about fifty minutes.

COUNSELLORS OR THERAPISTS

Persons who call themselves counsellors or therapists may have a variety of different backgrounds. Some of them may be social workers or psychologists. Others may have a master's degree in psychology. Although they have training in doing therapy, most of them do not do research.

In the US, here is also a special type of counsellor called a pastoral counsellor who specializes in treating people using a spiritual or religious orientation.

Mental health professionals exist to serve you, your child and your family. Work closely with your clinician. If you take advantage of his help and work hard, you and your child will probably find some relief.

chapter eighteen
THE ROLE OF THE GOVERNMENT

SO FAR WE HAVE concentrated primarily on things that parents can do to help their children. Now, we would like to discuss some things that we think may be helpful to children that parents alone cannot do – specifically, the ways in which the government may be able to improve the lives of children in this country.

People need to take classes and become qualified if they want to be doctors, bus drivers, or locksmiths. However, surprisingly, people are not required to have any kind of training for the biggest and most important job that they will ever have – being a parent. Given that you are reading this book, we know that you are interested in being a good parent and in educating yourself through available resources.

However, many other parents do not do this, perhaps because of poverty, lack of reading skills, or apathy. Some parents don't have realistic expectations about child-rearing. They do not understand how much work it is, how much time it takes, or that it is a twenty-four-hour-a-day job. They have not heard of colic and are puzzled when their newborn cries for hours at a time and cannot be pacified. This can cause problems, including child abuse.

The children of today will become the citizens and workers of tomorrow. Although we live in a capitalist society where profit is the bottom line, the government is responsible for the citizens of this country.

TEACHING PARENTING IN SCHOOLS AND COMMUNITIES

We propose that the government would benefit greatly from providing all students, starting in primary school, with education about child development and good parenting. Fortunately, some schools are progressive and do have such programmes. Most schools, however, have tight budgets and have to focus on basic academic education. Still, parenting information could be added to health classes at very little cost.

This education should continue at other points in the lives of future parents. For example, all men and women who are getting married should be required to take parenting classes. After the birth of a child, parents should definitely be required to take additional classes. These classes could focus on important issues such as normal child development and how to deal with various problems.

In addition, all families should have access to government-sponsored prenatal care. In our opinion, it is much more important for the government to spend money on these programmes than on building new roads.

If parents are well educated about how to raise a family, our children will have a safe and nurturing environment in which to grow.

IMPROVED OPPORTUNITIES

The government could also help fight child problems by providing early education and other services to children. Early stimulation can actually affect the way a child's brain develops. Opportunities like those provided by Head Start, preschool and day care may help stimulate early development. Pulitzer Prize-winning author Ronald Kotulak suggests that formal schooling should start before age five, maybe even as young as three.

We are also convinced that strong day-care services for children of working parents should be provided by employers in conjunction with the government.

Although funding such programmes at a national level may be expensive, we think, and the scientific community agrees, that in the long run it will save money that would later be spent for incarceration or mental health services. It would also help to make our workforce more intelligent and competitive in today's world.

IT TAKES MORE THAN A VILLAGE

We have all probably heard that it takes a village to raise a child. Actually, we think it takes a nation to raise a child. The government does many things for children, however, the government can do more to help *prevent* child problems from developing.

In this democratic country, all of these ideas are feasible. However, the government has to know that parents want these things to happen. Parents should avoid becoming complacent and assuming that they cannot help make changes in our society or that problems in our country are overwhelming or unsolvable. You can therefore further help your child by standing up for causes that are important to you and your family.

Get involved in your community and vote for candidates and laws that will help your family and neighbours. In addition, write to your Member of Parliament about issues affecting our children.

final thoughts

HAPPY CHILDREN: OUR JOY AND OUR HOPE

PERHAPS THE MOST important and rewarding role that any person can play is that of a parent who helps to shape a child's behaviour and personality. It is a taxing job; however, parents usually find it less overwhelming when they feel that they are doing a good job. This book emphasizes things that parents can do to become better at their job and that ultimately will make parenting easier.

As you think back over what you've read, we hope you'll remember first of all to take care of yourself and make sure that you are satisfied with your life. This will put you in the best position to be a loving parent. Also keep in mind that your relationships with others, including your spouse, are vital to the atmosphere you create for your child. A household filled with people who enjoy being together is certainly a healthy environment in which to raise a happy family.

The family is an important influence on a child and should be a source of support and comfort. Problems in the family can lead directly to problems in the child. If your family, or a member of your family, is going through a stressful period, review the five-step problem-solving method outlined in Chapter 5.

And finally, remember that you are the single most important person in your child's life and his or her primary role model. If you can spend a few minutes each day enjoying each of your children, you'll find that creating a happy family is one of the most pleasant of life's tasks. Good luck and enjoy.

REFERENCES

REFERENCES

These works were useful in preparing this book.

INTRODUCTION

Meyers, J. K., Weissman, M. M., Tischler, G. L., Holzer, C. E. III, Leaf, P. J., Orvaschel, H., Anthony, J. C., Boyd, J. H., Burke, J. D., Kramer, M., Stoltzman, R. (1984). Six-month prevalence of psychiatric disorders in three communities: 1980–1982. *Archives of General Psychiatry, 41,* 959–967.

Robins, L. N., Helzer, J. E., Weissman, M. M., Orvaschel, H., Gruenberg, E., Burke, J. D., Jr., and Reiger, D. A. (1984). Lifetime prevalence of specific psychiatric disorders in three sites. *Archives of General Psychiatry, 41,* 949–958.

Kashani, J. H., Beck, N. C., Hoeper, E. W., Fallahi, C., Corcoran, C. M., McAllister, J. A., Rosenberg, T. K., and Reid, J. C. (1987). Psychiatric disorders in a community sample of adolescents. *American Journal of Psychiatry, 144,* 584–589.

Kashani, J. H., and Ray, J. S. (1987). Major depression with delusional features in a preschool-age child. *Journal of the American Academy of Child and Adolescent Psychiatry, 26,* 110–112.

PART ONE

Kashani, J. H., Soltys, S. M., Dandoy, A. C., Vaidya, A. F., and Reid, J. C. (1991). Correlates of hopelessness in psychiatrically hospitalized children. *Comprehensive Psychiatry, 32,* 330–337.

PART TWO

Kohn, A. (1993). *Punished by rewards: The trouble with gold stars, incentive plans, A's, praise, and other bribes.* Boston, Mass.: Houghton Mifflin.

Walco, G. A. and Varni, J. W. (1991). Cognitive-behavioral interventions for children with chronic illnesses. In P. C. Kendall (Ed.), *Child and adolescent therapy: Cognitive-behavioral procedures*, 209–244. New York: Guilford Press.

Kashani, J. H., Rosenberg, T., Beck, N. C., Reid, J. C. and Battle, E. F. (1987). Characteristics of well-adjusted adolescents. *Canadian Journal of Psychiatry, 32,* 418–422.

Cornelius, G. and Casler, J. (1991). Enhancing creativity in young children: Strategies for teachers. *Early Child Development and Care, 72,* 99–106.

McDevitt, T. M. (1990). Mothers' and children's beliefs about listening. *Child Study Journal, 20,* 105–128.

Fisher, T. D. (1990). Characteristics of mothers and fathers who talk to their adolescent children about sexuality. *Journal of Psychology and Human Sexuality, 3,* 53–70.

Huston, R. L., Martin, L. J. and Foulds, D. M. (1990). Effects of a program to facilitate parent-child communication about sex. *Clinical Pediatrics, 29,* 626–630.

Schmitt, B. D. (1987). Seven deadly sins of childhood: Advising parents about difficult developmental phases. *Child Abuse and Neglect, 11,* 421–432.

Mitchell, C. E. (1989). Effects of apology on marital and family relationships. *Family Therapy, 16,* 283–287.

MacIntyre, J. C. (1990). Resolved: Children should be told of their adoption status before they ask: Affirmative. *Journal of the American Academy of Child and Adolescent Psychiatry, 29,* 828–829.

Meyers, J. K., Weissman, M. M., Tischler, G. L., Holzer, C. E. III, Leaf, P. J., Orvaschel, H., Anthony, J. C., Boyd, J. H., Burke, J. D., Kramer, M., Stoltzman, R. (1984). Six-month prevalence of psychiatric disorders in three communities: 1980–1982. *Archives of General Psychiatry, 41,* 959–967.

Walker, J. (1993). Co-operative parenting post-divorce: Possibility or pipedream? *Journal of Family Therapy, 15,* 273–292.

Mowatt, M. H. (1987). *Divorce counseling: A practical guide.* Lexington, Mass.: Lexington Books.

Hartin, W. W. (1990). Re-marriage—Some issues for clients and therapists. *Australian and New Zealand Journal of Family Therapy, 11,* 36–42.

Zigler, E. and Lang, M. E. (1986). The 'gourmet baby' and the 'little wild-flower'. *Zero to Three, 7,* 8–12.

Harris, I. D. and Howard, K. I. (1985). Correlates of perceived parental favoritism. *Journal of Genetic Psychology, 146,* 45–56.

Dare, C. (1993). The family scapegoat: An origin for hating. In V. P. Varma (Ed.), *How and why children hate,* 31–45. London: Jessica Kingsley.

Pillari, V. (1991). *Scapegoating in families: Intergenerational patterns of physical and emotional abuse.* New York: Brunner/Mazel.

Hansen, F. J., Stanilla, J. K., Ross, J. I. and Sinvani, C. (1992). Integrating child psychiatry and family systems approaches: A case of demonic possession in an eight-year-old boy. *Journal of Family Psychotherapy, 3,* 13–26.

Calladine, C. E. (1983). Sibling rivalry: A parent education perspective. *Child Welfare, 62,* 421–427.

American Psychiatric Association. (1994). *Diagnostic and statistical manual of mental disorders* (4th ed.). Washington, D.C.: American Psychiatric Press.

Thompson, C. L. and Rudolph, L. B. (1983). *Counseling children.* Monterey, Calif.: Brooks/Cole.

Weber, J. A. and Fournier, D. G. (1985). Family support and a child's adjustment to death. *Family Relations: Journal of Applied Family and Child Studies, 34,* 43–49.

Steinberg, P. I., Aufreiter, J., Merskey, H., Mount, J. and Rae-Grant, Q. (1989). The inability to name a child. *Canadian Journal of Psychiatry, 34,* 221–226.

Kearney, C. A. and Silverman, W. K. (1993). Measuring the function of school refusal behavior: The school refusal assessment scale. *Journal of Clinical Child Psychology, 22,* 85–96.

Epstein, J. S., Pratto, D. J. and Skipper, J. K., Jr. (1990). Teenagers, behavioral problems, and preferences for heavy metal and rap music: A case study of a southern middle school. *Deviant Behavior, 11,* 381–394.

PART THREE

American Psychiatric Association. (1994). *Diagnostic and statistical manual of mental disorders* (4th ed.). Washington, D.C.: American Psychiatric Press.

Kotulak, R. (1997). *Inside the brain: Revolutionary discoveries of how the mind works.* Kansas City, Mo.: Andrews McMeel.

Thomas, A. and Chess, S. (1977). *Temperament and development.* New York: Brunner/Mazel.

O'Neal, K. J. (1993). Anticipatory guidance: Alcohol, adolescents, and recognizing abuse and dependence. *Issues in Comprehensive Pediatric Nursing, 16,* 207–218.

U.S. Department of Education. (1991). *Growing up drug free: A parent's guide to prevention.* Washington, D.C.: U.S. Department of Education.

Kashani, J. H., Allan, W. D., Beck, N. C., Jr., Bledsoe, Y. and Reid, J. C. (1997). Dysthymic disorder in clinically referred preschool children. *Journal of the American Academy of Child and Adolescent Psychiatry, 36,* 1426–1433.

Craske, M. G. and Barlow, D. H. (1990). *Therapist's guide to the Mastery of Your Anxiety and Panic.* Albany, N.Y.: Graywind.

Kashani, J. H., Goddard, P. and Reid, J. C. (1989). Correlates of suicidal ideation in a community sample of children and adolescents. *Journal of the American Academy of Child and Adolescent Psychiatry, 28,* 912–917.

Darby, P. J., Allan, W. D., Kashani, J. H., Hartke, K. L. and Reid, J. C. (in press). Analysis of 112 juveniles who committed homicide: Characteristics and a closer look at family abuse. *Journal of Family Violence.*

BIBLIOGRAPHY

BIBLIOGRAPHY

Achte, K. (1991). Suicide prevention: Future trends. *Integrative Psychiatry, 7,* 230–233.

Allan, W. D., Kashani, J. H. and Reid, J. C. Correlates of anxiety. Manuscript in preparation.

American Psychiatric Association. (1994). *Diagnostic and statistical manual of mental disorders* (4th ed.). Washington, D.C.: American Psychiatric Press.

Ball, S. and Bogatz, G. (1972). A summative research on 'Sesame Street'.: Implications for the study of preschool children. In A. Pick (Ed.), *Minnesota Symposium on Child Development,* Minneapolis: University of Minnesota Press.

Bank, S. P. (1987). Favoritism. *Journal of Children in a Contemporary Society, 19,* 77–89.

Barkley, R. A. (1989). Attention deficit–hyperactivity disorder. In E. J. Mash and R. A. Barkley (Eds.), *Treatment of childhood disorders,* 39–72. New York: Guilford Press.

Barth, R. P. (1987). Assessment and treatment of stealing. In B. B. Lahey and A. E. Kazdin (Eds.), *Advances in clinical child psychology,* Vol. 10, 137–170. New York: Plenum Press.

Bedford, V. H. (1992). Memories of parental favoritism and the quality of parent-child ties in adulthood. *Journal of Gerontology, 47,* S149–S155.

Beitchman, J. H., Zucker, K. J., Hood, J. E., DaCosta, G. A. and Akman, D. (1991). A review of the short-term effects of child sexual abuse. *Child Abuse and Neglect, 15,* 537–556.

Bell, K. E. and Stein, D. M. (1992). Behavioral treatments for pica: A review of empirical studies. *International Journal of Eating Disorders, 11,* 377–389.

Belsky, J. (1988). The 'effects' of infant day care reconsidered. *Early Childhood Research Quarterly, 3,* 235–272.

Bennett, L. R. and Westera, D. (1994). The primacy of relationships for teens: Issues and responses. *Family and Community Health, 17,* 60–69.

Berger, K. S. (1991). *The developing person through childhood and adolescence* (3rd ed.). New York: Worth Publishers.

Bernhardt, G. R. and Praeger, S. G. (1985). Preventing child suicide: The elementary school death education puppet show. *Journal of Counseling and Development, 63,* 311–312.

Binder, A. (1993). Constructing racial rhetoric: Media depictions of harm in heavy metal and rap music. *American Sociological Review, 58,* 753–767.

Blagg, N. and Yule, W. (1994). School phobia. In T. H. Ollendick, N. J. King and W. Yule (Eds.), *International handbook of phobic and anxiety disorders in children and adolescents.* New York: Plenum Press.

Blair, S. L. (1992). Children's participation in household labor: Child socialization versus the need for household labor. *Journal of Youth and Adolesence, 21,* 241–258.

Bloome, D. (1985). Bedtime story reading as a social process. *National Reading Conference Yearbook, 34,* 287–294.

Blue, G. F. (1986). The value of pets in children's lives. *Childhood Education, 63,* 84–90.

Bray, G. A. (1986). Effects of obesity on health and happiness. In K. D. Brownell and J. P. Foreyt (Eds.), *Handbook of eating disorders: Physiology, psychology, and treatment of obesity, anorexia, and bulimia,* 3–44. New York: Basic Books.

Brodzinsky, D. M. (1984). New perspectives on adoption revelation. *Early Child Development and Care, 18,* 105–118.

Byrnes, D. A. (1985). 'Cipher' in the classroom: The invisible child. *Childhood Education, 62,* 91–97.

Buchanan, C. M., Maccoby, E. E. and Dornbusch, S. M. (1991). Caught between parents: Adolescents' experience in divorced homes. *Child Development, 62,* 1008–1029.

Calladine, C. E. (1983). Sibling rivalry: A parent education perspective. *Child Welfare, 62,* 421–427.

Chambers, J. H. and Ascione, F. R. (1987). The effects of prosocial and aggressive video games on children's donating and helping. *Journal of Genetic Psychology, 148,* 499–505.

Chapman, C., Dorner, P., Silber, K. and Winterberg, T. S. (1987). Meeting the needs of the adoption triangle through open adoption: The adoptive parent. *Child and Adolescent Social Work Journal, 4,* 3–12.

Clark, M. S. and Pataki, S. P. (1995). Interpersonal processes influencing attraction and relationships. In A. Tesser (Ed.), *Advanced social psychology,* 283–331. New York: McGraw-Hill.

Clemens, A. W. and Axelson, L. J. (1985). The not-so-empty-nest: The return of the fledgling adult. *Family Relations: Journal of Applied Family and Child Studies, 34,* 259–264.

Coddington, R. D. (1972). The significance of life events as etiologic factors in the diseases of children II. A study of a normal population. *Journal of Psychometric Research, 16,* 205–213.

Cohen, S. J. (1983). Intentional teenage pregnancies. *Journal of School Health, 53,* 210–211.

Colan, N. B., Mague, K. C., Cohen, R. S. and Schneider, R. J. (1994). Family education in the workplace: A prevention program for working parents and school-age children. *Journal of Primary Prevention, 15,* 161–172.

Coolsen, P., Seligson, M. and Garbarino, J. (1985). *When school's out and nobody's home.* New York: National Committee for the Prevention of Child Abuse.

Cooper, J. and Mackie, D. (1986). Video games and aggression in children. *Journal of Applied Social Psychology, 16,* 726–744.

Cornelius, G. and Casler, J. (1991). Enhancing creativity in young children: Strategies for teachers. *Early Child Development and Care, 72,* 99–106.

Correa, J. E., Gonzalez, O. B. and Weber, M. S. (1991). Storytelling in families with children: A therapeutic approach to learning problems. *Comtemporary Family Therapy, 13,* 33–59.

Crick, N. R. and Dodge, K. A. (1994). A review and reformulation of social information-processing mechanisms in children's social adjustment. *Psychological Bulletin, 115,* 74–101.

Crowell, J., Keener, M., Ginsburg, N. and Anders, T. (1987). Sleep habits of toddlers 18 to 36 months old. *Journal of the American Academy of Child and Adolescent Psychiatry, 26,* 510–515.

Cummings, E. M., Ballard, M., El-Sheikh, M. and Lake, M. (1991). Resolution and children's responses to interadult anger. *Developmental Psychology, 27,* 462–470.

Dangel, R. F. and Polster, R. A. (1988). *Teaching child management skills.* New York: Pergamon Press.

Dare, C. (1993). The family scapegoat: An origin for hating. In V.P. Varma (Ed.), *How and why children hate* (pp. 31–45). London: Jessica Kingsley Publishers.

DelGiudice, G. T. (1986). The relationship between sibling jealousy and presence at a sibling's birth. *Birth: Issues in Perinatal Care and Education, 13,* 250–254.

Dodge, K. A. and Crick, N. R. (1990). Social information-processing bases of aggressive behavior in children. *Personality and Social Psychology Bulletin, 16,* 8–22.

Donovan, D. M. (1990). Resolved: Children should be told of their adoption status before they ask: Negative. *Journal of the American Academy of Child and Adolescent Psychiatry, 29,* 830–832.

Dunn, J. (1992). Sisters and brothers: Current issues in developmental research. In F. Boer and J. Dunn (Eds.), *Children's sibling relationships: Developmental and clinical issues,* 1–17. Hillsdale, N.J.: Lawrence Erlbaum Associates.

Eisen, A. R. and Kearney, C. A. (1995). *Practitioner's guide to treating fear and anxiety in children and adolescents: A cognitive-behavioral approach.* Northvale, N.J.: Jason Aronson.

Elkin, M. (1987). Joint custody: Affirming that parents and families are forever. *Social Work, 32,* 18–24.

Elrod, J. M. and Rubin, R. H. (1993). Parental involvement in sexual abuse prevention education. *Child Abuse and Neglect, 17,* 527–538.

Epstein, J. S., Pratto, D. J. and Skipper, J. K., Jr. (1990). Teenagers, behavioral problems and preferences for heavy metal and rap music: A case study of a southern middle school. *Deviant Behavior, 11,* 381–394.

Epstein, L. H. (1986). Treatment of childhood obesity. In K. D. Brownell and J. P. Foreyt (Eds.), *Handbook of eating disorders: Physiology, psychology, and treatment of obesity, anorexia and bulimia,* 159–179. New York: Basic Books.

Farber, E. D., Kinast, C., McCoard, W. D. and Falkner, D. (1984). Violence of families of adolescent runaways. *Child Abuse and Neglect, 8,* 295–299.

Farr, W. F., Briones, D. F. and Aguirre-Hauchbaum, S. F. (1986). Impact on children: When one parent disparages the other. *Medical Aspects of Human Sexuality, 20,* 45–56.

Fawcett, J. (1988). Predictors of early suicide: Identification and appropriate intervention. *Journal of Clinical Psychiatry, 49* (Suppl), 7–8.

Feather, N. T. (1991). Variables relating to the allocation of pocket money to children: Parental reasons and values. *British Journal of Social Psychology, 30,* 221–234.

Finkelhor, D. (1984). *Child sexual abuse: New theories and research.* New York: Free Press.

Fisher, T. D. (1990). Characteristics of mothers and fathers who talk to their adolescent children about sexuality. *Journal of Psychology and Human Sexuality, 3,* 53–70.

Fitz-Gerald, M. and Fitz-Gerald, D. R. (1987). Parents' involvement in the sex education of their children. *Volta Review, 89,* 96–110.

Forehand, R. and McMahon, R. J. (1981). *Helping the noncompliant child: A clinician's guide to parent training.* New York: Guilford Press.

Furstenberg, F. F., Jr. and Cherlin, A. J. (1991). *Divided families: What happens to children when parents part.* London: Harvard University Press.

Gardner, R. A. (1984). Counseling children in stepfamilies. *Elementary School Guidance and Counseling, 19,* 40–49.

Gerbner, G. (1972). Violence in television drama: Trends and symbolic functions. In G. A. Comstock and E. A. Rubinstein (Eds.), *Television and Social Behavior.* Washington, D.C.: U.S. Government Printing Office.

Gordon, B. N., Schroeder, C. S. and Abrams, J. M. (1990). Age and social-class differences in children's knowledge of sexuality. *Journal of Clinical Child Psychology, 19,* 33–43.

Gordon, S. (1986). What kids need to know. *Psychology Today, 20,* 22–26.

Gouze, K. (1979). Does aggressive television affect children the same way? *Early Reports, 6,* 3.

Greydanus, D. E. (1985). The teenage girl who is boy crazy. *Medical Aspects of Human Sexuality, 19,* 120–124.

Halmi, K. A. (1987). Anorexia nervosa and bulimia. In V. B. Van Hasselt and M. Hersen (Eds.), *Handbook of adolescent psychology,* 265–287. New York: Pergamon Press.

Hansen, F. J., Stanilla, J. K., Ross, J. I. and Sinvani, C. (1992). Integrating child psychiatry and family systems approaches: A case of demonic possession in an eight-year-old boy. *Journal of Family Psychotherapy, 3,* 13–26.

Harris, I. D. and Howard, K. I. (1984). Parental criticism and the adolescent experience. *Journal of Youth and Adolescence, 13,* 113–121.

Harris, I. D. and Howard, K. I. (1985). Correlates of perceived parental favoritism. *Journal of Genetic Psychology, 146,* 45–56.

Hartin, W. W. (1990). Re-marriage – Some issues for clients and therapists. *Australian and New Zealand Journal of Family Therapy, 11,* 36–42.

Hartman, C. R. and Burgess, A. W. (1989). Sexual abuse of children: Causes and consequences. In D. Cicchetti and V. Carlson (Eds.), *Child maltreatment: Theory and research on the causes and consequences of child abuse and neglect,* 95–128. Cambridge, England: Cambridge University Press.

Hayes, M. L. and Sloat, R. S. (1988). Preventing suicide in learning disabled children and adolescents. *Academic Therapy, 24,* 221–230.

Hein, K. (1989). AIDS in adolescence: Exploring the challenge. *Journal of Adolescent Health Care, 10,* 10S–35S.

Hemmer, J. D. and Kleiber, D. A. (1981). Tomboys and sissies: Androgynous children? *Sex Roles, 7,* 1205–1212.

Honig, A. S. (1983). Television and young children. *Young Children, 38,* 63–76.

Honig, A. S. (1987). The shy child. *Young Children, 42,* 54–64.

Houts, A. (1991). Nocturnal enuresis as a biobehavioral problem. *Behavior Therapy, 22,* 133–151.

Hrynkiw-Augimeri, L., Pepler, D. and Goldberg, K. (1993). An outreach program for children having police contact. *Canada's Mental Health, 4,* 7–11.

Humphrey, H. and Humphrey, M. (1989). Damaged identity and the search for kinship in adult adoptees. *British Journal of Medical Psychology, 62,* 301–309.

Husain, S. A. (1990). Current perspective on the role of psychosocial factors in adolescent suicide. *Psychiatric Annals, 20,* 122–127.

Huston, R. L., Martin, L. J. and Foulds, D. M. (1990). Effects of a program to facilitate parent-child communication about sex. *Clinical Pediatrics, 29,* 626–630.

Hyde, J. S., Rosenberg, B. G. and Behrman, J. T. (1977). Toyboyism. *Psychology of Women Quarterly, 2,* 73–75.

Ingersol, G. (1989). *Adolescents.* Englewood Cliffs, N.J.: Prentice-Hall.

Jacobson, L. I. (1991). Material incentives in childhood and adolescence. In S. Klebanow and E. L. Lowenkopf (Eds.), *Money and mind,* 27–40. New York: Plenum Press.

Jalongo, M. R. and Renck, M. A. (1985). Sibling relationships: A recurrent developmental and literary theme. *Childhood Education, 61,* 346–351.

Kalba, K. (1975). The electric community. In D. Cater and R. Adler (Eds.), *Television as a Social Force.* New York: Praeger.

Kashani, J. H., Beck, N. C., Hoeper, E. W., Fallahi, C., Corcoran, C. M., McAllister, J. A., Rosenberg, T. K. and Reid, J. C. (1987). Psychiatric disorders in a community sample of adolescents. *American Journal of Psychiatry, 144,* 584–589.

Kashani, J. H. and Carlson, G. A. (1985). Major depressive disorder in a preschooler. *Journal of the American Academy of Child Psychiatry, 24,* 490–494.

Kashani, J. H., Dahlmeier, J., Borduin, C. M., Soltys, S. M. and Reid, J. C. (1995). Characteristics of anger expression in depressed children. *Journal of the American Academy of Child and Adolescent Psychiatry, 34,* 322–326.

Kashani, J. H., Orvaschel, H., Rosenberg, T. K. and Reid, J. C. (1989). Psychopathology in a community sample of children and adolescents: A developmental perspective. *Journal of the American Academy of Child and Adolescent Psychiatry, 28,* 701–706.

Kearney, C. A. (1995). School refusal behavior. In A. R. Eisen, C. A. Kearney and C. E. Schaefer (Eds.), *Clinical handbook of anxiety disorders in children and adolescents,* 19–52. Northvale, N.J.: Jason Aronson.

Kendall, P. C. (1991). *Child and adolescent therapy: Cognitive-behavioral procedures.* New York: Guilford Press.

Kernberg, P. F. and Chazan, S. E. (1991). *Children with conduct disorders: A psychotherapy manual.* New York: Basic Books.

Kiracofe, N. M. (1992). Child-perceived parental favoritism and self-reported personal characteristics. *Individual Psychology: Journal of Adlerian Theory, Research, and Practice, 48,* 349–356.

Kiracofe, N. M. and Kiracofe, H. N. (1990). Child-perceived parental favoritism and birth order. *Individual Psychology: Journal of Adlerian Theory, Research, and Practice, 46,* 74–81.

Kohlberg, L. (1981). *The philosophy of moral development.* New York: Harper and Row.

Kohn, A. (1993). *Punished by rewards: The trouble with gold stars, incentive plans, A's, praise, and other bribes.* Boston, MA: Houghton Mifflin Company.

Kourany, R. F. C. and LaBarbera, J. D. (1986). Baby-sitting: A milestone of early adolescence. *Journal of Early Adolescence, 6,* 197–200.

Langdell, J. I. (1985). How can parents deal with the problem of an adolescent's messy room? *Medical Aspects of Human Sexuality, 19,* 124–131.

Lask, B. and Bryant-Waugh, R. (1992). Early-onset anorexia nervosa and related disorders. *Journal of Child Psychology and Psychiatry and Allied Disciplines, 33,* 281–300.

Lerner, J. V. (1993). The influence of child temperamental characteristics on parent behaviors. In T. Luster and L. Okagaki (Eds.), *Parenting: An ecological perspective,* 101–120. Hillsdale, N.J.: Lawrence Erlbaum Associates.

Leung, A. K. D. and Robson, W. L. M. (1991). Sibling rivalry. *Clinical Pediatrics, 30,* 314–317.

McCall, R. B. (1990). Infancy research: Individual differences. *Merrill-Palmer Quarterly, 36,* 141–158.

McDermott, R. P., Goldman, S. V. and Varenne, H. (1984). When school goes home: Some problems in the organization of homework. *Teachers College Record, 85,* 391–409.

McDevitt, T. M. (1990). Mothers' and children's beliefs about listening. *Child Study Journal, 20,* 105–128.

MacDonald, D. B. and Parke, R. D. (1984). Bridging the gap: Parent-child play interaction and peer interactive competence. *Child Development, 55,* 1265–1277.

McHale, S. M. and Harris, V. S. (1992). Children's experiences with disabled and nondisabled siblings: Links with personal adjustment and relationship evaluations. In F. Boer and J. Dunn (Eds.), *Children's sibling relationships: Developmental and clinical issues,* 83–100. Hillsdale, N.J.: Lawrence Erlbaum Associates.

MacIntyre, J. C. (1990). Resolved: Children should be told of their adoption status before they ask: Affirmative. *Journal of the American Academy of Child and Adolescent Psychiatry, 29,* 828–829.

McMahon, R. J. and Wells, K. C. (1989). Conduct disorders. In E. J. Mash and R. A. Barkley (Eds.), *Treatment of childhood disorders,* 73–132. New York: Guilford Press.

Madanes, C. (1981). *Strategic family therapy.* San Francisco: Josey-Bass.

Malekoff, A., Johnson, H. and Klappersack, B. (1991). Parent-professional collaboration on behalf of children with learning disabilities. *Families in Society, 72,* 416–424.

Maniacci, M. P. and Maniacci, S. V. (1989). Parental values as parameters for limit setting in a democratic atmosphere. *Individual Psychology, 45,* 509–512.

Matter, D. E. and Matter, R. M. (1985). Children who are lonely and shy: Action steps for the counselor. *Elementary School Guidance and Counseling, 20,* 129–135.

Miller, C. S. (1984). Building self-control: Discipline for young children. *Young Children, 40,* 15–19.

Mitchell, C. E. (1989). Effects of apology on marital and family relationships. *Family Therapy, 16,* 283–287.

Mohar, C. J. (1988). Applying the concept of temperament to child care. *Child and Youth Care Quarterly, 17,* 221–238.

Mook, B. (1985). Phenomenology, system theory and family therapy. *Journal of Phenomenological Psychology, 16,* 1–12.

Mowattr, M. H. (1987). *Divorce counseling: A practical guide.* Lexington, MA: Lexington Books.

Myers, J. K., Weissman, M. M., Tischler, G. L., et al. (1984). Six month prevalence of psychiatric disorders in three communities. *Archives of General Psychiatry, 41,* 959–967.

Neubauer, P. B. (1983). The importance of the sibling experience. *Psychoanalytic Study of the Child, 38,* 325–336.

Nichols, W. C. (1985). Family therapy with children of divorce. *Journal of Psychotherapy and the Family, 1,* 55–68.

Nicholson, S. (1986). Family therapy with adolescents: Giving up the struggle. *Australian and New Zealand Journal of Family Therapy, 7,* 1–6.

O'Neal, K. J. (1993). Anticipatory guidance: Alcohol, adolescents, and recognizing abuse and dependence. *Issues in Comprehensive Pediatric Nursing, 16,* 207–218.

Pate, J. E., Pumariega, A. J., Hester, C. and Garner, D. M. (1992). Cross-cultural patterns in eating disorders: A review. *Journal of the American Academy of Child and Adolescent Psychiatry, 31,* 802–809.

Pietropinto, A. (1985). The new baby. *Medical Aspects of Human Sexuality, 19,* 155–163.

Pietropinto, A. (1985). Runaway children. *Medical Aspects of Human Sexuality, 19,* 175–189.

Pill, C. J. and Rosenzweig, J. E. (1984). Workshops for parents of learning disabled children. *Social Casework, 65,* 45–48.

Pillari, V. (1991). *Scapegoating in families: Intergenerational patterns of physical and emotional abuse.* New York: Brunner/Mazel.

Plionis, E. M. (1990). Parenting, discipline and the concept of quality time. *Child and Adolescent Social Work Journal, 7,* 513–523.

Plumb, P. and Cowan, G. (1984). A developmental study of destereotyping and androgynous activity preferences of tomboys, nontomboys, and males. *Sex Roles, 10,* 703–712.

Prochaska, J. M. and Prochaska, J. O. (1985). Children's views of the causes and 'cures' of sibling rivalry. *Child Welfare, 64,* 427–433.

Raskin, N. J. and Rogers, C. R. (1989). Person-centered therapy. In R. J. Corsini and D. Wedding (Eds.), *Current psychotherapies* (4th ed.), 155–194. Itasca, Ill.: F. E. Peacock.

Ribbe, D. P., Lipovsky, J. A. and Freedy, J. R. (1995). Posttraumatic stress disorder. In A. R. Eisen, C. A. Kearney and C. E. Schaefer (Eds.), *Clinical handbook of anxiety disorders in children and adolescents,* 317–356. Northvale, N.J.: Jason Aronson.

Rich, D. (1992). *Helping your child succeed in school: With activities for children aged 5 through 11.* U.S. Department of Education Publication No. 1993–331–295. Washington, D.C.: U.S. Government Printing Office.

Richman, N. (1988). The family. In N. Richman and R. Lansdown (Eds.), *Problems of preschool children,* 1–12. Chichester, England: John Wiley.

Richman, N., Douglas, J., Hunt, H., Lansdown, R. and Levere, R. (1985). Behavioral methods in the treatment of sleep disorders: A pilot study. *Journal of Child Psychology and Psychiatry and Allied Disciplines, 26,* 581–590.

Robins, L. N., Helzer, J. E., Weissman, M. M., et al. (1984). Lifetime prevalence of specific disorders in three sites. *Archives of General Psychiatry, 41,* 949–958.

Rubinstein, E. A. (1983). Television and behavior: Research conclusions of the 1982 NIMH report and their policy implications. *American Psychologist, 38,* 820–825.

Ryan, N. D. (1992). The pharmacologic treatment of child and adolescent depression. *Psychiatric Clinics of North America, 15,* 29–40.

Samalin, N. and Whitney, C. (May 1995). What's wrong with spanking? *Parents,* 35–36.

Schepp, K. G. and Biocca, L. (1991). Adolescent suicide: Views of adolescents, parents and school personnel. *Archives of Psychiatric Nursing, 5,* 57–63.

Schmitt, B. D. (1987). Seven deadly sins of childhood: Advising parents about difficult developmental phases. *Child Abuse and Neglect, 11,* 421–432.

Searls, E. F., Lewis, M. B. and Morrow, Y. B. (1983). Parents as tutors—It works! *Reading Psychology, 3,* 117–129

Skerrett, K., Hardin, S. B. and Puskar, K. R. (1983). Infant anxiety. *Maternal-Child Nursing Journal, 12,* 51–59.

Smith, M. L., Minden, D. and Lefevbre, A. (1993). Knowledge and attitudes about AIDS and AIDS education in elementary school students and their parents. *Journal of School Psychology, 31,* 281–292.

Spencer, M., Wilens, T. and Biederman, J, (1995). Psychotropic medication for children and adolescents. *Child and Adolescent Psychiatric Clinics of North America, 4,* 97–121.

Spillane-Grieco, E. (1984). Feelings and perceptions of parents of runaways. *Child Welfare, 63,* 159–166.

Stanwyck, D. J. (1983). Self-esteem through the life span. *Family and Community Health, 6,* 11–28.

Starker, S. (1990). Self-help books: Ubiquitous agents of health care. *Medical Psychotherapy, 3,* 187–194.

Steinberg, P. I., Aufreiter, J., Merskey, H., Mount, J. and Rae-Grant, Q. (1989). The inability to name a child. *Canadian Journal of Psychiatry, 34,* 221–226.

Stewart, J. T., Myers, W. C., Burket, R. C. and Lyles, W. B. (1991). A review of the pharmacotherapy of aggression in children and adolescents. *Annual Progress in Child Psychiatry and Child Development,* 519–539.

Sutton-Smith, B. (1993). Dilemmas in adult play with children. In K. MacDonald (Ed.), *Parent-child play: Descriptions and implications,* 15–40.

Sykes, M. (1993). *Suggestions for helping young children cope with disaster.* Philadelphia: Please Touch Museum.

Taffel, R. (1994). *Why parents disagree.* New York: Morrow.

Thomas, A. and Chess, S. (1977). *Temperament and development.* New York: Brunner/Mazel.

Thomspon, C. L. and Rudolph, L. B. (1983). *Counseling children.* Monterey, CA: Brooks/Cole Publishing.

Tierney, D. and Jackson, H. J. (1984). Psychosocial treatments of rumination disorder: A review of the literature. *Australia and New Zealand Journal of Developmental Disabilities, 10,* 81–112.

Tonge, B. J. (1990). The impact of television on children and clinical practice. *Australian and New Zealand Journal of Psychiatry, 24,* 552–560.

Trice, A. D. and Parker, F. C. (1983). Decreasing adolescent swearing in an instructional setting. *Education and Treatment of Children, 6,* 29–35.

U.S. Department of Education. (1991). *Growing up drug free: A parent's guide to prevention.* Washington, D.C.: U.S. Department of Education.

U.S. Department of Education. (1994). *Preparing your child for college: A resource book for parents,* Publication No. 381-886-20233. Washington, D.C.: U.S. Government Printing Office.

Valentich, M. and Gripton, J. (1989). Teaching children about AIDS. *Journal of Sex Education and Therapy, 15,* 92–102.

Van Aken, M. A. G. and Riksen-Walraven, J. M. (1992). Parental support and the development of competence in children. *International Journal of Behavioral Development, 15,* 101–123.

Vernberg, E. M., Beery, S. H., Ewell, K. K. and Abwender, D. A. (1993). Parents' use of friendship facilitation strategies and the formation of friendships in early adolescence: A prospective study. *Journal of Family Psychology, 7,* 356–369.

Vigilante, F. W. (1983). Working with families of learning disabled children. *Child Welfare, 62,* 429–436.

Wagner, M. E., Schubert, H. J. P. and Schubert, D. S. P. (1983). Family size effects: A review. *The Journal of Genetic Psychology, 146,* 65–78.

Wagner, W. (1987). The behavioral treatment of childhood nocturnal enuresis. *Journal of Counseling and Development, 65,* 262–265.

Walco, G. A. and Varni, J. W. (1991). Cognitive-behavioral interventions for children with chronic illnesses. In P. C. Kendall (Ed.), *Child and adolescent therapy: Cognitive-behavioral procedures* (pp. 209–244). New York: Guilford Press.

Walker, C., Kenning, M. and Faust-Campanile, J. (1989). Enuresis and encopresis. In E. J. Mash and R. A. Barkley (Eds.), *Treatment of childhood disorders,* 423–448. New York: Guilford Press.

Walker, J. (1993). Co-operative parenting post-divorce: Possibility or pipedream? *Journal of Family Therapy, 15,* 273–292.

Washburn, P. (1991). Identification, assessment, and referral of adolescent drug abusers. *Pediatric Nursing, 17,* 137–140.

Watkins, C. E. (1992). Birth-order research and Adler's theory: A critical review. *Individual Psychology: Journal of Adlerian Theory, Research, and Practice, 48,* 357–368.

Weber, J. A. and Fournier, D. G. (1985). Family support and a child's adjustment to death. *Family Relations: Journal of Applied Family and Child Studies, 34,* 43–49.

West, D. A., Kellner, R. and Moore-West, M. (1986). The effects of loneliness: A review of the literature. *Comprehensive Psychiatry, 27,* 351–363.

Woolfolk, A. E. (1991). *Educational psychology* (4th ed.). Englewood Cliffs, N.J.: Prentice-Hall.

Wright, J. C. and Huston, A. C. (1983). A matter of form: Potentials of television for young viewers. *American Psychologist, 38,* 835–843.

Yager, J. (1988). The treatment of eating disorders. *Journal of Clinical Psychiatry, 49,* 18–25.

Youniss, J. and Smollar, J. (1985). *Adolescent relations with mothers, fathers, and friends.* Chicago: The University of Chicago Press.

Zero to Three (1994). *Diagnostic classification: 0–3: Diagnostic classification of mental health and developmental disorders of infancy and early childhood.*

index INDEX